HAUNTING VANCOUVER: A NEARLY TRUE HISTORY

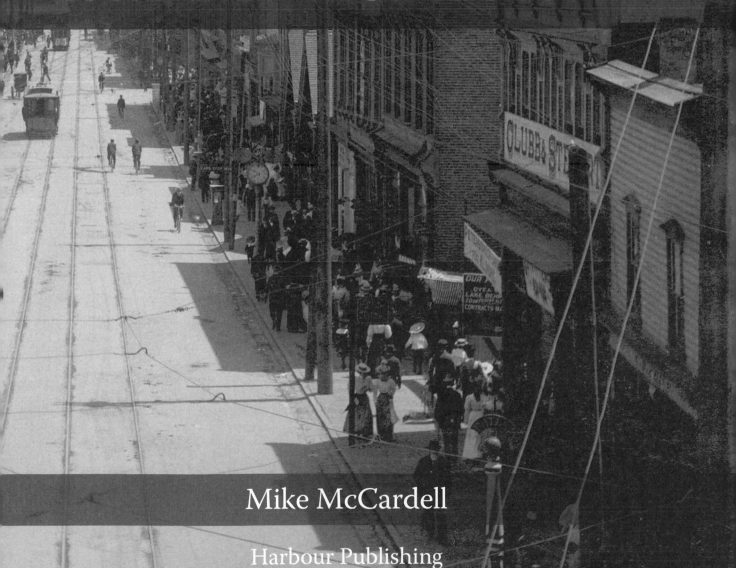

HAUNTING VANCOUVER:
A NEARLY TRUE HISTORY

Mike McCardell

Harbour Publishing

Harbour Publishing Co. Ltd.
P.O. Box 219, Madeira Park, BC, V0N 2H0
www.harbourpublishing.com

Additional image credits: Dust jacket photos of Mike McCardell and Engine 374 by Nick Didlick; Page 1—Stanley Park, ca. 1902. Photo by Richard Henry Trueman, City of Vancouver Archives AM1589-: CVA 2 - 139; Page 2—East Cordova, ca. 1890. Photo by Richard Henry Trueman, City of Vancouver Archives AM1589-: CVA 2 - 14. Endsheet photo by W.J. Moore, City of Vancouver Archives AM54-S4-3-: PAN NXXI.
Edited by Ian Whitelaw
Index by Nancy Wills
Cover design by Anna Comfort O'Keeffe
Text design by Roger Handling, Terra Firma Digital Arts
Printed and bound in Canada

Harbour Publishing acknowledges financial support from the Government of Canada through the Canada Book Fund and the Canada Council for the Arts, and from the Province of British Columbia through the BC Arts Council and the Book Publishing Tax Credit.

Library and Archives Canada Cataloguing in Publication
McCardell, Mike, 1944-, author
      Haunting Vancouver : a nearly true history / Mike McCardell.
Includes index.
ISBN 978-1-55017-606-3 (bound)
      1. Vancouver (B.C.)—History—Anecdotes. 2. Vancouver (B.C.)—
History—Humor. I. Title.
FC3847.4.M328 2013   971.1   C2013-904488-4

DEDICATION

It is sad if you have bad neighbours. They make going home uncomfortable.

I have good neighbours. They have turned a short part of a street into a village. They share meals and birthdays and grass cutting. They make going home a pleasure.

Their names? Barb and Jim with Isobel and Jimmy; Beth and Bruce with Kate; Caroline and Perry with Alice and James, whom they took into their home and who smiles a lot because of that, and Caroline's father, Claus, who directs the gardening; and Ron alone in his house at the end of the street, who is never alone.

They are doing what is in this story. They are the beginning of a society that will grow and spread, and someday others will share meals and birthdays and grass cutting because of them. That is why this book is dedicated to them.

It all starts so simply, at least when you are good to each other.

CONTENTS

Background photo: This is how the Hudson's Bay Post at Fort Langley looked in 1862. If you go on a tour around the Fort Langley National Historic Site today you will learn that in the spring the residents took a bath, put on clean clothes and then burned the clothes they had donned after their last bath the previous spring.

Royal BC Museum, BC Archives
A-04313

GIANT KILLER

The trees were giants, many of them over a thousand years old, before the men came with axes. In 1900 there were still a good many left but now they are virtually all gone.

City of Vancouver Archives AM1376-: CVA 1376-229

'm going to cut it down. By myself."

Impossible. Just totally impossible. I looked up at the massive cedar. It was about three hundred feet tall. On a cloudy day it went into the clouds.

"I hate it. I'm going to kill it. Me, alone. Kill it."

"Why?" I asked, because in my entire life I had never found a question that worked better.

"Because I want to walk here and this devil is standing in my way."

He was unquestionably self-confident, like most of the loggers, but this one added arrogance to his confidence.

Still, this battle was a bit overwhelming. Usually it took two men to slay a living dragon. One would find it hard on the hands.

The man was Alex Fraser, bragging, with a bit of madness in his eyes as he swiped a stone across the blade of his axe. But before I tell you what happened with Alex and the tree, let me introduce myself.

You are not going to believe this, but that's not my problem. My name is Jock Linn and I was one of the Sappers who helped with the birth of this colony, this province and this city—actually several cities.

In short, you owe it all to me and my friends.

You don't know about the Sappers? My poor friend, you've missed knowing about one of the greatest groups of soldiers ever, and I mean ever. I'll save that for another story but, believe me, had it not been for the 160 of us who did amazing things for your future you would now be living in America.

Okay, some of you think that would be better. You could go to Costco in Bellingham and get your milk cheaper. But you might be packing a gun and thinking it would save you if someone boarded your bus and pulled out a machine gun and you could plug him between the eyes. At least, that's one of the American dreams. And if it were not for my friends and me you wouldn't have the benefit of a universal health care system. So you owe your better health to us. We, the Sappers, saved you. You like being a Canadian, and we are the reason. But again, that's another story. Just hang in there.

In the meantime I want to tell you how I happened to be here in 1859 and to be here today when the border lineups to get to Costco in Bellingham are two hours long.

I was in an elite company of British soldiers who could dig and shoot, survey and march, draw blueprints for a town and plan a battle. We were the Royal Engineers, who could do anything.

Way back when, before your great-great-great-grandparents (don't try to figure it out; it was a long time ago) were born, the little Hudson's Bay outpost (that's Fort Langley to you) was being overrun by Americans. Americans can

James Douglas, the first governor of the colony of British Columbia, was the son of a Scottish planter and a free Creole woman from Barbados. He saved the land from being absorbed into the US.
City of Vancouver Archives Port P1536

be nice but this group had guns and whisky and gold pans and that's a bad combination in any nationality.

They also had American flags, which they were very proud of, and they flew these flags every time they camped and drank their whisky and cleaned their guns and talked about how rich they would be when they found gold in this foreign land.

The history of America before that had been, in short, that wherever Americans went the land became America.

Again, this is another story, but a fine employee of the Bay, a giant of a man named James Douglas, was frightened down to his Hudson's Bay boots, and almost nothing scared this man. (Don't worry, you don't have to remember his name. There won't be a test. This is history where you don't have to take notes or memorize anything.)

Anyway, Mr. Douglas was so worried about the sudden arrival of an army of Americans that he didn't bother telling his bosses at the Bay about it. If he had done that he would have gotten the usual results when management has a problem. There would have been a meeting; and then someone would have been appointed to do a study; and then there would have been another meeting to discuss the study. You've seen it happen. Meetings only give management a way of obscuring their inability to manage.

Douglas was a smart guy who wanted to get something done so he went straight to the top. He wrote to the Queen.

He posted his letter on a sailing ship and waited and hoped. He just prayed it would get there. It was a long trip, down to the bottom of South America, through the roughest waters on earth, then up the east coast of South America and then across the Atlantic to England. If that letter hadn't arrived at the palace on time, the betting is that the Americans would have taken over the land you now call your home.

But the ship docked and the Queen was so taken with Mr. Douglas's concern that she took his number one suggestion. Can you imagine someone in management doing that now? She made the place where you now live a British colony, and that meant to others who were not British, "Keep your hands off!"

She also needed a name for this place, and that was a problem. It had been called New Caledonia because that is what Simon Fraser had named it fifty years earlier when he was working for the Bay. He was hired to find a river that boats could use to get beaver furs from the interior to the coast. He found a river but no boats could get through it. He returned to Ontario as a defeated and broken man and went back to farming for the rest of his life. He died broke and pretty well forgotten.

The only things he left behind were a couple of names. The river he called the Fraser, which at least would make his mother proud, and the land, which had numerous Native names but nothing that sounded English, he called New Caledonia. The reason? He remembered that his beloved mother described her birthplace in Scotland as covered with trees. This new land looked the same. The Roman name for Scotland was Caledonia.

Simon Fraser looked around and said, "This is the New Caledonia."

And for the next half century that is what it was called. When the gold prospectors came here in their hordes they said they were coming to New Caledonia. It had a ring to it.

But when the Queen was about to proclaim New Caledonia as a colony of her very own, someone very smart hurried into her throne room and said, "Wait, Your Majesty. You can't do that. There already *is* a New Caledonia."

It was a small island in the South Pacific.

"We can't have *two* New Caledonias. If they went to war with each other we wouldn't know which one to defend."

I know all this happened because I was in England at the time as a member of the Sappers and we got the scuttlebutt in the barracks. The goings-on in the throne room were very important to us because when royalty made decisions we usually wound up digging trenches in the mud.

Queen Victoria was a wise woman; not very photogenic, but wise. She asked her aides for suggestions for another name.

They came up with none.

The ship was waiting on the Thames to go back with the proclamation. Every minute counted.

"Is there a river in this new land?" asked the Queen.

Someone checked a map.

"Yes, the Columbia."

"Then we will call it Columbia," said the Queen.

This was like *The Price Is Right*. A quick answer to a quick question. Meanwhile the tide was falling. The ship had to leave or wait another day.

"But the Columbia flows into the United States," said the aide. "That is a country that does not put Your Majesty's lovely portrait on its walls."

The Queen was pressed for an answer. Minutes were passing. The last rats were boarding the ship. It had to leave.

Then in a stroke of political genius she said, "We shall call it *British Columbia*."

That's one of those "I wish I had thought of that" moments.

Every company now is obsessed with branding. It doesn't matter what the company does; just get the name out there. Put it on baseball caps and jackets and car doors and billboards. The company may change what they sell but people will buy whatever it is if they see the name on whatever it is that they are selling, or so the executives say in their meetings.

The Queen was way ahead of them. She came up with a name that told you where it was, what it was, who owned it and who you would have to deal with in the complaints department if you didn't like it. Brilliant!

I know all this because right after she sent the proclamation on its way she called up our regiment and sent us on the next ship to British Columbia to make sure it stayed British. Lucky us. For most of us, that was the last we saw of England.

I came with that group. All of us were wearing itchy red jackets and carrying shovels and rifles and worrying about being shot by the aboriginals or the Americans or both. As soon as I got here I went for a beer.

But, no beer. No whisky. No pubs. No towns. No nightlife. What was wrong with this place?

I went for a walk in the forest and met someone sitting beside a campfire. He

We Sappers kept the peace, built the roads and mapped out the towns, and on days when we had nothing else to do we piled up mounds to indicate where the US-Canada boundary would be.
Royal BC Museum, BC Archives
C-08071

was wrapped in a blanket and stirring a pot that was hanging from a tripod of sticks. He offered me a drink. Do you think a Scotsman would refuse?

I drank. He talked with words I did not understand and I talked with words he did not understand. It was just like being home with some Scotch in a pub.

When I woke up he was gone and my head hurt. Again, it was just like being home. But a funny thing happened after that. I never again felt sick. I never felt pain. When I cut my finger it bled, but then it stopped and it healed, right before my eyes. When I got kicked by a horse I was knocked ten feet through the air, but then I got up and felt fine.

I never said anything to anyone. I went back into the woods but could not find the same spot where I met the old man.

Meanwhile, my life was good. The service was good. I didn't mind the endless hours and the miserable pay and the terrible conditions. It kept me from being bored.

A decade later the force was decommissioned and all the officers went back to England. I, along with most of the enlisted men, stayed. My wife had come from England and we settled at a creek across the big inlet that old George Vancouver had named after an ex-shipmate of his who had a rough life for a while.

This is the only surviving photograph of me, John Linn. Taken in 1865 with my wife, Mary (née Robertson), it hung on a wall in our little shack in North Vancouver and almost no one saw it—but weren't we a beautiful couple!
City of Vancouver Archives
AM54-S4-2-: CVA 371-1257

Poor Harry Burrard was accused of incompetence. That is not good for your naval career, but he was a friend of George Vancouver. They had been shipmates together when they were young. After Burrard's screw-ups at sea, George wanted to do something good for him so he named a large, newly discovered body of water after Burrard. It is always good to have something named after yourself.

Later Harry Burrard met a young woman from a very rich and influential family. Her family name was Neale. They were married and he changed his name to Burrard-Neale to make the father of the bride happy. Soon after that Harry was promoted to admiral, proving that incompetence has less importance when your father-in-law is rich.

Anyway, we Linns settled at the mouth of a creek on the north shore of the inlet and raised two boys and four girls. The boys did not do well. One held up a general store on Savary Island in 1893 and was finally hunted down by police. Found guilty of the murder of the store owner and his assistant, he was hanged in New Westminster the following year. His younger brother killed himself by cutting his own throat rather than be caught by the police for another crime.

And this is where history and family stories are always changing. When she was a little old lady, one of the younger girls in the family said that her brother had died of "throat problems." That was very kind of her; not true, but kind.

But I am happy to say after I died the creek was named after me. Burrard got an inlet; me, a sergeant, I got a creek. That would not be bad except they spelled it wrong. Someone changed the "i" to "y" and Lynn Creek, my claim to fame, has forever been misspelled.

There was one other thing. When I died I did not die.

Okay, you may find that hard to believe. Say whatever you want to say, it doesn't matter. They put me in a pine coffin and loaded it on a small boat and rowed me across the inlet—and I got up.

I still get goose pimples thinking about it. It is pretty freaky (that's the way they talk now), but I mean I just got up and no one saw me and I followed the wagon to the Sappers' cemetery in New Westminster. Part of the way there I hopped on the back and got a ride. Apparently, I thought to myself, even ghosts get tired.

I watched them bury me and they put a small stone on the ground over my head. I was thinking if I was down there I could not see it. At least it was spelled right: Linn. That's it, nothing else to report about my funeral.

They all went away. My friends and fellow Sappers and my wife left. I walked into New West and had a beer.

And then another strange thing happened. Everyone could see me but they did not know me. They talked to me and heard me but even those whom I had seen before didn't suddenly say, "Hey, what are you doing here? You're supposed to be dead."

I had been over on the north shore for years and had grown a long, shaggy beard.

By the time I was dead I looked way different from my army days. There was only one photo taken of me and my wife but that was years ago when I was clean shaved. There was no Facebook or TV so no one from my past knew what I looked like.

A few decades later I shaved and got a haircut and looked quite spiffy. See, once again, I guess we all see what we want to see, and I have looked that way ever since. Anyway, that's enough about me. Either you believe my story or you don't, but I know what is true and what is not.

However, another thing, more important than whether or not you believe me, was that I needed a job, and protecting the world for England and building roads and wearing an itchy red tunic was not what I wanted to go back to. The easiest way I knew of making a living was as a reporter. You don't really do anything. You just watch others do things and then tell someone else what they did.

Heck, I could do that. Anyone could do that.

Over the last century and a half that is what I have done. I have been a reporter for small newspapers and big television stations, and in truth I have never lifted anything heavier than a pen or a microphone. And they give me money for it. I wish I had known that before I was a Sapper.

And that is why I was watching Alex Fraser sharpening his axe. It was my job. Alex, by the way, was no relation to Simon. There were many Frasers around then, and most of them were from Scotland. They talked to each other but not many others could understand them because of their accent.

What I can tell you about Alex is he saw those beautiful old trees as the enemy, as did most who were coming to this land. The quicker you could cut them down the quicker you could put up a shack and plant a garden and get going with civilization. And the best part of getting rid of the trees was that you could sell them after you cut them down.

This was once a land of giants but the skid roads that were built to drag them out soon became pathways, and by the time these had become streets the giants were gone.
Photo by S.J. Thompson, City of Vancouver Archives AM54-S4-: St Pk P223

The only difficulty was the trees were the biggest living things on earth and a man was not. But Alex had gumption.

He swung his double-headed axe and hammered the blade into the bark. It took a nibble out of the ancient tree. He swung again and took another nibble.

"It is bad and I am good," he said.

Or he said something very close to that. I can't find my notes.

People thought the same of whales back then. They were evil. One of them swallowed Jonah and the story was in the Bible and that was enough to tell folks that whales were bad and it was okay to kill them. This was so even if they hadn't read the story in the Bible, which said Jonah was swallowed because he did not do what God told him to do and God sent the whale to teach him a lesson. What folks knew was the whale swallowed Jonah so let's go forth and kill whales.

So men with spears killed all that they could hunt down. They killed so many that the oceans came close to running out of whales. The killing only slowed down when other people said whales were good. But those people were called weirdos.

Thank goodness for the weirdos.

The whales and the trees led to a song of the hippie years. You remember "Big Yellow Taxi?" Joni Mitchell writing and singing, "They paved paradise and put up a parking lot." She also said "They took all the trees, put 'em in a tree museum, and they charged the people a dollar and a half just to see 'em."

That was one of the anthems of the people with long hair. They wanted to save the world. Bless them. The world needs more of them. And I bet you a beer you didn't know that Joni Mitchell was Canadian and that song was big in Canada before the US.

If you did know I'll buy you the beer. But I'll warn you, there will be other questions and other bets before the night ends.

Anyway, Alex hacked away until he had cut a slot in the bark right about his shoulder height and then he jammed a board into the hole. Then he climbed up on the board and started chopping again.

It was amazing that he could balance himself on that piece of wood. It stuck out about three feet from the bark and was only about nine inches wide. You should try that sometime. Put a board on the ground and see if you can swing an axe without moving your feet, without falling off the board and without chopping off your leg.

That board was the floor of Alex's workshop. All the loggers did that because big old trees are much wider at the base than they are a few yards farther up and no one wants to chop through more trunk than they have to. That's why you see notches in the stumps of the old trees in Stanley Park.

Alex then cut another hole, again about the level of his shoulders, and jammed another board into it. He climbed up to the second board and started cutting again. He was now almost ten feet off the ground, balancing on a piece of wood and chopping away at a giant that had lived in this spot for about eight hundred years. WorkSafeBC would have spasms about that now.

I watched a lot of men cutting down those old trees and sometimes wondered who had it harder, the tree or the man. A lot of men died when they did not get out of the way quickly enough when the tree fell, or they broke their legs jumping off, or they cut off their hands or feet if they fell and landed on the axe.

Almost all the trees were cut down and man is still here.

I know you think that is bad. You who are living now love trees. Some of you even hug them, and you stop logging companies from working.

It wasn't like that in the old days. No, sir. Anyone hugging a tree would be crazy. Women were for hugging. Trees were for cutting. Trees were everywhere and we knew we would never run out of them. Getting rid of them was a duty. If we did not cut them down, where would we have started putting up your cities?

The same with salmon. There were so many in the creeks in the fall that we could just pitchfork them out and use them for fertilizer.

And if we hadn't caught enough of them to put into cans and sell, along with selling the wood from the trees, there would have been no Vancouver. Back in the old days there was nothing else to sell.

The lesson for today: no trees, no salmon, no Vancouver. Period.

But it's funny that now we have a city called Vancouver, we have just about run out of the fish and trees that made it possible. We are hoping computers can replace the trees and we complain that our fish come from farms. We are a strange species.

Anyway, I just want to tell you that Alex worked on that tree with passion. He was sort of crazy, but no one would call him that because he was strong and crazy.

The betting started early.

"Can't do it. I say you can't do it. I bet you can't."

I don't remember who said that, but almost everyone did.

It was not easy to slay a giant. Chop a hole, stick in a board, climb up, balance on the board, then work a saw endlessly back and forth or swing an axe—and try not to miss. The home of this magnificent old fellow would later become Broadway and Waterloo.

City of Vancouver Archives
AM54-S4-: Log P11

"I will. Just watch," Alex said.

"Yes, but how long will you take?" Someone else asked that.

About five men were standing around the giant tree with Alex. Each of them had cut at least one hundred giants, but they all worked with a partner. A few of them had stretched out in the open cut of a tree for a photographer. The idea of the pictures was to show a man comfortably relaxing in a crevice that would turn him into mush in a second if the tree leaned forward. The men are smiling. Gutsy men.

Actually, just working in the woods was more dangerous than dozing in the chopped-out space in a trunk, but pictures sometimes make the story more dramatic than the story actually is. Television later proved that.

"One week," Alex said. "I will have it on its side in one week."

"Impossible," they said. They knew how long it would take. One week with two men, maybe, if they were good men.

The wager was made. It was the traditional bet.

Alex chopped and chopped. He chopped all morning, then climbed down and ate a lunch of smoked salmon and bread and beer. The beer was flat. He carried it in a clay jar.

Then he climbed back up and chopped, each cut digging in a slice, followed by another cut that chipped out the slice. He could hear in the almost silent forest the chopping of others. Someday they would get rid of these beasts and have a nice place to live.

He chopped until dark and then walked through the woods to his shack near the water. Many of the loggers lived in a camp but Alex wanted some comforts of home.

He had built it himself from scraps from the nearby sawmill. Mostly he made it just to get out of the rain. No windows, one door, a stump for a chair and one for a table. Just enough room left over for him to lie down on pine boughs on the ground on which he had a woollen blanket.

Since I have been around for a long time I can tell you that it is sad Alex did not have a deed to that spot. Of course no one had a deed then. Pity, because that little shack was right at the front doors of where the Pan Pacific Hotel is now.

Alex was from Scotland but had come here from California after he missed the gold rush in the warm valleys there. Then he learned he had missed the gold rush in the soggy valleys of the Fraser Valley. The next step was the Cariboo but that was cold and far and Alex was tired of moving. He was way past thirty, he guessed, and knew his life would soon be over. He wanted to settle down.

He was drinking beer in the saloon-filled town of New Westminster when someone told him he could cut down trees and get paid for it. The only problem was he would have to live in the remote tiny village of Gastown where there were no women, no lodging, no cooks and lots of rain.

"Sounds good to me," he said. He didn't mean it; he just needed a job.

In a few months he had become a Paul Bunyan, without knowing who Paul Bunyan was. Alex even did the sawing by himself—one man pushing and pulling on a two-man saw—and he did it while standing on a board stuck in a hole in the tree. He couldn't move either foot backward or forward. Today loggers stand on the ground and use chainsaws on trees that you could wrap your arms around. Alex used a handsaw on trees that would have taken ten people to give it one hug.

It's a shame he didn't have a good public relations company behind him. Nowadays almost anyone who does anything better than others can make a small fortune off it. A good logger today can wind up on the cover of a loggers' magazine, with endorsements.

"Bet you can't do it," said Alex's friends.

He was getting two dollars a week from the sawmill. He was not getting anything extra for doing this alone. But on the other hand there was nothing else to do. Remember: no women, no restaurants, no bowling alleys, no church, just beer at Gassy's. And there was that bet that Alex wanted to win.

On the seventh day I walked back to the tree. It was hard to believe. He was almost done. Another hour of sawing and next would come that scary cracking sound followed by the terrifying fast falling and the earth-pounding, ground-shaking thud. I am not overstating that.

But the part that rattled me most was that the tree might fall the way Alex planned it or it might twist and fall to the left or right. The only safe place was to be far away, and Alex wasn't.

"Looks like you are going to make it," I said.

"You didn't doubt me, did you? I want to win that bet."

We talked by me shouting up and him shouting down. He was standing on the equivalent of a ten-foot-high diving board.

"There, a couple more and done, look out."

He dropped his saw to the ground, turned around on the board and pulled up the axe that was tied to a rope tied around his waist. Then he swung that sharp piece of metal and *thwack*. The sound was solid. The sound was strong. He dug out the axe and swung again, digging deep into the back side of the crevice. Then again. And again. I backed up, then backed up some more.

Each cut brought the giant closer to its end. Each cut came closer to Alex jumping and running.

He swung again but just as his blade cut into the wood flesh the cedar began to lose its balance and started to twist. An explosion of wood splinters burst from the cut. Alex jumped. It was almost double his own height and both he and the tree were falling together. He hit the ground and fell down with a scream. The tree was coming down on top of him.

Every one of the gigantic trees that were cut down had its own history, and this one temporarily became a real estate office! Later this was the place you'd come to go shopping at the Hudson's Bay.
City of Vancouver Archives AM1477-1-55-: CVA 1477-418

He rolled to his side, then rolled again and the mammoth power of stored-up centuries of wood and water slammed into the earth an arm's length from his head.

It really wouldn't have mattered if it had hit his head or any part below his head. I would have just dug a hole under him and covered him up.

"Alex, Alex, are you alive?"

He yelled in pain, then said, "Yes, help me. I twisted my leg or my foot."

I pulled him up. It was so close. It was just like the last seconds of so many of the trees—and of the loggers who did not make it that arm's length away.

He leaned on my shoulder and hobbled through the woods and all the way he kept saying, "I did it. I did it. I won the bet."

At Gassy's saloon there was shouting and praise. Men were squeezed into the tiny room but they made space for Alex. They even pulled a stump inside for him to sit on.

"Here's your winnings," they said, and put down a tin mug of beer in front of him.

That was always the wager. There was nothing much else to win or lose.

And that was the first story I wrote. I did it with some ink and paper I got from the Hastings Store and I nailed it to the door of Gassy's place.

I thought it was pretty good for a first attempt.

"LOCAL MAN SLAYS DRAGON."

At the end of the story I said it was a tree. See? There is always some truth in journalism.

Anyway, poor Alex had actually broken his ankle, and maybe his knee as well. There were no doctors and he never knew, but whatever it was it didn't heal correctly and he was out of work for the rest of his life. There were many like him. He lived by hunting deer. One day he went into the woods with his rifle and never came back but he was always known as the man who cut the tree by himself. Sixty years later the Hudson's Bay store, which is now owned by an American company, was built where the tree had stood.

Inside the store is a small section that sells Canadian souvenirs, many of which are made in China. Most are made of plastic.

When the logging was done, the wasted tree slash was twenty feet deep in places and when it dried it became a bomb waiting for a spark. That bomb burned down the baby city of Vancouver.

City of Vancouver Archives
AM336-S3-2-: CVA 677-516

WHAT WE DID FOR YOU

t is time you learned about us, the Sappers, the people who gave you endless border lineups and higher taxes.

Sorry for that. We weren't perfect.

Think back to the year 1858. I know you can't do that, but I can. I was there.

We were a special unit of the British Army. We were the Royal Engineers and we were proud. Our history dated back to the medieval French who devised a devious kind of warfare. When they were storming a castle with cannons they would be out in the open while the enemy in the castle was protected. Out in the open was not a good place to be.

So the French would dig a zigzag trench that was difficult to hit from the castle and the French would pull their cannons ever closer until they could fire at the castle walls. They called the trench a *sappe* or something close to that, which was an old French word for a spade, which really doesn't make too much sense when you are describing a trench but who is going to argue with an old Frenchman?

The British and Canadian armies still have Sappers, as do the Israeli Army and the US Marines and they don't go around questioning the French on what the word means. The only western army that no longer has Sappers is the French. The Foreign Legion has *sapeurs*, but not the national army. You will have to ask someone in France to explain that.

It's not quite the view you get today from the corner of Seventh Avenue and Main, but this is how False Creek looked in April 1887.
City of Vancouver Archives
AM54-S4-: Van Sc P60

Anyway, there were 160 of us when we landed at Queensborough, which was just a spot on the side of a hill near a river. Nothing else was there. The first order the Queen gave was to change the name to New Westminster. She did not like the name Queensborough and since she was the Queen she could do that.

The 160 of us had a simple task. We were to keep thirty thousand mostly unsavoury, smelly and unsober gold miners peaceful, to build roads for them and others to travel on, to map out towns and to build a fortification on the banks of the Fraser in order to blow apart any American ships that might come and try to take over. And in the process of making that fort we built New Westminster.

Idle hands are the devil's workbench, we were told, but the devil couldn't work on us. We were never idle.

Have you ever driven along Kingsway to get from Vancouver to New West? You are welcome. We built it, through the forest, and we did not have Metrotown to do any shopping on our coffee breaks, which we did not have either. And you know North Road that goes from New West to Port Moody? We built it. If we were around now we would be the shopping mall kings. Lougheed Mall gets half its customers from North Road.

We also had to patrol an area larger than Germany and France combined. The Germans and the French had trouble doing that.

During our off-hours we did the dishes in the camp.

Back to those miners. Some still think that they were like the Hollywood version; a little grumpy and a little philosophical, with bushy beards and barrows and lots of jokes.

Wrong, wrong, wrong. Anyone as soft as a Hollywood image had his gold stolen by the ones who were just plain criminals. James Douglas, the man who sent the note to the Queen to save this place from the Americans, called the gold-seeking hordes "the dregs of society." He was right. Anyone who had any nobility of mind quickly had it knocked out of them when it came to who got the gold first. And they had guns and we had no laws to tell them they could not use the guns.

Among the gold seekers were competing gangs from San Francisco who had had no trouble beating up each other there and had no trouble doing the same here.

Our job was to stop them, and mostly we did. I think they were afraid of our red tunics.

Those scarlet jackets were the part that I disliked the most. We had to wear that itchy wool all of the time. The officers could change into civilian clothes when they were off-duty but not us. They said if we ever deserted we would be easier to spot in bright red.

Now who would think of deserting? Low pay, poor conditions, and on top of that we were not allowed to prospect for gold. We could only protect those who did. Again I ask, who would think of deserting?

My wife joined me after a short time. Many of the other men also had wives, so when we finished with our duties we had the pleasure of going home where the early version of the honey-do list was waiting.

Five years later the gold had run out in the lower Fraser and the detachment was disbanded. Every Sapper was offered a free trip back to England. All the officers, including the famous Colonel Moody, went back but almost all the enlisted men stayed here. The lower-ranking soldiers are the soul of the earth. They do the fighting, they do the digging, they do the dying. They are not like officers, who get catered to, but it's the officers, especially the ones closest to the top, like Colonel Moody, who get the credit. The same happens in every company or office. Get used to it.

But after we had helped the pioneers, we became pioneers. Now the future was ours.

It was a good life. As I told you we lived at the mouth of a creek on the north shore of Burrard Inlet and they later named it after me. And then I died and was buried in the Sappers' cemetery in the area of New Westminster that is still called Sapperton.

"Oh, my gosh," someone who lives there is now saying. "So that's how the place got its name."

If you are anywhere on the mainland of BC you can trace the history back to me and my buddies in our red tunics.

I was buried not far from Gassy Jack. But as you know, something happened and I am still around. You have your doubts, I know, but if I wasn't how would I know that they misspelled my creek? They called it Lynn Creek, which comes out of Lynn Canyon, which is in Lynn Valley, which has tens of thousands of people living there. They are all living in a place named after me. Except my headstone says Linn.

We all make mistakes.

America had George Washington, Vancouver had Jack Deighton. Seen here in the 1880s, Gassy Jack was so named because of his propensity for talking constantly.
Royal BC Museum, BC Archives
D-07873

GASSY JACK

ow there was a character. There were so many characters around then, but Jack was the king of character.

He had a giant stomach, from beer. And a giant laugh that seemed to come from his stomach. But what I liked most about him was his business sense. He was an early Jimmy Pattison—brilliant, fearless and imaginative. He started with nothing and in the end started almost everything.

In Jimmy's case, he started a used car lot and wound up owning a phone book of businesses. In Jack's case, he started with a saloon and wound up giving birth to a city. He did not really own it, unless you consider the creator of something as its owner.

You probably know the story because everybody knows about Jack, but in case you want a refresher, the story is like Jack and the Beanstalk, except this was Jack and the City.

Jack Deighton was operating a steamboat when he arrived in New West, but that was before I met him. By the time we were introduced he was running one of the saloons on Columbia Street. I don't remember how many saloons there were but honestly I only remember one general store and every other door led to a bar with beer and whisky.

There was no wine. Just beer and whisky. The only place you could get wine was in that hoity-toity town of Victoria where you would think you were in England. New West was a man's town. No wine.

Back to the story.

Jack was doing well because there was no end to the miners still coming through, and they all wanted beer and whisky. The saloons were open twenty-four hours a day, except on Sunday of course. That is unless you went around to the back door and swore you were just coming from church.

Jack had quit the boat business hauling miners up the Fraser because his legs and feet were swelling up. But I think he quit because he would rather stay in one place and drink beer than be on a boat drinking beer. On a boat you might run out.

Besides beer he had this one other passion. He talked. You know someone who talks constantly? Someone who gets one story out after another and then laughs at his own stories and then turns to a different crowd and keeps talking but just as you think you can escape he turns back to you and continues the story? You know that person? That would be a descendant of Jack if there was one, which there might or might not be.

I asked him once why he never stopped talking.

"Because I sound so good," he said.

"Actually, I didn't realize I talked so much," he added. "I thought I was the quiet type. Just a word here and there. But I once met an old woman who really could talk. She set a talking record of twenty-four hours without stopping. And when she got through she said… do you know what she said?"

I shook my head.

"She said, 'I forgot to tell you something.'"

He laughed. He laughed at everything he said. If the stories didn't drive you crazy his laughter did. And then you grew to like it and want more.

"Did I tell you about the time I escaped from bandits in Mexico?"

"Jack, you were never in Mexico," I said.

"Of course I was. That was after I travelled across America and got tired of the way they talked and I wanted to go somewhere where they weren't ruining English." He laughed again.

What we used to say back then about anyone who talked a lot was that they were full of gas. You now call them an attention-seeking chronic obsessive-compulsive conveyor of mindless monologue. Full of gas was better.

And because he was full of gas we nicknamed him Gassy. No one had to guess what he was about.

Anyway, he used his savings to open a saloon that he called the Globe, which was named after Shakespeare's favourite theatre because he felt his stories were as good as the Bard's. In fact, his might even have been better because he played all the parts in whatever story he was telling.

But about 1867 business was slowing. The goldfields of the Cariboo were drying up and so were the miners. And then his wife got sick. She was a Native woman for whom he would do anything.

You know how you go to the walk-in clinic when you are not feeling well? Well, besides whisky, there was only one cure for everything that hurt you back then. The hot water in the hot springs. If you had achy bones, aching head, stomach problems, or problems with your wife or your husband, there was only one cure. The hot baths. The only problem was, the water was a two-day wagon ride away. You know it today as Harrison Hot Springs and you can get there in two hours from Vancouver.

For Jack and his wife, and for everyone, the ride would mean a five-day trip if you only spent one day getting the cure, and that would never do. So you would spend two days or three days soaking in the creeks while the steaming water flowed over your aching legs or stomach or back. And because it felt so good you would spend another day and then you would say, "I feel better."

Of course you felt better. You had just spent two or three days not worrying about your back or legs or husband or wife and there was never a better cure for nearly everything.

But while Jack and his wife were soaking up the good feelings I was back at his Globe saloon drinking a beer, and I realized Jack had made a big mistake. This was the morning of July 4, 1867. It was American Independence Day and Jack had left his business in the hands of a friend who was American.

You know how you now say OMG? This was OMG!!!

"Drinks on the house," said Jack's friend to both his American and Canadian friends. No one would be left out. I was Scottish and he still slid one over for me.

"That's kind of you," I said. "But won't Jack mind?"

"Jack? I'm sure he would do the same," said Jack's friend.

I did not think so. Jack was friendly, but not dumb as a doornail, which his American friend apparently was.

By the time the sun was setting on the Fourth of July on Columbia Street

In 1873 Columbia Street, New Westminster, the location of Gassy Jack's Globe saloon, looked peaceful enough, but six years earlier a friend was giving away all Jack's beer and liquor and changing the history of Vancouver.
Photo by Philip Timms, City of Vancouver Archives AM336-S3-2-: CVA 677-284

in New Westminster, the Canadians and Americans and Englishmen were staggering from wall to wall, except for the ones lying unconscious on the floor.

Jack was in a wagon with his wife slowly clip-clopping back to his business, feeling refreshed and content and looking forward to getting back to work.

OMG!!!!

Jack's exact words were stronger, but my head hurt too much to make a note of them. That was the morning of the Fifth of July and I was still somewhere between the walls of his saloon, along with many other new friends I had met the night before.

"What the…???"

Jack did not finish that. His American friend who had taken over the bar was trying to pour a beer for him to welcome him back, but there was no beer coming from the spigot.

"What…?"

Jack could not speak. He opened his mouth but nothing came out. That would be like a dam suddenly shutting off a mighty river with nothing getting by. This was not good.

He looked at the whisky bottles that he kept behind the bar. The few that were still there were empty. The ones that weren't there, well they weren't there.

There were several beer barrels on their sides on the floor. He nudged them. They rolled. Barrels with beer in them don't roll.

I opened my painful eyes far enough to see Jack trying to breathe.

He walked over to the cash drawer behind the bar. He looked around at the bodies on the floor, the barrels on their sides and the bottles without content and opened the drawer.

"Aggggaggggg!"

I think that's what he said.

"Aggggaggggg!" he repeated, but this time it was louder.

He pulled out the drawer and turned it upside down. Nothing came out.

This time I held my ears.

The word that came next was very loud and very long and hard to describe. But it did go right through my fingers and through my ears and collided somewhere in the middle of my head. This did not make me feel good.

Jack turned around and walked out. He never came back. And here is where history turned on its pounding head.

Carrall Street
copyright applied for

GASTOWN

 day or two later, when the pain in my brain had subsided and I had sworn on everything holy and unholy that I would never do that again, I met Jack standing in the middle of the street talking to a group of men.

If Jack was talking I knew everything was the way it should be.

I squeezed into the crowd and heard the name "Edward Stamp."

The maple tree at the corner of Carrall and Water Streets became known as the "Meeting Place." Edward Stamp suggested to his friend Gassy Jack that he open a saloon here, which would make the men working nearby in Stamp's sawmill very happy.

Photo by H. Devine, Vancouver Public Library 1098

Jack said that Mr. Stamp had heard about what had happened and had a suggestion. The news that Gassy Jack's Globe was trashed travelled fast. It does not matter what century it is, news like that always gets more coverage than the important things like the workings of government. A bar drying up gets bigger headlines than the birth of a bill to regulate banking, even though the banking is much more important.

At least that's what the emails say.

Anyway, Jack had met Mr. Stamp years earlier on one of Stamp's business trips to New West. You know who Edward Stamp is, right? He is another one of those people without whom Vancouver might have started fifty years later and then we would be fifty years behind and there wouldn't yet be any skyscrapers downtown, no World's Fair, no Olympics and no breakdowns on the SkyTrain. We would have to wait half a century for all that.

But in case you missed that lesson in your history class, Edward Stamp left England and went to San Francisco looking for a way to make his life better. Then he left San Francisco and came here for the same reason. Eventually he hoped to get it right.

He knew about the gold but saw the trees and like every good businessman saw gold in what was available. Cut the trees, sell the wood back to San Francisco and retire rich. Easy.

Edward Stamp tried to set up a sawmill at Brockton Point, in what is now Stanley Park. When the tide took away his logs he moved further east and there began a sawmill that began a town that began a city.
City of Vancouver Archives
AM54-S4-: Port P264

If you go to Brockton Oval in Stanley Park and walk the seawall you can see a little plaque on the ground with his name on it. That was the spot where he said, "Perfect, we will build our mill here." It had trees and ocean water on which to move the trees. What else could a person want for his sawmill?

Actually, it was even better because there was fresh water nearby. Have you ever gone to Beaver Lake in the middle of Stanley Park? That would supply the fresh water for the steam to run the saws in the mill. You can't do that with salt water.

So Mr. Stamp hired some men to cut down trees and dig an aqueduct from the lake to the spot where his mill would be and he sent away to England for the parts to build the mill. There was no FedEx then and he figured it would be almost six months before the blades and boilers arrived.

Meanwhile he ordered the men to cut and cut.

You know those cricket games that are played in the park now? They owe it all to Mr. Stamp's men with axes.

They also owe their playing field to a misjudgment by Mr. Stamp. He had his men dump all the trees in the water of Burrard Inlet, where they could wait for his mill to be ready, along with all the other trees that had been cut down. There was the beginning of a fortune floating just off the edge of the land where his mill would go.

And then something happened that still happens. There is a narrows on the inlet, which is why that spot is called the narrows. It is the first narrows of the inlet so it is named the First Narrows. You seldom get more creative than that. That is why the Lions Gate Bridge was built over that spot, because the crossing was narrower there.

Somehow Mr. Stamp forgot about the narrows, a bit like building a car and forgetting the rear wheels. Whoops.

Occasionally, during an extremely high or low tide, the water moves through the narrows faster than a cricket game. It is more like hockey, on a power play. And fast-moving water, which is called a riptide, has the strength to undo the dreams of someone who thought he would get rich.

The tide took his logs and carried them out to sea.

"Darn."

I was there and I heard it. Edward Stamp was a gentleman. He had just seen his entire fortune float away and all he said was "Darn."

I liked him for that.

He went for a long, long walk along the water's edge until he came to another narrows. That would be the Second Narrows. If we named our children like that the first would be called First and the second would be Second, and no one would ever have to ask who was older.

Anyway, Mr. Stamp turned around and walked back until he found a spot right between the first narrows and the second narrows and said, as he did the first time, "Perfect. We will build our mill here." This time he was right.

The spot was at the foot of what is now Dunlevy Avenue. If you went down to what used to be the main police station at 312 Main Street you would be only four blocks from the mill.

Edward Stamp got the rights from the new and tiny government of British Columbia to sixteen thousand acres of land on which to cut trees. If you want to cut down a tree in your own backyard you now need the permission of the

government, plus you have to plant another tree to replace the one you are cutting, but for a relatively small business fee, Mr. Stamp got permission to cut down half a million trees and in the process cleared the way for the east side of Vancouver. He also opened an opportunity for a new business: stump removal.

The point of all this is that he had one rule. Okay, he had many rules for his workers. Come to work, do your job, go home and come back again. But it was hard to enforce those rules because it was nearly impossible to get men to work for him there because his mill was basically on the back side of the moon.

Men with no gold and hungry for work heard about the sawmill, but where was it?

"You're kidding. Where's that?"

And once they got there, where would they sleep? And where would they eat? And most important, where would they drink?

That last question was a stunner, a brain number, a puzzle without solution, because that was Edward Stamp's number one rule: No drinking on the job.

That was insane. This was an age fuelled by alcohol. Everyone drank, on and off the job. The British Navy floated on rum. The British aristocracy ruled by gin. And I must tell you about the Americans when they all lived in colonies and what gave rise to their crazy idea to take on Britain in a war of independence.

You have heard of Johnny Appleseed? He was an American legend. Unlike me, he never really existed, but basically every single American colonist had an apple tree in his yard. That's a lot of apples, and they were doing more than just making pies with them.

There was very little whisky because it was hard to get. There was almost no wine because they had not yet learned to pair the wretchedly bad almost-vinegar that they got from grapes with anything edible. And there wasn't much beer, because you had to have a field to grow wheat and then you had to chop down the wheat and give some to your wife to make bread and after all that work who wanted to start a new batch of ale?

But apples were different. They fell on the ground. You put them into a barrel and let them rot. Then you drank the swill that oozed out of the rotten apples and you felt better. At least for a while.

You could also feed your pigs with the apple mush that was left over and make them very happy. Have you ever seen a staggering pig? Okay, I know the people against animal cruelty will condemn me, but I am just the messenger. Staggering pigs were a big diversion in the late 1700s.

And then you hung up a ham in your kitchen/living room/dining room/bedroom when you had company. Everyone had ham and everyone had cider. Lots of cider.

Then you and your friend could cut pieces off the ham and sit around chewing the fat while you talked about a revolution.

Then you would chew some more fat and have another cider, and another. The American Revolution was brewed by stomachs filled with fat and brains giddy with apple cider. How do you think an insane notion like war with a superpower happened? Over tea?

That's another history lesson you will not be tested on.

Now back to Edward Stamp and Jack Deighton. Sorry, I am talking almost as much as Jack.

Edward Stamp had a mill that needed men. He had met a man who had the means of attracting them.

I was there when the proposal was made. It was like the egg and the sperm coming together to make a child, except here we had an industrialist and a bartender coming together to make the future.

It almost sounds gay since it was two men, but that is a later chapter. By the way, do you know who Davie Street was named after? Just wait.

Anyway, I was there when I saw Edward Stamp and Jack Deighton talking on Columbia Street.

"I have an idea," said Edward. "There is a place that is hungry, thirsty, dying for beer and whisky."

"Go on," said Jack, who was not going to be suckered in on a Ponzi scheme.

"There is a new sawmill on the Burrard Inlet. It will have many men working there as soon as I can figure a way of getting them to move there."

"Continue," said Jack.

"It's not much. Just mud and rain and trees and cold and bears and cougars and lonely men."

"What would I do there?" asked Jack.

"Open a saloon," said Edward Stamp. "I am noted for picking perfect places."

So Jack, who was out of money and out of beer and out of business, got his wife and his brother-in-law and his dog into a large rowboat.

Oh, there was one thing more. He had one barrel of whisky hidden in a shed. It was sort of like his RSP, except he had to cash it in early. And if you have not started saving yet for a time when everything is gone, take a lesson from Gassy. His future, the future of your city, your condo, your cappuccino on Robson Street rested on that barrel.

Gassy did the dreaming, his brother-in-law did the rowing, and his wife did the directing.

They floated down the Fraser past a few stragglers of men walking the other way along the banks of the river. They were looking for gold in one direction, Jack in the other. I always thought there was a lesson to be learned in that, but I'm not sure what it is. Maybe it is just that the direction does not matter, just what you do when you get there that counts.

"Turn right at the end of the land," she said to her brother who was rowing. "That looks like a good spot to put a university someday," she added.

Then her brother started rowing down to Richmond.

"No, my right, not yours."

"Now, turn right again at that bulge of land. My right."

Always knowing which way is right is what makes a woman such a calming influence while directing.

She looked up. "If that was a park we could have a picnic there," she said to her husband.

"What's a park?" he asked.

"Never mind. Go back to sleep."

"Right there is where we should stop," she said to her brother.

I was there, waiting for them to come ashore. I hiked across country and beat them. I was not carrying a barrel of whisky, but I was hoping to get some when they arrived.

I asked Gassy's wife how she knew this was the right spot. She said she could see the boundary of the end of the mill right there. She was pointing to a large stake in the ground with a red flag tied to it.

That would be about where Gore Street is now. Don't worry if you can't picture it. She could and that is all that mattered.

Edward Stamp had told them it would be a good idea to open a saloon just outside the boundary of the mill. That would be right here, about a short throw of a stone from the stake.

Gassy asked me and a few other men watching them pull in their boat if we could help. It would not take much time and we would get whisky if we worked.

Count me in.

"Let us construct a friendly little place of business right here," said Gassy.

It was next to a maple tree.

"When do we get the whisky?" I asked.

"When you are finished," said Gassy.

He was just as smart as Edward Stamp.

We worked fast and in half a day had a shack standing that could hold eight or ten men, so long as they were standing.

Then Gassy gave us our pay, all the whisky we could drink in one sitting. With empty stomachs and exhausted backs from working so fast it did not take long for the whisky to knock us over so that we were no longer sitting or standing. And you cannot drink more if you are lying down. Gassy got a lot of work for very little pay.

The sawmill workers came and drank and Gassy sent his brother-in-law back with the cash to buy another barrel and added a barrel of beer to the list.

Soon, very soon, he had steady customers, at least they were steady until they left his new Globe saloon. In a short while shacks were being built close to his place and a little town was growing up. The fellows called it Gassy's town, which quickly got shortened to Gastown.

In case you did not know, now you do. But I know you knew all along how it got that name.

Gassy Jack was happy: he had started a new career and money was flowing

Jack didn't look half bad from down here. He lived with beer, whisky, brawls and the birth of a city. He didn't have time for botox.

City of Vancouver Archives AM1435-: CVA 1435-482

in. Edward Stamp was happy: he had no trouble enticing men to work for him because now they had a way of spending their pay, which of course meant they had to keep on working.

What you might not have known about Gassy Jack is that his loving wife died soon after he opened his new saloon. But she was a thoughtful wife, at least by the standards of the mid-1800s. She left to him her twelve-year-old niece to keep him warm at night. The twelve-year-old, named Madeline, had a baby before she was thirteen.

And business boomed. The blades in the mill were spinning, the men were working, and the liquor was flowing. A town was popping up just behind the saloon. It was six acres from end to end, which means it went from what is now Carrall and Water Streets, just where Gassy's statue is, to Cambie Street. You could walk across town in ten minutes. But it was a town. And a town needs a name. And there was a government that felt it was the duty of the government to give it that name.

"What are we going to call it?" said one of the government people in the capital of New Westminster.

"How about Stamp Town, or Deighton Town?" said the people of New West. "Ed and Jack are the reason it is there."

But the government people said, "No, those are not dignified. We need a name of importance. We also have to flatter somebody who is important."

I know all this went on because I was in the official room where the important people sat around a table trying to think of someone even more important than themselves to name a town after.

"There is the governor in charge of the colony, Lord Granville," said one of the men in New West. "He would like to have a town with his name."

"But he has never been here," said the people.

"Overruled," said the important men in the official room. "Granville it will be."

So the new town of Granville was born and the streets were laid out and now that a government was involved there was a problem.

The wonderful, communal, boisterous Gassy Jack Deighton's saloon, which was the womb in which a great city was growing, was right in the middle of a street that had not existed the day before.

The man who was at least half-responsible for the town being here was told to demolish his saloon and move. I felt bad for him. He was cheated. But I did not realize how smart he was. He turned disaster into triumph, and that is why I love this man.

Gassy Jack knocked down the tiny saloon and bought—yes, he had to "buy"—a piece of land a few steps away. It was at the southwest corner of Carrall and Water Streets.

He built a two-storey hotel and bar that had a billiards room and rooms for rent upstairs and a balcony that overlooked the maple tree in the square that was slowly being called Maple Tree Square, the spot where you could find good beer and a good bed in Gassy Jack's Deighton Hotel.

And you won't believe what happened next. Or probably you will. Crime was coming to Gastown. There were robberies and holdups and fights and all manner of bad things going on. That happens, I have noticed. When you put together alcohol and men you get the results of alcohol and men.

Jack and a few of the newcomers asked the government to *do something*. And believe it or not, because I still don't believe it, the government listened and *did something*. It hired a man to be the constable and keep the peace.

He was Jonathan Miller, who was a big man. He was cutting down trees in what would become Stanley Park when some men from the government asked him if he would like to be chief constable of Granville.

"Who will I have to be chief of?" he asked.

"No one. You will be chief and you will tell you what you want you to do."

Jonathan Miller thought it over. Then they said they would pay him more than he would make chopping trees.

He took the job and the first thing he wanted was a jail. The government built a solid log enclosure just behind the Deighton Hotel. If you go back behind the statue of Gassy Jack now you will be in the Gaolers. That is where the jail was. Some people say it was on another street but, there again, that is a problem with history.

It was dark. The streets had no lights but when Miller took someone to the clink for the night he knew exactly where he was going.

Gaol was the English word for jail and when many of the drunken Americans were taken to the gaol they said, "Good, I was afraid I was going to jail."

When Gastown got gentrified the city mothers and fathers kept the name Gaol but added Mews after it. A *mews* was an old British word for a pretty little back lane behind the stables, which they thought would greatly soften the name of Gaol. In short it was now a pretty little jail. And now lawyers buy their expensive condos in Gaoler's Mews, which makes sense since they make most of their money keeping crooks out of the gaol.

Miller did not lock the rooms when he arrested anyone for drunk and disorderly conduct or for theft. He just told them to stay there. They knew if they left, Miller would hunt them down and deal with them behind a tree. It was better to wait in the gaol, even if they did not know what a gaol was, until he decided to let them go free.

For the real bad cases he put their legs in irons. It worked. Unlike today, he never had anyone he locked up back out the next day doing more crimes.

And this is when I became a crime reporter. It was exciting. All my work before this had been writing on scraps of paper and nailing them up on Gassy's front door. The stories were about trees getting cut and gardens being planted but how many stories can you do on the same subject before your readers get bored? Some of the readers in the saloon were asking me, "Can't you get us some real news? We are tired of all this warm and fuzzy stuff."

And their wish was about to come true.

Small newspapers were starting up and I got a job reporting on the seedy side of town, which was Gastown.

My biggest story was the Battle of Jericho. This is the story as I wrote it, and the story behind the story, the story of how it was covered. This was more exciting than being a Sapper.

Jonathan Miller looked gentle in his later years, and he was, but as Vancouver's first cop he was so towering and tough he didn't even bother to lock the jail. No one would have dared try to escape.

City of Vancouver Archives
AM54-S4-: Port P471

Dateline: Jericho. Two unscrupulous thieves in a boat tried to make off with goods they had stolen from miners when they were spotted by Chief Constable Jonathan Miller.

Miller saw them rowing to shore near Gassy Jack's saloon.

"I thought they were going to sell the hot goods to unscrupulous buyers. I hope this practice does not continue into the future."

But the pair of thieves saw Miller and turned their boat around and started rowing feverishly away.

Miller deputized another man and the two of them commandeered a rowboat.

This reporter wanted to be part of all of the action and jumped into the boat and helped row. It was a chase scene and I was chasing.

"I thought the press was supposed to be an impartial observer," Miller said to me.

"This is called 'investigative reporting,'" I said. "I am now inventing it and I am getting my hands dirty while digging into the story."

"But your hands are not getting dirty," said Miller. "At the worst, they will get wet. You reporters are always exaggerating."

Anyway, we followed the thieves to Jericho, which was where Jerry Rogers was living and working. That is why it is called Jericho, Jerry's cove. Jerry, who

Jericho Beach, seen here in the 1890s with the paddlewheel tug Richmond *offshore, was the scene of Constable Miller's pursuit of the Gastown thieves. The bad news? The thugs got away. The good news? They never came back.*
Photo by Bailey Bros., City of Vancouver Archives AM54-S4-: Be P41

was a very well-known logger and a man who took no guff from anyone, must have been out that night, because he would have told those young crooks a thing or two. And if Jerry, who always carried a two-headed axe, told you a thing or two you probably would not forget either of them.

By the time we pulled our boat onto the beach the bad guys were lying in wait. They fired a rifle at us.

"What?" I thought. "This is Canada. Thieves are supposed to be nice."

Bang. Bang again. This was serious business. Shooting at a police officer, worse shooting at a reporter, would not go well for them in court, especially if they had good aim.

If you have ever been shot at you know how far you can push your face into the sand. You also know how you can lose control of your bodily functions. That was embarrassing.

The thieves escaped. I learned their names were Brown and Shipley. But they left behind their stolen goods. That was half the battle. And I think after their close call with the law and the press they might have turned to a life of honesty, because they were never heard from again. Sometimes a good scare may be better than a bad punishment.

The "Battle of Jericho" made the front page. There was only one page to the paper, but when a reporter gets top billing he gloats. Reporters are not very deep but they are human.

A few years later my good friend Gassy Jack passed away. He was forty-four. He was buried just down the hill in the cemetery from me and if he ever comes back I'll take him to Gastown for a couple of beers. He won't believe his eyes. And he won't believe that statue of him either.

"Was I that ugly?"

"No," I will say, and I'll be right.

Gassy's son died just six months after his father, but his young wife lived until she was ninety in the North Vancouver Indian reserve just across the water from Gastown. I don't believe she ever went back to Gastown, not even for a visit. So sad.

The area we now know as Jericho was originally called "Jerry's Cove," named in honour of the well-known logger Jerry Rogers. This photo of him was taken in the 1870s.

City of Vancouver Archives
AM54-S4-: Port P401

LOGGING ENGLISH BAY.

NO STINKIES ALLOWED

veryone was welcomed in Gassy's saloon. As they say in Quebec, where some of the loggers came from, *mais oui!* But of course.

Everyone drank beer, *mais oui!* Everyone had some coins to spend that came from the mill, which was eating up the forests that would become a city. *Mais oui.*

It all sounds so poetic.

In the late 1890s oxen were the kings of the woods, and people gained status by their relationship to the beasts. Those who poured fish oil over the skid roads to make logs slide more easily were definitely on the bottom tier.
City of Vancouver Archives
AM54-S4-: Log P5

But I liked to talk to the men who were not allowed in. Actually, I wanted to talk to them because they were the outcasts and I have always found the outcasts had better stories than the in-fashion people. The only problem with the outcasts was you could not understand their stories. That is still true.

But there was Joshua, who had come from a religious family in California. He rejected their religion and sought gold. He did not find gold. He thought that was a heavenly punch in the nose for his rejection.

He went to the mill near Gassy's saloon and took the bottom job on the bottom of the ladder at the bottom of the totem pole. There is no other way of describing it. This was not a job that was hard to fill. He was hired as a Pig Man.

His job was to walk along the skid roads that were being carved through the forest and pour fish oil on the small logs that the giant logs would slide over. Easy job. Except the fish oil grew rancid before the day was out and the oil Joshua used was a week old or more. And it smelled.

No, that is not the way to describe it. It stank. It was wretched. It made you gag.

And it was in Joshua's clothes and hands and hair and boots.

"Go outside and drink your beer," said the men inside the saloon.

Poor Joshua.

I saw him sitting on a stump near the saloon and went to talk with him.

Ugh. Down stomach, down. He was stinking.

I tried breathing through my mouth.

"Hello."

That was all I could get out.

"Thanks," said Joshua. "No one talks to me."

I was thinking I would be one of those no ones, except I wanted to know about his job.

"I brought you another beer," I said. "Tell me what you do. But first I must tell you I am a member of the press and everything you say will be sensationalized as much as possible for my benefit to find a buyer for your story."

He sipped. He said: "I am an outcast. Even the oxen don't like me, but I make their lives so much easier."

He said he walked behind the oxen and poured fish oil, fish grease, fish guts, fish heads, anything fishy on the logs that went across the paths cut through the woods.

"The others get paid so much more. Take the teamsters. I hate those guys. All they do is keep the oxen moving and they get the most. I mean they are at the top of the scale. They are crooks."

"Careful," I said. "You can't accuse anyone of anything unless you can prove it in court."

Joshua looked at me in an odd way. "What's a court?"

Okay, we had one thing down. Teamsters, with their four-foot-long poles with nails in the end that they poked into the rear ends of the oxen to make them move, were the best-paid men in the forest.

This was before Jimmy Hoffa got big raises for men who held onto steering wheels and got mechanical horsepower to move large trailers long distances.

There is something about a teamster that means, "Don't mess with me; just give me more." It worked back then. They kept the oxen moving.

Poor oxen. They had to pull unbelievably heavy loads of trees to the mill. Ten of them at a time would be hooked to a half-dozen sixty-foot sections of tree trunks, each weighing more than any power on earth could move, except for an ox with a nail jabbed in its rear.

After the teamsters came the fallers, the men who spent their lives chopping and sawing and then risked their lives when the tree fell. They looked at the teamsters and said, "No way could I get those oxen to move."

The way to wealth often depends less on the energy you put in than on the image you put out. Teamsters were heavy on bravado, and loud. The fallers were just exhausted.

Next in the pay scale came the mill workers, those who went to work every day that they were not too drunk to make it to their post. They pulled on the logs and put them in their right slots and pulled the ropes that made the saws move and hoped their fingers were not in the way.

They made only half of what the fallers got, who made much less than the teamsters. Moral? Don't take a job on an assembly line or, if you do, invent a new way to get the goods to market.

But at the bottom of the pay scale was the Pig Man.

"It is all I deserve," Joshua said to me.

"No, you could make a new life for yourself. You could get an axe or a stick with a nail in it and move right up."

I was hoping to inspire him but as is the case with most people who are somewhere that they don't want to be, he was convinced that that was his place and he could not escape.

The skid road that he was greasing to make it skid better later became East Hastings Street. Other skid roads became Georgia and Granville Streets. But I was most interested in Joshua, the man with the name from the Bible, who thought his miserable condition was preordained and was what he deserved.

I thought about that 150 years later when I was reporting on some of the folks who were living on the new skid road, which now has a thirty-kilometre-an-hour speed limit because the local citizens cross the street without looking. These new inhabitants of skid road were stinking and staggering and living for the next injection of drugs.

"What's wrong?" I asked.

"I really want to be like one of those people in the BMWs who drive by but I am stuck in this stinking hole."

Many of them said that.

"Why don't you leave?" I asked.

"Can't," they said. "We are stuck here. It's what we deserve."

"Why?" I asked.

"Because we screwed up our lives and this is all we have."

I asked the same thing of many people who were drinking too much and snorting too much cocaine and who had jobs they hated.

"Why don't you change?" I asked.

"Can't," they said. "We are stuck here."

"Did you ever try?" I asked.

"No. There's no point in trying," they said. "There is no way out."

I asked Joshua the same thing. "Why don't you get one of those sticks with the nail in the end and say you want to learn to be a teamster?"

"Are you kidding?" he said. "I could never do that. I am stuck right here, greasing the skids and drinking beer outside the saloon."

I have to tell you I have been doing this job of reporting for more than 150 years and besides the laptop and the iPhone not much has changed in what the subjects of the stories are. I see those who are stuck at the bottom saying they can't move up because… and then they stop. "I don't know why I can't move up, but I just can't. You don't understand."

On the other hand I have seen a few who have changed, and they all say, "I wish I had done this sooner."

All of them who have left the skid roads that are everywhere and in every time have said the same of those who have stayed: "They get very comfortable there, and they always have everyone above them to hate. It gives them something to live for."

Pity.

VANCOUVER: THAT'S QUITE A NAME

 told you how the town got the name Granville. In case you missed the chapter it was because the politicians wanted to flatter the colonial secretary in Britain who was named Granville and who was a lord even though he had never been here and might even have had a problem finding his namesake on a map.

The Hotel Vancouver was built and knocked down, then built and knocked down again. Each time it moved to a new location. The CPR executives were afraid new owners would compete against them with their old hotels.
City of Vancouver Archives
AM336-S3-2-: CVA 677-21

47

Then came William Cornelius Van Horne. I liked this guy. I liked him as much as I liked Gassy Jack. In fact, I loved this guy. Don't get any ideas; I loved him in a reporter kind of way because I learned so much from him. The people of Port Moody hated him, but heck, we can't please everyone.

He, an American, is the reason British Columbia is not part of America.

Van Horne was from Dutch ancestry, but he knew little about that. He was born in America and he knew his father wanted him to be a lawyer.

But William loved trains. So he went to work for the railroad. That was when he was fourteen. What did you do when you were fourteen?

I know that's a stupid question. Times are different and there is school and video games and after-school activities and more video games and who the heck asked you at fourteen what you wanted to do? On the other hand no one asked William either and he got a job on the railroad. He did everything. He cleaned, he fixed, he did fourteen-year-olds' jobs. And he worked hard. And in time he moved into management. And in more time he got an offer to work in a foreign country for the newly formed Canadian Pacific Railway.

He did not need a passport. But he quickly rose up to be president of the CPR. No one cared that he wasn't a C.

This was a time when you rose up or failed based on what you could do, period, much like what I see today, despite those who say that it's not true.

Anyway, William was the head of the CPR at a time of great tribulation. The people of the Pacific coast, after which the railroad was named, wanted to have the railroad come to the Pacific. It seemed obvious to them. In fact, it seems obvious to me even now, a century and a half later.

The people in the west said if they did not have a connection with those in the east then they would join those in the south. Washington and Oregon and even California were closer to British Columbia than Ontario or Quebec.

"Give us a railroad or we will salute the stars and stripes." Even the English people were saying this, though they tried to hide their accents when they said it.

William felt the pull of the land of his birth. He felt the patriotic strings singing to him. The idea of the western part of Canada joining the US would be good for his home and native land.

On the other hand the joining up of the east and west of Canada would be good for his wallet.

Huummm, he thought. He probably thought for two or three seconds before he said: "Build the tracks to the Pacific."

This was one of Canada's greatest achievements. The steel rails were joined and the mountains were blasted away and the hills were levelled and the Chinese workers were killed.

That part of the story we often leave out. There were many white men who were blown apart too, but mostly it was the Chinese. Back then we figured if the Chinese wanted to live here badly enough they would not mind dying when they got here.

Anyhow, without going into the darker parts of the history, the railroad was finished and the tracks ended at Port Moody. They ended there because the road that the Royal Engineers built ended at Port Moody and that was because Burrard Inlet ended at Port Moody.

All the incoming sailing ships dropped their anchors at Port Moody. The saloons were open in Port Moody. Rosa's Spaghetti House would one day be open in Port Moody and there would be a lineup every night because her cooking was good and her prices were low.

And the people of Port Moody were happy—until William got off the train in Port Moody.

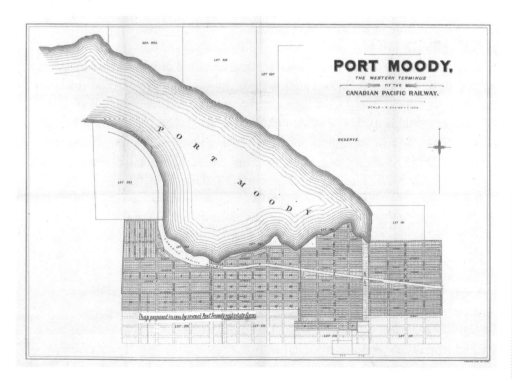

Port Moody was going to be the western terminus of the Canadian Pacific Railway before Van Horne chose to locate it in Vancouver—on something of a whim.
City of Vancouver Archives AM54-S4-: Out P706

"Not much of a town," he said.

I know because I was there. I saw William look around like someone who had just gotten off an airplane at a dream vacation spot and had seen only a bunch of shacks and a flashing motel sign.

"This is not what the travel agent told us," he said.

He asked a friend what else there was to see and I went along for the walk. After a day and a half of hiking farther west, past the sawmill, past Gassy's saloon… actually we did not pass Gassy's saloon. We went inside and invested a few hours of social research into the future of the land.

By the time William came out of the bar he had made some new friends for life and decided this might be the best place in the world to live.

He asked his friend, Lauchlan Hamilton, to get a boat and show him around. Lauchlan worked for the railroad. He was the land commissioner, which meant he was in charge of all the land that the railroad went through, which meant the more tracks William laid down, the more land Lauchlan had to play with. Lauchlan would do anything for William, including rowing a boat.

I got in and we rowed out past where the Nine O'Clock Gun is now. We rowed far out into the inlet. We rowed until Lauchlan got tired, but that did not matter because William was enthralled.

"This is *beautiful*," he said.

That is a direct quote. I know, because instead of rowing I was taking notes.

"We should bring the railroad out to here," he said, looking back at the shoreline.

That was all it took. There was no meeting of the executive board of the railroad. There was no consultation with the stockholders. William looked at the view that the SeaBus passengers now have and said, much like God is said to have said in the book of Genesis, "This is good. I like it. We'll keep it."

But God was not quite so greedy. He just said it was good and he let the people have it. William said it was good but wanted to keep much of it for his company.

He asked Lauchlan what this place was called?

"Granville," said Lauchlan.

"That's dumb," said William. "Who's Granville?"

William was told about Granville, and then the American head of the Canadian Pacific Railway said, "When our trains stop here it will become a great city and a great city needs a great name, not, what did you say it was called?"

"Granville."

"Dumb name. He's a nobody."

Both Lauchlan and I watched the big man think.

"Who is the most famous man in the world?" he asked.

"Jesus?" said Lauchlan.

"Colonel Moody?" I said. He was the leader of the Royal Engineers.

"*No!*" said William. "It is George Vancouver."

"Of course," we said, because we did not want to disagree with William Van Horne when we were out at sea and the Kitsilano Coast Guard base had not yet been built or disbanded.

"Captain Vancouver was English, wasn't he? He was here once, wasn't he? He is famous, isn't he?"

William was listing qualifications faster than I could take notes.

"Well, let us name the city that will be here Vancouver," he said.

And that was it. By the time we rowed back to Gastown the entire city then and forever would be called Vancouver. No, there was no white paper, green paper, plebiscite or focus group. Mr. Van Horne, president of the CPR, said what he wanted to say and that was it.

I did not want to tell William the rest of the story of Captain George Vancouver. When someone is high on a thought it is never a good idea to tell him the other side of the story.

The Captain Vancouver story happened before I was born, but during my off-hours as a Sapper I did a lot of reading and it is amazing what you can learn from books.

Poor George Vancouver. He was a hero when he returned to England from his third trip to the west coast of North America, but you know how quickly fame can fade. Ask a politician or a television anchor.

Several of the men he had brought on board his ship held a grudge against him. They did not like the way they were treated. Usually the captain just shrugs his shoulders and says, "Buck up, fellows, that's the way it is on a British Royal Naval Ship where discipline is god, after God of course and Sunday morning services."

Captain George Vancouver died out of favour, forgotten and destitute, but luckily for him his legacy lives on in the city that bears his name. That really only happened because William Van Horne did not like the name Granville.
Royal BC Museum, BC Archives
PDP02252

But one of those who did not like being reprimanded was Thomas Pitt, the Second Baron Camelford.

His father was the First Baron Camelford and a member of the House of Lords, so the Second Baron was definitely in the upper, actually the upper-upper, class.

George Vancouver had worked his way up from lowly beginnings to be captain of a ship, and being captain over the upper-class baron who served on his ship was not an easy task. It wasn't easy for either of them.

However, Pitt the Baron wanted to go to sea and he ended up under Captain Vancouver. That spelled trouble in a boat.

Here is a list of some of the things the uppity British baron did:

In Tahiti he tried to trade a piece of broken barrel hoop for the favours of an island woman. The barrel hoop was stolen from the ship. Not only was that an insult to the girl (he could have at least offered an unbroken hoop) but offering anything and stealing anything were strictly against the captain's orders.

That was because when you combined barrel hoops and seamen with young, largely naked women things happened. In time you had a mutiny on the ship, like that one named the *Bounty*.

So no barrel hoops.

And the baron was flogged, which is what you do on a ship even if the flogger is a lowly captain and the floggee is a highly placed baron. The rules of the Royal Navy were that the captain was required to flog anyone who pilfered anything.

The baron did not care about the rules. He was mad and a mad baron is like a mad hatter with a title.

And then, off the coast of what would become British Columbia, Pitt the Baron tried to trade some trinkets with the Natives. That was another official no-no. Flogged again.

And then the baron was playing some upper-class tomfoolery with another officer and he broke a piece of glass that was used for navigating. Flogged again.

You can see how their relationship was less than ideal.

And finally, the baron was caught deep in sleep while he was supposed to be on watch. There is no crime at sea more serious. You can run into things, like an island, and sink the whole ship.

The baron was locked in irons.

Vancouver had other things to do, such as keeping his ship shipshape, mapping the West Coast and being diplomatic to the Spanish, who were doing the same thing, and he did not have time to deal with this young aristocrat. He found another ship going back to England and sent the baron on his way, along with a letter to the admiralty that did not say nice things about the baron.

In this reporting business I still find it strange how the seedy side of a story gets more coverage than the important events.

However, on with the seedy, because we want to sell papers:

Back in England Vancouver stepped off his ship a hero. Everyone loved him. He had made the world more understandable.

But, did he know that Thomas Pitt, the baron whom he had flogged, had a cousin who now was the prime minister of England? Of all the luck. The PM sent out negative press releases about the returning captain. It was like attack ads, and they turned many hero worshippers against their hero.

Then Thomas Pitt the Baron sent George Vancouver a letter insulting him and challenging him to a duel.

Vancouver said that he had done on the ship what was required of him, and he turned down the chance to shoot or get shot, stab or get stabbed.

"Come on, grow up," is what he wanted to say, but he said, "If you don't like what happened, let us go to court."

Instead, Thomas the Baron stalked Vancouver and assaulted him on a London street corner.

You know, if only they told you this stuff in school you would stay awake in your history lessons.

Anyway, the assault was stopped by a constable. Can you imagine that poor policeman trying to stop a fight between a cane-swinging aristocrat and a captain of the Royal Navy? They don't get paid enough.

The baron had friends in the press. Back then they could be bought, which gave future generations a bad name; the stories piled up and Vancouver was shunned. Vancouver's brother went hunting for the baron and beat him into a pulp and that resulted in more scandals, all accusing George Vancouver as the evil one. A few months earlier he had been the number one action figure; now he was a bum.

He could not fight back against the money of the Camelford family. He seldom came out of his house. He got sick and died, less than three years after returning to England. He was buried in near obscurity.

Luckily for us, you don't see any of that in the statue of Captain Vancouver behind city hall in Vancouver. There he is, tall and brave, pointing his finger at the city with his name. We still like you, George.

As for the name of the man who brought him down, well, I am happy to tell you it disappeared.

Thomas Pitt, Baron Camelford, went on with a life of fighting and lawsuits and pushing people down stairs and planting ugly stories with his reporter friends about his other friends.

Then one day he heard that another royal captain had been badmouthing him to a woman who was Pitt's mistress. This woman had been the captain's mistress before Pitt stepped in. Those daytime soap operas have been going on for a long time.

The two men wound up in a duel and there *is* justice in the world. Baron Camelford got shot through the chest and his spinal cord was severed, but he did not remain a paraplegic for long. He died three days later.

There was no known heir and the title of Camelford became extinct.

What's more, after he was buried someone stole his body. It was never found. That's the kind of ending I like.

But I did not want to tell William Van Horne that story. He was happy naming the city after a hero, and that is the way it should be. Had it not been for that decision in a rowboat Captain George Vancouver's name would still be mentioned, but probably just in a history class and then forgotten.

In case you can't get to the Hotel Vancouver, here is William Van Horne, president of the CPR, who made several momentous decisions that were to have a lasting impact on the City of Vancouver.
City of Vancouver Archives
AM54-S4-2-: CVA 371-450

If you would like to see a picture of William Van Horne one is on permanent display in the lobby of the Hotel Vancouver. That is because the hotel was one of the original CPR hotels, which the railroad built on acres of property it was given for every inch it moved the train across the country. It was a very good deal.

He is quite distinguished in his photograph, but knowing him as I do I know he would be furious if he learned that the Hotel Vancouver's name was altered when it was bought by a new company. Is there nothing sacred? Is branding more important than tradition? Of course.

Instead of the Hotel Vancouver it is now the Fairmont Hotel Vancouver. That makes the Fairmont people happy.

But I think George would still be proud—and surprised.

NAME THAT STREET

here is another story about names that I love. It's called "I Really Think I Am Very Important and How Can I Remind You of That?" or simply "Name That Street."

The fellow with us in the rowboat, Lauchlan Hamilton, was working for William Van Horne, and he was pretty high up in the chain of being important.

Okay, he had to row the boat but at least he was *in* the boat so you know where he stood—or sat.

Hamilton set up his camp on the south side of False Creek in 1886. Faced with a jumble of cut forest he planned the streets and avenues of a great city. I make fun of him for naming a street after himself, but he did an amazing job.
City of Vancouver Archives
AM54-S4-: Dist P36

He was the land manager for the CPR, which meant if the railroad had land he was the manager of it, and the CPR had a lot of land. The Canadian government had given the company twenty-five million acres of Canada for building a set of narrow tracks across the country.

One of the duties of Lauchlan Hamilton was to lay out some new streets in the new city and name them. He was thirty-three years old.

On his very first day with a survey spike and a notebook he went into the forest a half-hour walk to the west of Gastown and said, "This is where we will officially begin the city."

"Why here?" I asked.

"I like it," he said.

"But why here? Why not over there?"

"Are you a reporter or a critic?" he asked.

"Okay, you got me. But I was still wondering why you picked this spot in the forest to start a world-class city."

Lauchlan Hamilton looked at me as if I was the dumbest creature on earth. Okay, not far from the truth, but why here?

"I have no idea," he said. "But we have to begin somewhere and next to this tree is as good as next to that tree."

He drove in the spike and made a note in his book.

"What are you going to name the street?" I asked.

Lauchlan looked around. Here he was in the middle of a forest. Have you ever been in the middle of a forest? You are lost even if you know where you are. You feel tiny. You feel insignificant. That is how Lauchlan and I felt.

"Well, all the big names have been taken," he said. "But I have an idea."

He scribbled in his notebook. I had no idea what he was going to call the number one street in the new city of Vancouver. It might be Smith or Jones. But no. It turned out that Lauchlan Hamilton was a man of strong self-appreciation.

He had the television reporter's syndrome of wanting to be seen. Some TV reporters cannot go through a day or a story without standing in front of the camera and saying what would have been better said over pictures of whatever it is that they are talking about.

Lauchlan Hamilton was a young man in his thirties when he laid out the streets of Vancouver. The street that began where he first drove in his survey spike he named Hamilton.

City of Vancouver Archives
AM54-S4-: Port P291

It is called the Stand-Up, and reporters love it. It is when they get to say, "Look at Me." They are talking about politics or floods or famine or death, but the most important part of the story is when they stand in front of the camera and talk.

Some reporters will apply makeup before they do a stand-up. It is strange to watch someone in front of a burning building slip into a car and touch up the face before coming out to stand in front of the flames.

"Two people died in this tragedy tonight. The neighbours are heartbroken."

Then, to the cameraman, "How did I look?"

If you assume that it is a woman, yes, but men are just as bad. "Get me into every shot. I want the audience to know that I am here, caring and feeling and being part of the story."

Of course Lauchlan Hamilton did not have a camera or a television station to make his presence known. So he improvised.

"I will call this first street in the new mega-world-class city that will grow here, I will call the street so that everyone will know where it all began, I will call it... [he paused for effect but there were only trees and me waiting for his next word] *Hamilton* Street."

Gee, where did you get that name from?

If you go to the corner of Hamilton and Hastings, on the side of a building you will see a plaque dedicated to Hamilton that says, "In the silent solitude of the primeval forest he drove a wooden stake into the earth and commenced to measure an empty land into the streets of Vancouver."

But as with many who seek fame there is often a downside.

Lauchlan Hamilton would have freaked out if he had known that the city's most famous hemp shop, where marijuana is the only topic and inhaling is the goal, is only a few steps away from where his name went up on a pole.

DAVIE STREET

here is another street that I love to visit. This one turned out just the way it should.

If I say Davie Street to you, you get a picture of men holding hands with men. And women holding hands with women.

How did this happen? I don't mean how did the hand-holding happen. That is not even a question anymore. But how did Davie Street become the hand-holding street where the hands that are holding hands are the same as the hands they are holding?

My editors in the old newspaper kept saying I can't say that because it doesn't make any sense, but I say I get the picture.

There is a lot of hand-holding on Davie. It is a warm and loving street. There are pink bus stop shelters and rainbow flags and Hamburger Mary's and other places where the hands that serve you are the same as the hands they will be holding later, after work.

Now go back, to about 125 years ago. That is five generations. It is your great-great-great-grandfather. You probably don't know if he strolled on Davie Street.

But there was a politician who did, before it was called Davie Street. He had three first names, which he always used: Alexander Edmund Batson. He told his friends to call him A.E.B., which was hard to say. I just called him Alex.

And his last name? I bet you guessed. It was Davie.

And Davie liked to hold hands, with men.

But he lived in an age when people like him in England went to jail for doing that. In a bad bit of timing he was born in England, but in a good move his parents got on a sailing ship and came to Canada and ended up in British Columbia.

I've got to tell you that kind of hand-holding was not looked on fondly here either, but at least you did not go to jail for it. On the other hand there were social norms, and Alex got married and had four kids. There are many hand-holding people who have the same story.

And then he became a lawyer. He was the first man to get his entire law education in British Columbia. That was amazing because only twenty years earlier—you can remember back twenty years—there were no lawyers on the mainland of British Columbia.

The lawyer business was important because the next step for Alex was in politics and he became the Attorney General under Premier William Smithe. He has a street named after him, too.

Alexander Davie was a brave man. Being premier of the province was easy, but can you imagine admitting you are gay in a town of lumberjacks?
Royal BC Museum, BC Archives
D-07869

That all sounds like the typical story of a politician, except Davie was gay, openly gay with gay friends. He was gay in a town of lumberjacks and railroad men. This was not easy.

I had coffee with him one day and asked how he survived.

"Be nice," he said.

I thought he was referring to my question.

"I am nice," I said.

"I'm sure you are, but I mean I try to be nice to everyone, even the ones who are not nice to me."

I met some of his friends and they all said Alex was a nice guy, nice in the nicest way. He was kind, thoughtful, smart, good-looking and helpful.

He and his friends built a small clubhouse far from the noisy and hard-drinking part of town. It was on a street with no name, but it was on Lauchlan Hamilton's map of what he wanted the city to look like. That map is still around; you can find it by looking up the CPR 1887 Plan for Vancouver.

If he were here now, Alexander Davie would lead the Pride Parade past the street with his name and then run back to cheer those at the end. He is the unofficial patron saint of the street that has become a village.

Photo by Stephanie Vacher

Hamilton had mapped out streets and avenues on what would become downtown Vancouver and the West End. There were no survey spikes in the ground, but the streets were on the map. Some were just ditches cut through the forest. Some were skid roads that would become major streets.

Davie and his friends went to one of the smaller streets, just twenty-five feet wide but peaceful and safe. It was a short walk from False Creek. That was the home of their clubhouse.

Then things changed drastically in Davie's life. The premier died in office and Davie was offered the job. Great, what a wonderful opportunity, except he was sick. I have no idea what he was sick with but he was sick. He took the job but almost immediately went to California to recuperate. He tried to run the province through letter writing.

He came back almost a year later but he was still sick, and he died shortly after that. He was forty-one.

It was a remarkable thing that he was not shunned, even after death. The fact that he was gay and did not hide it did not come into consideration when it was decided a street should be named for him, but which street?

Davie's friends had no trouble telling the politicians which street. They had improved their clubhouse and the street on which it sat was named Davie.

Except for a few farmers who worked the land that was named after them, almost no one had ever seen or walked on the street that carried their name.

Davie not only walked on his own street but it is the only one in Vancouver that took on the character of its namesake. His clubhouse was across the street and a little to the west of where Celebrities nightclub is now. The club was the first openly gay nightspot in British Columbia. Davie would fit right in.

BEER AND MORE BEER

et's get back to a more universal subject than sex and politics and street names. Let us talk of beer.

Did you know beer was the first alcoholic drink in the world? I read that somewhere so I know it is true.

It is easier to throw a handful of weeds and grass and seeds into a pot and add some water and wait than it is to cultivate grapes.

The Egyptians built their giant, pointed funeral homes fuelled with beer. How do you think they got all those slaves to keep on hauling rocks up the incline? It wasn't all the whip. It was beer.

Wine came later with the discovery that fruit could do what weeds did. Fruit produced more alcohol so it grew in favour quickly but beer was still number one. In fact, after water, beer is the world's favourite drink. It even beats tea and coffee.

But back to the story of beer and Vancouver.

After Gassy built his saloon and later his hotel, the main thing on his menu was of course beer, and he could not keep going back to New West for more of it.

What's more, the street behind his bar was filling up with more bars. That is where you see the Old Spaghetti Factory and the souvenir shops now. They were all, as I have said, open twenty-four hours a day—and they needed beer.

Some wise investors saw the need and took advantage of it. History, like a city, like a person, grows according to how someone sees something that needs to be done and does it. Simple.

Building a brewery was not hard. Finding the main ingredient was. The main thing in beer is water. Just ask anyone in the men's room after a night of drinking it.

And as you know, the water must be just right: the best, the purest, the clearest, the cleanest and, don't forget, the wettest. Just listen to the ads of some beers today. "Mountain water makes it best." Or "Desert water makes it best." I don't think there is a desert water, but if there was it would be the *best*.

Truly, what is needed is a supply that does not dry up. The new village had many streams and creeks but during a hot summer—when the dry, thirsty throats demanded the most—some of those creeks and streams gave the least.

But the Royal Engineers were there to save the day. Yes, once again, we Sappers were there when you needed us.

We had built a road almost from the doorstep of Gassy's saloon to the capital in New West. We called it Westminster Avenue. You call it Main Street. It joined up with the New Westminster Road, which you call Kingsway. We had built that a few years earlier.

And would you believe it, right at the point where the two roads met was this

Opposite page: Beer at work, beer after work. These employees of Doering and Marstrand Brewery in Mount Pleasant are relaxing with all the essentials of life—a barrel of beer, shotguns, dogs and a stuffed eagle. In 1890 seven breweries were operating at the same time near Broadway and Main Street.
City of Vancouver Archives
AM54-S4-: Dist P18

Photo by Stuart Thomson, City of Vancouver Archives AM1535-: CVA 99-1404

Busy workers load up trucks with crates of beer from the Vancouver Brewery. One of the most popular local beers was called Cascade, the name being the winning entry in a contest held by the Red Cross Brewery. The prize was $50, enough to put a hundred bottles of beer on your wall.

wonderful creek that flowed all year long, even in the hottest of beer-demanding summers.

The brewery investors said that would be the perfect place to go to work. They named the flow of water Brewery Creek. Brilliant. At last a name that meant something and was not named after a politician. Seven, count them, seven breweries went into operation around the creek and they, like the saloons they supplied, turned out beer twenty-four hours a day, seven days a week, even on the Sabbath.

The workers said they would get to church as soon as the last barrel was filled.

And speaking of barrels, cooperages opened not far away on False Creek. One good idea often leads to another.

One of the brewery buildings is still there. It is now a beautiful boutique and condo at Scotia and 6th Avenue. It is a nice place to visit and to think that this is where so many great ideas came from, followed by so many headaches.

Men pack bottles of beer in a Vancouver brewery. Thanks to the thriving brewing industry, business was booming for the barrel makers at False Creek.
Photo by Stuart Thomson, City of Vancouver Archives AM1535-: CVA 99-3071

And down at Gassy's I would listen to the loggers and mill workers sipping their beer and discussing the finer characteristics of the brew.

"You can taste a hint of salmon in this," one said.

"It has a lovely lingering bouquet of bear scat," said another, "and I can almost taste a hint of raccoon handwashing. The water from Brewery Creek is what makes this beer the *best*."

It is such a shame now. Brewery Creek has asphalt on top of it and buses and cars drive over it. You who were born too late will never know the subtle body that rabbit droppings can give to your beer. Pity.

I got to witness the construction of a bridge for the Canadian Pacific Railway in the late 1800s. Chinese workers were given the most dangerous jobs. Despite the prejudice against them, their work helped the railroad company build something that was nearly impossible.

Royal BC Museum, BC Archives
D-01440

THAT OLD CHUG-ALONG

f you grew up in Vancouver anytime before Expo 86 and you went to Kitsilano Beach you probably climbed on that old locomotive in the parking lot.

It was Engine 374. You could see that engraved right in the front. It stood on rails that were just long enough for its wheels. It stood in the rain and the snow, and on any days when it was not raining or snowing it stood under the feet and fingers of kids who climbed all over it.

It was wonderful fun but it was falling apart; a sad ending for the steam engine that saved Canada.

I know everyone in school learned about the first spike and the last spike, and that the people in British Columbia were going to leave Canada if they did not have a train that connected them with the rest of the country, but did you know that the railway was almost not built?

It cost huge amounts of cash to build the longest train line in the world and the CPR had run out of money. William Van Horne wanted to keep going because his company was getting such a good deal. They were given twenty miles of land on both sides of the tracks all the way across the country in return for laying down the steel, but no matter how much money they were going to get they could not finish the project. The cash they had raised and borrowed and squeezed out of investors was gone. Most of the money they owed was borrowed from the Government of Canada, which means from the people.

I was doing a series of stories on building the railroad when William Van Horne heard the news that they were broke.

"We can't raise any more. We can't borrow it. There *must* be something we can do." Then he said to someone, "Give me that newspaper."

He read the headlines and his eyebrows went up. There was a major rebellion going on in the territory of Saskatchewan. He had never been to Saskatchewan. The rebellious people were the Métis. He had heard about them, but he could not remember ever meeting one.

"That is the answer," he said.

I could see his genius at work. He had a problem and he figured out a solution, even though the solution would be very bad for some people.

"It says here in the newspaper that the government will have great difficulty putting down this rebellion because they can't get troops there."

He smiled.

"I will get them there," he said.

The only problem was the tracks going near a place that would later be called Winnipeg were not yet finished and those that were in place had never been tested.

"Finish them," he said.

If you think Canada never had a king you are only technically right. It had William Van Horne, an American, who acted as though he had a crown.

The tracks were finished within a few days and Van Horne told the prime minister to send his army on the new troop train to Saskatchewan. He did, and in a record nine days the guns of the government were there.

Poor Louis Riel, who had led the rebellion, was hanged for treason in 1885. That was not a good ending for him, but the Canadian government was so thankful to Van Horne that all the debt he owed the government was forgiven.

That part of the history of the CPR is written in small print.

There is another part of the building of the railroad that is not in the headlines of the CPR history. I was on the line when the work was being done and this is not something you joke about.

The white men who worked on the railroad were getting between $1 and $2.50 a day. Out of that they had to pay for their own food, their clothing, their medical care and their transportation from wherever they slept to where they were working. Rotten conditions.

Van Horne was not in the business of charity.

After a hundred non-stop days of back-breaking work (they had no days off) they were lucky if they had fifteen dollars left over.

Tough. But the Chinese who worked alongside the whites were paid half those wages. It was basically the same as being black in Alabama in the 1930s. About half the workers were Chinese, so Van Horne was making a big saving there.

At the end of a hundred days they had only a few dollars to send back to their families in China, which was the reason they had left home and travelled across an ocean to come here.

But there were other problems with being Chinese. If there was dynamite to be put into a cave to blow it up to make a tunnel, guess whose job that was? If you had to climb out over a cliff to string a cable, guess whose job that was?

And if you were killed, the officials of the railroad would not inform your family. They would tell the other Chinese to bury you alongside the tracks and forget you.

As for the young boys who were Chinese, well, someone had to hold the spikes while someone else with a twenty-pound sledgehammer would lift that hammer up high and then come slamming down with all his might. Usually they

Tunnels were blasted for the Canadian Pacific Railway mainly using Chinese workers. It is sad to say, but they were considered dispensable by the railroad employers.
Royal BC Museum, BC Archives
D-01477

hit the spike, but not always.

What I really enjoy nowadays is to report on the computer science and economics classes at the universities, which are almost all filled with Chinese students.

I'm supposed to be impartial but I like to say, "Right on."

Anyway, the train that made the people in the west happy and kept them in Canada reached Vancouver on May 23, 1887. At the front of it was Engine 374. That same engine is now in the Roundhouse Community Centre in Yaletown. It is the same engine that was at Kits Beach. But now you can go to the Roundhouse and climb up to where the engineer and fireman worked. You will not only be touching the past, you can touch your own past and pretend you are a kid again.

If I were a history teacher I would teach all my classes beside the train.

There is one other thing. You know that the Roundhouse is located in Yaletown. Here's the question. Why is that area called Yaletown?

Answer:... Well, not so fast. I don't want to make this easy for you.

Engine 374 pulled the first passenger train into Vancouver on May 23, 1887. Had it not been for that engine chugging into the city the citizens would probably have voted to join the US.
Photo by Major James Skitt Matthews, City of Vancouver Archives AM54-S4-: Can P6

First come with me back to one of my favourite towns. Have you ever driven up the Fraser Canyon? No, of course not. You go on the Coquihalla Highway. Quicker, but no soul. No history. On the canyon highway, which we Sappers helped to build, you pass through Yale. Only one in a thousand of you stops because honestly, there is nothing in Yale except a cemetery and a museum.

But when I was there it was the biggest city west of Chicago and north of San Francisco. And not only was it big, but it was bad. Really bad. There were bars on every corner and more bars between the corners. There were brothels and there were fights and there were murders. There was gold and there were guns and there were more fights and more bars.

Yale was at one time the biggest city west of Chicago and north of San Francisco. When the railroad repair shops were moved to Vancouver the people who went along named their part of the new city Yaletown.

City of Vancouver Archives
AM54-S4-: Out P706

You get the idea. It was not Disneyland. Actually, you may not get the idea because there is no place like Yale anywhere in Canada today. That was in the 1880s. Gold was flowing in from the mines, the railroad had its repair shops in Yale and the beer and whisky sellers made a fortune. You can see why the cemetery is still one of the lasting memories of the town.

However, eventually the city fathers in Vancouver wanted the railroad to move its main operations into the city and offered the CPR even more land in return for the move. The railroad took the offer and that is why there is a roundhouse in the middle of the city. Along with the trains, the CPR workers moved down and built their shacks next to the warehouses and repair shops and named the area after the only other place they knew: Yaletown.

When the railroad left the town of Yale and the gold petered out, the biggest, baddest hot spot in the country faded away. Now you drive through it, see a gas station and a motel, and keep on going.

It is right about there that your kids start saying: "This drive is boring. There's nothing to do."

I can only tell your kids that if they stepped through the doors of history they would be dodging bullets, looking at men and women doing things their parents would not let them look at, seeing beer barrels rolling down the main street and watching the Hanging Judge trying to keep the peace.

They would never again say history is boring.

THE HANGING JUDGE

y the way, do you know about him? He was a good buddy of mine. They called him the Hanging Judge because he did that sometimes, but sometimes he would fight day and night, even going without sleep, to free someone who he thought was innocent, even when others swore he was not.

And one thing I know for sure is he would look at the justice system now and say, *"What the heck is that??"*

Judge Matthew Baillie Begbie, Chief Justice of BC, treasured his brief times for relaxing. For twelve years he was the only judge in the colony, travelling by horseback and by foot, sleeping in a tent and holding court in forests and mining camps.
Royal BC Museum, BC Archives
B-05748

I can imagine him now with his judge's robes in a knapsack, sitting in the back row of a fancy, expensive modern courtroom, shaking his head in disbelief.

"How can a trial go on for six months?" he would ask me. "The crime only took six minutes."

"Lawyers," I would answer.

"And how come this case is going to trial now? The crime took place six years ago?"

"Lawyers," I would answer.

He would get up and walk out of the courtroom into the corridors filled with: "Lawyers? Are all those people lawyers?" he would ask.

"Don't answer," he would tell me.

Matthew Begbie seldom listened to lawyers. He was a judge. The job of a judge was to judge after he listened to the people involved. He made allowances if they were stumbling, bumbling inarticulate miners with a threadbare vocabulary, and he cut through the foam if they were men who could spin a fascinating yarn with flowery, exciting speech.

He listened, he thought, he decided.

I met him shortly after I arrived in this new land with the Royal Engineers. We, as I have told you, were here to keep the peace and build the roads and do a thousand other things. Judge Matthew Begbie was sent from England to decide right from wrong, which was a much harder job than I had.

It was 1859 and there was trouble in Yale over gold. Gee, there was a surprise. Two groups of American miners from California were having a dispute. It was not only about gold. It was about a black American who had been invited to the Christmas dance in town and neither group wanted blacks to be at any function. It was also about the fact that these two groups had been trying to kill each other back in San Francisco, and it was about who could bribe the local Justices of the Peace.

It was also about Canada not being able to handle problems in its own country and so the country should be taken over by America. So thought the Americans.

In short, it was an unholy mess. The black man was in jail, even though he had done nothing wrong, and the two feuding groups had charged each other with various crimes. Both sets of charges had been laid before the Justices, who had been bribed.

Anyway, Judge Begbie put his judicial robes in a knapsack along with his black cap (he wore that when he sentenced someone to death) and we set out, first on foot, then by canoe, then on foot, then by canoe. It was snowing. Judge Begbie kept going.

"Come on, fellows," he said to us Sappers. "Can't you keep up?"

He had been educated at Oxford and had been on his way to becoming a very important lawyer in London when someone asked him if would take the post of Judge of British Columbia.

"Where is that?" he asked.

He was shown on a map.

"What's there?"

"Trees, miners, gold and rain."

"What about culture, entertainment, theatre, dinners and ladies?"

"No. None of the above," he was told.

"Okay, I will try," he said.

He became the first judge of the colony. His territory went from New Westminster to Kamloops. He walked the distance. Occasionally he rode a horse, sometimes he was in a canoe, but usually he walked.

He carried a tent and that became his travelling hotel. He fished for his dinner. When he got to a mining camp where there was a dispute he used a tree stump as his high court bench. He listened, deliberated and decided. He was justice as it should be.

If he was wearing his black hat when he sat down on the stump everyone knew the verdict. That hat was the single most powerful symbol in a land nearly as large as Europe.

Over his career he sentenced twenty-seven men to hang. Anyone who killed anyone else was hanged. Simple. Did he send anyone who was innocent to the rope?

We don't know but he did not think so because even as a judge he fought for the rights of everyone.

He already spoke French, Spanish and Italian but when he came here he

The people of BC called Judge Begbie the Hanging Judge, because that was part of his job, but he was also fair and would fight for the rights of Native Canadians and Chinese when others would not.
Royal BC Museum, BC Archives
A-06955

learned several aboriginal languages and, even though it would be frowned on by his colleagues in England, he allowed witnesses and Natives who were in court to swear on anything they believed was sacred. It did not have to be the Bible.

I liked this man. He saw what was right and what was wrong and he decided. Unlike today, he did not say he would deliberate on a case for a month and then give a verdict that would take a half-hour to deliver. He listened, he looked, he deliberated and made his decision all on the day of the trial. How is that for speedy justice?

Right or wrong, it worked, and when I was with him in Yale he did the same. One day of listening to the feuding Americans and he made his judgment. He freed the black man who had been accused of nothing more than being black and he fined one of the Americans from California for obstruction of justice. Then he fired the Justices of the Peace who had been bribed. No shots were fired and no one complained. His self-confidence was so strong that what he said was final.

No appeals. No tying up the court for years. Everyone went back to looking for gold because, like children, they had been told who was right, who was wrong and what they should do.

He loved the judging and he loved the land. The only thing that the judge missed was gossip. He wrote to a friend in England and he asked for gossip because he said there were only men here and the society needed women to make things interesting. This was not like email. He had to wait six months for an answer.

He lived his social life by his letters and meanwhile he gave out justice in a way not seen since. I know if I could take him into a courtroom now he would gag.

"Ten years for murder? But he will get out in seven. Seven years in a cell with cablevision?"

Luckily for him I won't take him there.

Cordova St.

THE BIG FLAME-OUT

 "This is the modern way of cutting trees," the man with the axe said to me.

We were standing at the edge of a roughly five-hundred-acre ancient forest. The trees were so thick the sun did not get to the ground. Behind us was Burrard Inlet. A little to our left was Gastown, though the upper crust were calling it Granville because they didn't want people to think they lived in a place that was built on beer.

Just five weeks after the fire that burned everything to the ground the city was coming back. Businesses were being rebuilt by volunteers, and the Hastings Mill, which amazingly was spared from the flames, donated its lumber to anyone who asked. The buildings here are on Cordova Street looking west from Carrall.
City of Vancouver Archives
AM54-S4-: Str P7.1

"First we cut some of those smaller trees, the ones that are only about three hundred years old. Babies," he laughed.

"In the old days we would cut right through them but this modern way is so simple and fast."

I did not trust this. I knew modern ways were not always so good. It was simpler to load a rifle from the breech, but it killed many more men than the slower way of loading from the muzzle. Is that good or bad?

The logger chopped one tree, then another, then another. We talked about the weather and how it had been so hot and dry for so long.

"Things are changing," he said. "I think all the smoke from the mill is pushing away the rain."

Could be, I thought. The smoke certainly had pushed away the clean air.

Then, while a couple of his buddies chopped away on one giant tree—a mammoth monster that might have been growing for a thousand years—my friend went on chopping at the baby trees.

Just as a side note, because I have been around for a while, outside of a few parks there are no trees left in the province that are as big as those he called "babies" back then. In fact the trees that are left are really embryos. But back to the story.

"So we partially cut these and those and those over there."

He pointed to a wide semicircle of forest.

"And we line them up. This is very scientific or mathematical or something with a big word."

Whatever the word, he was aiming so that the giant of a tree would fall on two huge but slightly smaller trees. Then those trees would each hit two more trees as they fell and those four would smash into eight more and before they lost their energy those eight could bring down as many as sixteen more. If everything went well a total of thirty-one trees could come down with a single stroke of the saw. Of course they never got that perfect score but it was still a marvel of calculation.

"Actually, we've been working on this for a few days," he said to me. "I didn't want to keep you waiting, you being an important newspaper reporter. I want you to see this so you know what the future of logging is going to be."

I took out my notebook but only to make him feel important. So far my notes would be "chop tree, line up tree" and I did not want to waste a page writing that. Trees were easy to come by, paper was not.

GEO. GIBSON   ALD. GRIFFITHS   ALD. BALFOUR   ALD. DUNN   J.J. BLAKE   ALD. HUMPHRIES   G. F. BALDWIN   DR. McGUIGAN
CITY SOLICITOR   CITY TREASURER

In the wake of the fire a makeshift tent became City Hall for a council meeting in September of 1886. It was half a stunt and half for real, but it was one time that politicians got high ratings. City of Vancouver Archives AM1477-1-S5-: CVA 1477-419

"So how do you like the new city?" I asked.

"What city?"

"This one. The one you are standing in."

"This is a city?" he asked. "Since when?"

"Two months ago. Granville is a city. City council, government, politicians, the works. No taxes yet, but just you wait."

He looked bewildered.

"A city? Can we still get beer?"

Yes, he could get beer, a tall schooner for a nickel, still twenty-four hours a day. Making money was more important than making rules on beer drinking. And there was a lot of money to be made. Only a year before, you could buy a building lot in Gastown for sixty-six dollars. Then the CPR announced they would run their tracks right into the new city.

That sixty-six dollar investment became a two thousand dollar piece of property almost overnight.

Folks had been pouring into the new townsite for months. New buildings were going up with the wood still sticky from sap. The beer was flowing and the real estate was growing while my friend in the woods was chopping.

The place where he was standing would later be Burrard Street where it meets False Creek. What he was looking at would later be the steel and glass buildings of downtown Vancouver.

"As I was saying," he said, "we have a modern way of clearing these trees."

His buddies told him the big one was ready to go.

"Get back," he said to me. "In a minute no one in there is going to be alive."

He told his friends to give the big one the last few strokes on the saw and then came the crack that I had heard so many times before as a giant's shin bone was broken. But instead of just one tree falling it hit half a dozen others in a row, which instantly started crashing to the earth. Before they hit the ground they hit others and right before my eyes, like dominoes in a rolling thunder louder than anything I had ever heard, including cannon fire, a vast field of what had been forest went smashing to the ground.

The dust, the dirt, the screaming of birds that followed the slow return of silence was awe inspiring—or awful. It depends if you had a conscience or not.

"Pretty good, huh?" he said.

The sky was there up where the sky should be, but now we could see the sky, through the smoke. In two minutes part of a forest was gone.

"We could have this whole place cleared in a couple of weeks," he said. "In the old days it would have taken years."

"But half of those trees, no, not half those trees, *most* of those trees are wasted. They can't go to the mill. They're shattered."

He shrugged. "Doesn't matter. You don't really think we are going to run out of trees, do you?"

Sadly, I have to tell you, again because I watched all this, the practice of logging by bowling ball became the way of the woods. Every society since the start has had the same saying: "We grow too soon old and too late smart." You don't have to ask why.

We went back to the city for a beer. My friend was happy.

A few of the big trunks were cut up and pulled out by oxen. The rest, the slash, the wasted wood and leaves and twigs, was twenty-five feet deep in some places. And as we had talked about just a few minutes earlier, it was hot. Day after day, as sometimes happens now in the summer, the sun came out full bore and the earth heated up and even though there was smoke in the air the air was hot and dry and the rain did not come.

And then more trees were felled the same way.

This Ronald Steam Pumper, attended by men of the Volunteer Fire Brigade outside No. 2 Firehall on Seymour Street, is an example of the firefighting equipment of the 1880s.
Photo by Bailey Bros., Vancouver Public Library 19789

The only way to get rid of the slash was to burn it. This would be safe because men and oxen, mostly the oxen, had pulled the debris into piles. Just start one of them burning and in a few hot hours the pile would be smouldering ash. Then start another one. Okay, sometimes start two of them at once because nothing is going to happen.

The air was thick with air that you could not breathe, but so what? It was always thick with smoke. Sometimes it was thicker, but at the edge of the woods, out where nature was still pristine next to a brand new city, who would complain that they couldn't breathe?

It was a Sunday, a few days after I had seen the new method of logging. It was June 13, 1886. There were women and children now living in some of the newer houses. They had brought furniture with them to this new land where their families would have a new beginning. In fact, they had brought everything they could bring with them: rare photos, family bibles, keepsakes from their grandparents.

There was money to be made with the railroad coming and gold being discovered again in the north and the sawmills working within walking distance of home. And the air would not always be smoky.

While they were in church one of those little slash-burning fires got slightly out of control. Then it got largely out of control. Then a railway crew started fighting it, but what could you do? Throw dirt on it? It was close to the roundhouse they were building. The roundhouse was where the Roundhouse Community Centre is now.

Dry, burning wood was rising in the air from the fire. It was like a fire in a fireplace where sometimes you see newspaper rising when it first starts. Only now chunks of burning wood were rising. Then the best thing in the world happened to the fire. It got windy. Wind is like music for a fire. It makes the flames dance. And then the rising chunks of burning wood flew to the next pile of trees and slash. Then more burning wood rose in the air and the wind blew it to the next pile.

In too short a time to do anything, even though there was nothing they could do, slash piles were burning everywhere and their flames were reaching out and joining hands to become one giant fire. The wind became a gale and flaming chunks of wood the size of split logs were carried into the sky to come bombing down on dry piles of slash near the new homes.

The piles near where Victory Square is now exploded into fire. That was a three-minute walk to the newest of the new homes—but no one was walking. Those who were anywhere near were running and screaming and grabbing children. There was no time to get anything from any home. The fire was now moving faster than a man could run.

Those caught by the howling monster did not catch on fire; they vaporized. The same with houses. There was no igniting and burning. There was only an explosion and the house was gone.

Many ran to the water but the heat was so intense they could only breathe by holding their faces close to the surface.

A man driving a horse and wagon was caught while trying to turn around. Both he and the horse were cremated alive in the middle of the street. Three men who worked for the railroad volunteered to fight the fire. They were never seen again.

The day after the great fire of 1886 a few photographer friends of mine were able to find enough unburnt equipment to take this picture. Almost everything was gone.

Photo by J.A. Brock and H.T. Devine, City of Vancouver Archives AM1477-1-S5-: CVA 1477-416

A black man, a bartender at the Sunny Side hotel, grabbed a woman and her son and carried them to safety. He said his name was Joe.

There is no record of how many died. The fire was over in less than an hour and basically every structure except for a few outlying buildings was gone. There was nothing left.

Many of the homeless refugees were picked up by canoe and tug from the Mission Reserve across Burrard Inlet. The water was coated with blackened wood. Others found their way to the water of False Creek. None of the citizens of this new city now had any possessions other than what they had in their pockets.

The next morning help came from New Westminster. Blankets and food and water were given to the survivors. The Hastings Mill, which had entirely escaped the flames, emptied its store of everything for the people. The biggest immediate need was to treat the burns. Mud was the only remedy.

But the next morning beer also arrived from New West. It, too, helped soothe the pain.

The manager of the mill donated all the lumber in the yard free of charge for rebuilding the city.

If anything like that happens today, even ridiculously smaller in scope, there are inquiries, investigations, allegations, charges, countercharges, lawyers, white papers, green papers, cover-ups, press releases, press conferences and despair.

Not so with the people who built this city. In little over a month things were back to normal.

Outlining the tragic events of 1886, this map was pieced together years later with help from survivors who remembered that fateful day. Major J.S. Matthews noted that one lady who saw the fire from a small boat in Coal Harbour described it as "A grand but awful sight." In truth, it was hell.
Photo by Major J.S. Matthews, City of Vancouver Archives AM1562-: 75-54

Joe Fortes wears his trademark enormous smile at English Bay in 1905, with the buildings of the West End visible in the background. Joe was the city's first black man and the amazing thing was that, even in a white society, he was so popular no one noticed his colour.
Photo by Philip Timms, City of Vancouver Archives AM336-S3-2-: CVA 677-440

OLD JOE

e could have taught some priests so much. He was Catholic and he could have saved the Pope a mess of headaches and some really bad press.

He was also an athlete and he could have taught some coaches so much.

82

But no, they did not learn anything and Joe went about his life being one of the neatest, coolest, friendliest oddballs in the city, possibly in the history of the city, with no one learning anything from him.

And *no*, he was not a restaurant owner. I mention Joe Fortes to some of my friends now and they say, "Good place to eat."

No, no, and *no*!

Scratch my balding head; how can some intelligent people not know some of the great people who lived such a short time ago in their own city? I say "intelligent" people because they watch a lot of TV and they know who survived on the island and which news anchors are pregnant. You have to have advanced TV degrees to reach that level of knowledge.

Two people who work for the biggest of the TV stations in Vancouver, one of whom is in management, did not know Joe Fortes did anything except sell oysters in a fancy restaurant just off Robson Street.

I rest my case. I am not sure what my case is, but the bottom line is watch less TV, read more and consume some history. It is better than potato chips.

Back to Joe. His parents wanted him to be a doctor. Many parents have the same wish for their kids. Some of his relatives in the Caribbean were doctors.

"Seraphim, we want you to be a doctor and save lives."

That was his mother speaking. They named him Seraphim from the Old Testament in the Bible. It meant he was an angel, a guardian angel.

But Seraphim wanted the sea. Many young boys, and now girls, want to go off to foreign lands to see what they can see. It is exciting and adventurous and you don't have to spend a lot of time in school like you do to be a doctor.

Seraphim went to sea and his parents were crushed. "He will never save anyone's life," they said.

They probably also said, "What are we going to tell the neighbours?" but that is only a guess.

Seraphim went to England on a sailing ship. He learned to pull up the sails and scrub the deck and load the coal and he was happy, which should have made his parents happy, but parents who want a doctor for a child are often not happy if their prescription is not followed.

Through occasional letters Seraphim learned how unhappy he had made his parents, which was not good for his well-being. There is a lesson in that: if you are a parent don't make your kids unhappy just because they don't do what you want them to do. If you don't let them go free you have a robot instead of a child.

Seraphim left England heading for Panama City in a wooden ship with its belly full of coal. The coal would be used to keep the steam engines going that were digging the Panama Canal. This was only ten years after Gassy Jack had died, but Seraphim had never heard of him or the city that would be his home for life.

He and the other sailors unloaded the coal, which was done by hand, which is exhausting, sweaty, endless work. It is also the kind of work that turns arms into limbs of steel.

Then they loaded rocks into the ships to act as ballast in place of the coal. More sweat, more steel in the arms.

Then they sailed for Granville, way up the coast, to fill the ship with lumber. The job of a ship is never done. If you want to know what life was like then, jump into the cab of a long-haul trucker now. He never stops. If he is not moving and carrying something he is not making any money. The only difference is a trucker seldom gets any exercise and dies young because of his job while a sailor on a wooden ship never got anything but exercise and died young because of his job.

But between Victoria and the town called Granville, the ship Seraphim was on went through some fog, the same fog that we get now, but there was no radar or foghorn. The ship hit some rocks at low tide and almost sank.

It was towed into the harbour just outside the Hastings Sawmill and Seraphim got off the ship. It was the last time he would go to sea.

He got a job in the mill and immediately met a foul-mouthed, big-armed bigot who worked at the mill. There was some pushing and swearing and threatening and all the stuff that leads to a no-good ending.

The manager of the mill said they would have to settle their dispute with a fist fight, outside the mill.

That is where I met Seraphim. I had heard about the fight and wanted to cover it for the mill's newsletter.

In one corner was the foul-mouthed bigot. Lord, he was a nasty man, and he was big. Big like one of those tree trunks that were being sliced up in the mill. Big like you don't want to mess with him. Big like, BIG. And he smirked a lot. And he said things about Seraphim's skin colour that were not nice.

The ring was made by the hundred men who surrounded the two men without shirts and the ring was getting smaller every second.

The bigot spread out his arms and laughed. He had never been beaten in a fight.

Seraphim looked up and did the only thing he could. He smiled. When you smile you are either unbeatable or crazy.

I was at the ringside. I saw the smile. I thought this fellow was crazy. He is going to be pulverized and all he does is smile? Crazy.

This was a bare-knuckle fight. There was no referee. The three-minute rounds were timed by someone looking at his pocket watch, if he looked. Someone else held an iron pan and a hammer and banged it.

The two men went at each other, knuckle against knuckle against jaw against stomach. The big man, seen as the white man in the ring who was predestined to win, swung a wild right. Seraphim ducked. Then Seraphim came up with a right to the jaw. You could hear the crushing sound when fist met bone and teeth.

And then you could see the big man falling back into the crowd.

It made him angry.

He came at Seraphim like an elephant or a tiger. Actually, like an elephant *and* a tiger, even though no one had ever seen either of those. But the claws were out and the weight was there.

Seraphim ducked again, just in time, and drove his right fist into the stomach of his enemy. It went in deep. That was one of the hands that had loaded the coal on a ship and then unloaded it and then replaced the coal with large rocks.

The big man doubled over and then fell.

Seraphim waited for him to get up. That was odd. Usually in these fights when someone was down the next move was to pick him up by his hair and then batter him into the ground again.

Seraphim waited. And when the big man got up and put up his fists, Seraphim hit him with a left to one side of his head and then a right to the other.

The big man went down. He did not get up again.

I congratulated Seraphim and said he would make the headlines the next morning.

"I feel sorry for that fellow," he said. He spoke with a strange accent. It was the first time I had met anyone from the Caribbean. "He wanted to prove something and he failed."

"Oh, Lord, Seraphim, are you serious? You beat a miserable guy and you feel sorry for him?"

Headline the next day: "David Thumps Goliath and Feels Bad." I was still learning to write and thought clichés were good.

But aside from that, I can only tell you that after the fight Seraphim had no problems. He was never again mocked or insulted. He had a reputation now, which was one fist of iron and the other of steel. Pity he did not write a song about that.

Then came the matter of his name.

No one had ever heard a name like that and no one wanted to be the first to use it. You can't simply accept someone who is new with a strange name. What would your friends think? They might accuse you of being friendly with him and say that if you are friends with him you can't be friends with us. You know how nutty we humans are.

Imagine if you invited someone who wore a face-covering home for dinner. Your neighbours might think you were accepting them as they are and then what?

On the other hand you might say, "Guess who's coming to dinner?" and win an Oscar.

Just before Seraphim arrived in Vancouver there was an American songwriter named Stephen Foster. I went down to Ohio to meet him and I thought he was a neat guy. He was turning out hits like a one-man song factory.

Many were about the sweet life of the Old South. Many spoke of how loving and loyal and kind the slaves were. And the songs praised the beauty of the cotton fields. Stephen Foster had hit on an idea that sold very well.

He wrote more than two hundred songs, most of them big sellers.

He had only two problems; actually only one problem and one funny quirk. The problem was he was drunk most of the time. Somehow between bottles he could get out another song and then he'd black out for another day or so.

The quirk was he knew nothing about the South, old or new. He was only in it once and that was on a riverboat during his honeymoon. What he wrote about was what people wanted to believe—kind old happy black folks knowing their place in life and kind white folks who were always kind to the black folks.

This was such a good way of seeing things that Stephen Foster was called the Father of American Music.

And then he opened another bottle. His wife left him.

He wrote about Old Black Joe, who had left the old cotton fields for a better place.

And he opened another bottle. He moved to the Bowery in New York when it was the Bowery after which Main and Hastings was designed. He died there when he was thirty-seven. He had less than a dollar in his wallet.

But his music was still sung everywhere for the next hundred years, meaning for the next hundred years black people were expected to be nice and quiet and ride in the back of the bus and listen to songs about how good their lives were.

"Old Black Joe" was one of the most popular songs. It was sung by white kids in New York City elementary schools a hundred years after it was written, many of whom had never seen a black person except those washing dishes in the back of a diner.

And it was sung in the saloons in Gastown because there was no CRTC saying you could only have a certain percentage of foreign songs allowed per beer per bar.

"We will call you Joe," someone said to Seraphim. And then he wisely added, "If you don't mind."

Seraphim did not and Joe Fortes was born in his twenty-second year. He got a job as a bartender and despite all that temptation around him he did not drink. He was a devout Catholic and he went to church in Holy Rosary Church every Sunday.

But one day he went for a walk and found the ocean.

He looked at English Bay and thought this was better than a bar. The water was cold, but oh, it felt so good, he said. It was not like home, but it was not like Gastown and so he stayed. He put up a tent right in front of where the Sylvia Hotel is now and started on a happy life.

Throughout the 1890s this was Joe's home on English Bay. He lived in this tent until he found a shack nearby. A water fountain with his image on it now stands in Alexandra Park, close to his last home.
City of Vancouver Archives
AM54-S4-: Port P1725

He taught kids how to swim. He taught scores, then hundreds and more hundreds. The part of the story where he could have touched a kid improperly? Never happened. The part where he invited a kid home never happened. No, sir. He simply taught them to swim and went home and smoked his pipe. He did not know that one day he could be fined for smoking on a public beach.

If he was a priest there would have been no one coming along later to complain about the secret things he did. That never happened either.

After the tent he lived in a shack, which was more of a cottage, on the beach. *Shack* if he was black, *cottage* for whites, same building. But then came slum clearance, so it was definitely a shack. The city was growing and wanted to eliminate people living on the beach so they set fire to the homes that were there.

Except, what did they do when they came to Joe's?

He was the most popular person on the beach. To the city, the people said, "No. You cannot destroy his home."

Joe asked the mayor to spare him. The mayor was smart. City workers put his home on some skids, hooked them to two large horses and dragged Joe's cottage to the other end of the beach where Bidwell Street is now. Same view but away from the crowds. Sometimes city hall can do something right. Joe lived there for the rest of his life. There is a plaque on the ground in the middle of a grove of trees where his home stood.

He not only taught kids to swim, he also saved them and their parents from drowning. Swimming was not high on the list of things a person did during the reign of Queen Victoria. It was a rare adult who would strip down enough to go in the water but some did, and some did not know what to do when they got there and some of them started slipping under the surface.

Along came Joe. He is officially credited with saving twenty-six lives. That is quite a few, but unofficially he saved hundreds.

Joe teaches a woman to swim in English Bay in 1905. There are still many people who can look at this and say, "Joe taught my grandma how to swim and she taught my mother and she taught me." Photo by Philip Timms, City of Vancouver Archives AM336-S3-2-: CVA 677-421

However, a terrible tragedy happened one day when the tide was the lowest it had ever been. That is not a technically accurate fact—reporters never get those right—but the tide was so low people said they would walk to Japan.

Two young women tried it. Then the tide came in. They were caught in the undertow and dragged down. Their heavy, modesty-minded swimming clothes did not help them.

The kids on the beach called for Joe. He ran, he dove in. He swam and then went under as far as he could. He came up for air and went down again. Then again. And again. He would not stop searching, even when the sun went down.

Others on the beach finally pulled him out when his strength was gone. He sat on the sand most of the night crying.

Boaters with grappling hooks snagged the bodies the next day. One of the women had just been married.

Joe was angry. It was the only way he could deal with his emotions. The beach had become his home and the bathers were his family, and fathers protect their children. He had let them down.

He asked, actually he demanded (and when Joe demanded something he got it), he demanded that he be made a special constable so he could order people not to go in the water when it was dangerous.

He got the position, special constable with a pistol and a badge. Not bad for a lifeguard.

The beach was getting crowded. Actually it was packed, so crowded that some people were going to a new beach in Kitsilano. It was not the discovery of a new beach that was amazing but the growth of Vancouver. It was like a teenager on steroids, which would be illegal but that is how fast the city was growing.

I don't know if you were in Vancouver before Expo 86, but if you were you saw an explosion of growth. The rundown, abandoned, empty industrial shores of False Creek are now a towering forest of condos. Where no one lived before, now hundreds of thousands of people with tiny dogs walk on seawalls with upper-crust views.

And throughout the rest of the city, houses are coming down and condos are going up. Before Expo there were no traffic reporters. Now there is a twenty-four-hour non-stop traffic reporting radio station, and usually the news is bad.

Well, all of this is nothing compared with what happened to Vancouver between Joe's arrival on the muddy streets of Gastown and the time he stood smoking his pipe at his home in its new location.

When Joe first saw the beach it was surrounded by forest. That was in 1885, one hundred years exactly before construction started at Expo 86.

When Joe first saw the beach he had walked there through the forest. There were no homes south of Robson Street. Davie Street had a clubhouse where the friends of Premier Davie could hold hands, but there was no street.

By the time Joe's home was moved in 1905, the crowds were coming by streetcar along Davie Street and Robson Street. Houses were lining every street in the West End. The rich people had moved there and were now moving out because it was so crowded. They were going to the new rich area in Shaughnessy and their old mansions were being turned into rooming houses.

Joe executes a spectacular dive into English Bay in 1906. He was there every day. Joe was to English Bay what the Sappers were to British Columbia: everything.
Photo by Philip Timms, City of Vancouver Archives AM336-S3-3-: CVA 677-591

In twenty years the city had exploded with people. There were shops on every main street. The mill and the railroad and the forests and the salmon were drawing men with families. Schools were opening and candy shops were becoming popular.

"It wasn't like this in the old days," some of the old-timers said. "Back then if you wanted a steak for dinner you shot a deer. Now you have to go to a store to buy a piece of meat. Life is too easy."

One of the things Joe never complained about was the lack of black people to talk with, though there were almost none. He had met one couple, but the husband died soon after. Joe remained friends, but just friends, with his widow. Then she died.

He was friends with one of her daughters and he told her that when he died she should get his coat. He told her she would never have to worry about the future because he had sewn all of his savings into the lining.

I learned this from Lisa Anne Smith, who spent ten years researching Joe. She could have just asked me, but she didn't know me then and she did it all with books and newspaper articles, which goes to show that books are good for something. She also talked to a bunch of old folks who were children when they were taught to swim by Joe.

Not one of them had a bad thing to say about him. No one accused him of anything. That is where the church and some sports coaches could have learned something. Joe was good, and that is all there was to it.

Lisa is a member of the Native Daughters of BC, Post #1. Before I met her I thought she would be stuffy and conservative. When I met her I slapped myself in my prejudice. She was laughing and lively and smart and bubbling with excitement about Joe.

"I really have great respect for him," she said. Then she added, almost sheepishly, "I think I channelled him."

I think she was right, because everything in her book, *Our Friend Joe*, was right on. Trust me, I know.

But I did learn about Joe wanting to give the daughter of his friend all his money. That was nice of him.

He died in Vancouver Hospital on February 4, 1922, a week short of his fifty-ninth birthday. The daughter of his friend was at his bedside. When they went to look through his belongings in his cottage no one could find his coat. It is one of those bad things that happen even to good people.

The funeral was mammoth. It was a civic funeral reserved for dignitaries, not lifeguards. In fact, only one other person who was not in government ever received the same respect—Pauline Johnson, whom the next story is about.

Ten thousand people lined the streets of the city. There was a service in Holy Rosary and the congregation sang "Old Black Joe." I think he would have taken it as a compliment. I hoped that his mother was seeing this. Her son who did not become a doctor had saved many lives.

He is buried in Mountain View Cemetery and his headstone simply says: JOE.

Near where his cottage stood is a water fountain with a picture of him in copper. There are words written on it, too: Little Children Loved Him. It is sort of creepy today, but at the turn of the nineteenth century it had a good and deep meaning.

In 1986 when the city was celebrating its first hundred years the Vancouver Historical Society was looking for the one person who gave more to the city than anyone else, the one who gave it character and love, the one who gave it a soul. They chose Joe and named him the Citizen of the Century. And although he was a sailor, bartender and lifeguard, he never worked in a restaurant.

LOST LAGOON

A thriving, peaceful aboriginal village lay between Lost Lagoon and Coal Harbour for centuries before the park was made and the causeway built.

City of Vancouver Archives

AM54-S4-: St Pk N4

 take a walk around Lost Lagoon almost every week. It is one of the finest outdoor parts of the city. You have high-rises on one side, a forest on the other and countless dead people along the shore.

Those are all the ashes of the dearly gone away. Before you die in Vancouver it is customary to tell your friends that your secret wish is to have your ashes spread around Lost Lagoon. It has to be secret because it is against the law and someday a cop is going to bust right into a funeral procession and say, "Halt. Step away from those ashes."

No, that is not going to happen. Not really. Can you imagine the front-page headline in the *Province* the next day: "Police Kill Fun at Funeral." The poor cop will have to attend sensitivity classes on how to understand ashes and the chief will have to apologize to someone who is not here.

Better to just let the ashes fall. The only problem with that is there are so many remains of departed souls being left where the ducks climb out of the water that the park's workers have a secret mission every month or so to shovel up the ashes. Otherwise they would become so slippery that the gardeners might fall into the water while they are tending to the vegetation at the edge of the lagoon.

The bad part of that is the water is so polluted that the gardeners could go on long-term disability, which would increase the city's debt. Death is not good for balancing the city's budget.

I was floating around this lake in a canoe with my old friend Pauline Johnson a while back. Okay, it was the beginning of the last century but as I get older time goes by faster.

"I think I'll write a poem about this," she said.

Pauline had written many poems, but I wasn't interested in that. I just liked looking at her because she was so pretty. She was half Indian—that is what they called Native aboriginal First Nations people back then—and half white, which is the only thing whites have ever been called. Whites have so much less colour in their speech and their lives than just about anyone else. That gives them more time to search for the colour in others.

Anyway, I was happy to be looking while she was paddling. She was wearing a very loose-fitting summer dress that was much more inviting than the trees and birds, so I kept admiring her nature.

Sorry. I am getting distracted.

"This is my favourite spot to paddle," she said, "but it is such a shame that it disappears sometimes."

"Do you mean we might run out of water and have to park?" I asked.

"No, white man," she said. "I am fully in control."

Darn, I thought. She had never been married and I had been a widow for fifty or sixty years. I was just getting into my prime. But Pauline did what she always did—she thought about her poetry.

She had made a pretty good living touring the US and Britain with her poems. Of course her performance made the poems even better. When the curtain went up she would come out onstage wearing Indian clothing. You know, the buckskins, feathers, beads and moccasins that white folks thought all aboriginals wore.

The people loved her. This was around the same time that old Buffalo Bill Cody was touring the States with his Wild West Show. After killing most of the Indians and putting the rest of them on reserves that were like prison camps, the white folks could not get enough of them. They wanted to see real Indians, the noble savages who lived close to nature and could kill a buffalo with their bare hands.

There was no way to prove this since the white men had killed all the buffalo with their guns for the sport of target practice. But it was good to think an Indian was theoretically superior in one way now that he was officially inferior in every other.

The white mind is a hard thing to unravel.

Anyway, sweet Pauline would recite her poems of trees and trail mix to a mesmerized audience who could not believe that an Indian could be so beautiful and so smart and look so good in feathers.

Then for the second act she would change into a Victorian dress that went to the floor with ruffles and covered everything except her fingers and her face.

And she would recite her poems of refined English life with references that could have come from the Queen and were understood by the women in the audience wearing dresses that covered everything except their fingers and their faces.

They loved her everywhere, except in the world of dating.

"But mother, father, I love her. I don't care about her colour."

"Go to your room, Horatio, and don't come out until you have that evil, ridiculous, nonsensical and most of all embarrassing thought expunged from your childish mind."

Pauline Johnson was beautiful and bright and sweet. Okay, I liked her a lot. So did most of Canada even though she was also advocating for indigenous rights when that was difficult to do.
Chiefswood National Historic Site, Six Nations of the Grand River

"But mother, I am forty years old. I can make up my own mind."

"Go. And don't mention her again. Just think. If you had children, what would we do then?"

"But mother, I still don't know how to make children."

"*Go!*"

And Horatio went, along with all the other men. So the way I figured it, Pauline was saving herself for me.

"I love this lagoon," she said again. "I shall write a poem about it. What should I say?"

Well, as you know, I was used to writing short sentences with some sensationalizing. That is what reporters do. The flower did not die in the fall. No, sir. A good reporter writes: The flower fell to the hostile invasion of biting winds. And always he must quote someone saying, "This is the coldest autumn in sixty years."

That sells more papers.

The only thing I could suggest to Pauline was to describe the lagoon. "What did your ancestors call it?"

"My ancestors did not live here. My father was a Mohawk. Actually, he was half Mohawk and half white but they still called him Mohawk."

I told Pauline that in the US if a black man and a white woman had a baby then that baby would still be black even if the baby was only half black, even if he became president. That, of course, would be impossible, I added.

But then if that black man who was really only half black met a white woman and they had a baby it would be only a quarter black but they would still call it black.

And if that black baby who was only a quarter black grew up and met a white woman and they had a baby it would *still* be called black, even though it was only a sixteenth black. That is unless he or she looked white, and then he or she would be white until he or she tried to be president and then someone in some weirdo political party would dig up some family history to prove he or she was hiding his or her black ancestry and therefore was unsuited to be president. That will make sense to those who carry guns into the voting booth.

"That's crazy," Pauline said. "But we kind of have the same thing here. You can have only a drop of Indian in your system and gallons of white, but white folks will still say you are Indian."

I told her that means that someday her descendants would not have to pay tax for cigarettes even if they did not look like Indians.

"That's terrible," she said. "Cigarettes are bad for everyone."

She was a smart woman. Anyway, we got back to the poem and the lagoon and I asked again, "What did the old folks who lived here call it?"

"They said it was the water that disappeared sometimes because it flows out at the other end at low tide."

She used a long Indian word and then said, "They were very clear in their meaning. If the water disappeared then they said the water disappeared. And if a chief was cheating on his wife they said the chief was cheating. They did not say the chief had moments of despair when he went off to a hideaway in Bellingham to consider his future."

"So why don't you write about the water going away?" I asked.

Pauline, whose Mohawk name Tekahionwake literally means "double-life," often played on her half-European, half-Mohawk heritage in poetry performances.
Chiefswood National Historic Site,
Six Nations of the Grand River

She was doing the paddling and I had nothing to do but lean back and look at her and then at the blue sky. It was a beautiful blue sky. I thought I could write a newspaper story about it. I would say, "The blue sky was threatened today by clouds that could appear any minute and kill the blueness."

That would sell papers.

"How about the Lost Lagoon?" Pauline asked me.

"Not bad," I said. "But do you think people will remember it?"

We went around the lagoon a few more times and then hugged before saying goodbye. That was one good hug. I carried the memory for the rest of my life, which means I still carry it.

She wrote the poem and kids learned it in school.

Not too long after that Pauline passed away. I don't like to say she died; that is too abrupt. Breast cancer. Poor girl. Poor world. Poor me. She had so much to give.

Anyway, they did not spread her ashes around the lagoon. No one did that then because, just as she wrote, sometimes the lagoon disappeared and how do you spread ashes around something that is not there? Instead they buried her ashes near the Tea House, which was the most fashionable spot to eat back then. Come to think of it, the Tea House is still the most fashionable spot to eat. I'll tell you about that later. Meanwhile, if you drive down to Third Beach you will pass her grave at the very top of the gentle slope that goes down to the parking lot.

There is a fountain hidden in the trees with a dedication to Pauline. It is very peaceful. I have gone there many times and said: "Pauline, everyone in Vancouver knows the name Lost Lagoon. You were a genius."

Then I go away before I tell her that almost no one remembers her name. Once she was the most famous of all Canadian women and of almost all Canadians, men or women. It is sad when it happens to poets. On the other hand it also happens to television anchors, much to their shock, and that is a blessing.

But more about Lost Lagoon. That is one big oddity. While Pauline was very sick and dying, the city of Vancouver was turning her lagoon and the land around it into a park. Many people asked: "What's a park?"

They were told it was a place with trees where you could go and commune with nature.

They said, "The *whole world* is full of trees and what does 'commune' mean?"

They were right. Even though most of the trees inside Vancouver had been cut down, there were still endless forests outside the city. And those trees were for cutting down, not communing with. Communing was something you did in church, even if you did not understand it.

But the lagoon Pauline paddled around became the entranceway to the park. This was not good for the lagoon. Later we called it the unintended consequence of an action. That means that when you do something, even when you think you know what you are doing, you actually have no idea that the something you are doing is going to screw up other things. That's one of God's jokes.

That happens in politics and grocery shopping. You go to buy eggs because you think you are out of them, but no, you still have a dozen in the back of the fridge that you did not know about and now you have two dozen eggs and you have to eat a lot of them before they expire and you get an overdose of cholesterol and die.

And it happens in politics when you say you will defend the folks in Afghanistan and Iraq and Mali and the Congo and suddenly you have no soldiers left at home to help people with flooding. The people at home then vote for someone else and your dreams of helping the people of the world die. And the people of the world also go on dying and the flooding becomes a scandal. It happens.

To make this beautiful area a park they needed a road to get into it. So the

The main entrance to Stanley Park effectively blocked off Lost Lagoon. Oyster shells from a nearby aboriginal midden were dug up and used as the bed for the new road.
City of Vancouver Archives
AM54-S4-1-: S-5-1

powers-that-were said, "Build a road." Powers-that-be like to pronounce things that are difficult to do, and then take the credit for doing them.

The new city employees of the new city went to the closest source of road-making material they could find and dug it out. They knew it was left by the Indians. That did not faze them. This pile of shells and pottery and trinkets from past civilizations was handy and that was good enough.

They dug it up and dumped it onto the outlet of the lagoon. In one step they destroyed the history of the people who lived here long ago and strangled the only lagoon in the city, the only one with a name and a history and an attachment to a famous person.

"Good job," they were told. "Now our names will go on the papers," said the powers-that-were.

But now the lagoon had no in-and-out flow, which is the way a lagoon breathes. Think what happens when a person's in-and-out flow of air is cut off; for instance, when you are strangled around the neck by someone who really does not like you. It's a scientific fact well known through history: no in-and-out air, no more you.

Did the builders of the road into the park miss this lesson in school? They built the road, cut off the flow of water and… how did that happen? The lagoon died.

The fish that had swum then starved and the oysters starved and the frogs starved and they all died—and you know what happens to fish and other creatures after they are dead for a while.

"We don't want a park that stinks," said the people who came to the new park. They were also the people who voted for the people who made the park. Suddenly they saw the people they voted for wasting their money and not doing what they said they would do. It would be like building a very expensive ferry and then finding out it cannot sail across the water.

The powers-that-be said it was not their fault. They always say that. It was the fault of the engineers, the road builders and the park people and maybe it was nature's fault for not making fish that could live without eating.

The powers-that-be told their underlings to figure out a way to get water into the lagoon and out of the lagoon before they were voted out of office. Politics, life and lagoons are always a race against time.

The underlings suggested that a pipeline be placed between the lagoon and the ocean or the bay or anywhere where it could replace what God had figured out long ago.

"Build the pipeline to the beach," some city worker said. "It makes sense. It's close by."

The politicians looked at the plan and said, "Are you crazy? That is the second beach that our voters will swim at. You don't want a big pipe dumping out dead fish around the toes of our fine citizens."

"What is the first beach?" a city worker asked.

"English Bay, you idiot," said one of the politicians. "You know the place that Captain Vancouver claimed while he gave the Spanish the banks way out of town?"

"Did the Spanish like that?" the city worker asked.

"They said peace and tranquility beat crowds and noisy Polar Bear swims any day. We had no idea what they were talking about but then they were Spanish and what could you expect?"

"So the second beach is near the lagoon that is no longer a lagoon?" the city worker asked.

"Correct. By the way, I hope you have a union to protect you because workers are expected to work, not think. We do the thinking."

"Can I please ask one tiny, insignificant question?" asked the worker.

"If it is insignificant I can answer it," said the politician.

"What is the name of the second beach?"

The politician thought, and conferred with the other politicians and thought some more and said: "It is clear, isn't it? Second beach is Second Beach and it shall be hence and forever."

That is when my pencil broke. I was covering this little meeting of the dead lagoon issue and had been taking notes. But when the deep thought of a politician was thrown out into the world my humble pencil could not contain itself. The point snapped off.

"Would you repeat that?" I asked the politician.

"Who are *you*?" asked the politician.

"A reporter," I answered.

The face of the politician turned a strange colour. "You are recording my words?"

"Yes, sir."

"Everything I say?"

"Yes."

"Out, get out of here. We can't allow those on the outside to know what we are doing on the inside especially if it will affect those on the outside. If we do not have secrecy, how can we have reliable and open government?"

I was escorted out by other city workers who were told they could not talk to me about anything that would affect them or anyone else. And that began the custom of secret gatherings of politicians called in camera meetings.

I had to look up that one. *Camera* came from the old Romans who got it from the Greek word for a vault, which was a safe and often secret place to store things. In the seventeenth century in Italy and Spain it came to be applied to a council chamber in which secret decisions were made.

That is also where our word *camera* came from, but for politicians it means a place for hiding what's inside, not showing it. Politicians never push the shutter or let in even a glimmer of light.

Anyway, back to the lagoon, which was still festering and stinking. The decision was made to build a pipeline from the stagnant water filled with dead fish to Burrard Inlet and through that marvellous human invention fulfill the needs of nature.

The tide would come in and flow through the pipe and fill the lagoon with fresh water and new fish and then the tide would go out and flush out the old, smelly stuff.

"Excuse me, politician, sir. I am that city worker you met a few months ago."

"Yes, I am busy. What do you want?"

"The pipe to the lagoon is clogged."

"Well, clean it."

"We have, over and over and over."

"Well, clean it again. We will meet in camera and make a decision. And whatever you do, don't tell anyone about this, especially any reporters."

"But everyone knows, sir. The lagoon stinks again."

"Well, put a full-time special crew on to clean the pipe around the clock. We will spare no expense to keep the people happy and to prove we are right."

I knew about this because of an interview with someone who was there but who requested anonymity for fear of being fired before his pension started.

Cleaning the pipe did not work. Actually, no one would work on it to clean it because that meant going in it to clean it and you didn't want to go in there.

The next step was to completely drain the lagoon, close off the pipe at both ends and cover the whole thing with dirt. Hey presto: you now have Pipeline Road, which is good because without that there would be no way to get to the Miniature Railway or the lights at Christmas. See, everything turns out for the best.

And then the storm drains from the city were redirected to fill up the lagoon with fresh water.

"See, with just a little engineering we fixed everything," said the politicians.

Now you have a fresh-water pond that is no longer a lagoon, so polluted that fish no longer swim in it and lined with the ashes of dead people, as one of the city's most-visited attractions.

But the name Lost Lagoon is still there. Pauline would be happy, sort of.

PS: I promised to tell you about the Tea House restaurant. Well during World War II cannons were installed just outside the restaurant to shoot Japanese boats that might come to invade the country. The restaurant was the dining room for the officers in charge of the cannons.

They would sip tea and look through the windows at the men arming the big guns and say, "Jolly good. We will get them if they come." Meanwhile, the men who were ready to fire the cannons ate in the rain. It was just like being a Sapper.

Now Japanese tourists eat at the restaurant and say, "Lovely view. You can see all the ships bringing Japanese cars here."

CENTRAL PARK, BURNABY

t is not in the centre of the city, as you know. Central Park in Burnaby is on Boundary Road, which is the boundary between Vancouver and Burnaby.

If anyone were to name the park now it would be called Boundary Road Park, or Burnaby's Park Real Close to Vancouver.

102

I'll tell you how it became Central Park. It's a love story.

David Oppenheimer was Jewish—and German. This was long before it was very bad to be both of those but it was still not too easy being both so he left Germany with his four brothers. They were going to get rich in California by finding gold.

The only problem was, by the time they got there most of the gold was already found. They moved to British Columbia looking for gold. Too late again.

So they did a very smart thing. They started selling axes and shovels to the miners who still believed they could find the winning lottery in the ground.

At the job of selling, the Oppenheimers did very well. They became rich but despite that they continued to be about the nicest guys you could meet, especially David.

In fact he was so well liked that while he was living in Vancouver the people of this fine village decided he would be a good man to put in charge. Some of the leading citizens said to him, "Would you like to be mayor? We guarantee the job."

Can you imagine any politician today getting that kind of offer?

No one ran against him and David Oppenheimer became the second mayor of the city. He took no salary and when guests of the city had to be entertained he paid for it.

Can you imagine any politician doing that today?

He did a lot of good. He helped create the fire department and got drinking water from the Capilano River into the city and started the building of a city hospital. But his most passionate love was to give the city more parks.

This he did by buying hunks of land and giving them to the city to be used as parks and playgrounds.

I hate to repeat myself, but can you imagine any politician today… you know the question *and* the answer.

I met him before he became mayor. He was positive, outgoing and generous, but lonely. He had been a widower for several years after his wife of twenty years had died.

Born in Germany in 1834, David Oppenheimer made his way to Canada via the US and became what one local newspaper described as "the best friend Vancouver ever had."

Photo by Major James Skitt Matthews, City of Vancouver Archives AM54-S4-: Port P1789

Then, on a business trip to San Francisco, he met Julia Walters. He looked, she looked, he looked again. You can fill in the rest. But there was one problem. She was from New York and wanted desperately to go back.

"I don't suppose you would like to visit Vancouver?" he asked her.

"Is it farther from New York?" she asked.

"Just a bit," he fibbed.

She told him what she missed most about New York was the new, beautiful Central Park. It was a place where you could escape from the city without leaving the city.

But despite that, and because of that eyes meeting eyes thing, she agreed to visit Vancouver and then she agreed to stay for a while.

Shortly after that David asked Julia to climb into a one-horse buggy for a ride out in the country. Of course just about anywhere you went was out in the country, but David had a plan. They rode out of Gastown on Westminster Road because it was the way to New Westminster. You can't get lost on roads that tell you where they are going. GPS without the satellites.

Westminster Road was later changed to Main Street, which should tell you that you are in the centre of town, except Main Street in Vancouver is not. Ontario Street is the centre of town, to which the people in Ontario say, "But of course." They think they are the centre of the world so they should be the centre of Vancouver.

But David was not thinking about streets. He had something else on his mind. At Kingsway they made a left. That is still the route to New West. We Sappers had laid the foundations of both of those roads to get to the capital of the colony.

Did you know the Romans conquered the world by building roads? Once they had roads, they could get messages delivered from anywhere in the world to Rome in just the time it took someone to run a couple of thousand miles. That was much faster than going through the forests and swamps. And the Roman armies could get anywhere in no time flat when they had a road to march on. It was the first internet of the world.

I promise no more detours on this trip, even if I think of something else to say. Promise.

The only thing David was hoping to conquer was a heart. After a jolly little jaunt during which they talked about the weather and life and then the weather again, David stopped the buggy. He helped Julia climb down and walked with her to a tree stump.

"Close your eyes," he said.

Then he pulled back a large piece of cloth that was covering a sign.

"Open your eyes."

"Oh, David."

The sign read: CENTRAL PARK.

"This is for you."

Soon after that they were married. They lived an extremely happy life. They had one daughter with whom they frequently had picnics in Central Park.

The park had been a military reserve owned by the government for the purpose of supplying trees to use as spars and masts for the Royal Navy. By the time David bought it and gave it to the city much of the old-growth trees were gone and new trees were springing up, just like in the park in New York.

The park remained Central Park after Burnaby was created and the boundary was drawn right at the edge of it.

David loved his wife a great deal. She died a few years before him. It was her wish to be buried in New York.

When he passed away, he of course had left instructions that he be buried next to her. She had shared his home with him, he would now share eternity with her in her home, not too far from the other Central Park.

SQUIRRELS AND A CANNON

 hile we are talking about the park I have to tell you about that noisy old cannon. First of all, what people in their right mind would have signs up as you enter the city that said: "Nuclear Weapons Free Zone" and then shoot off a cannon aimed at the city every night?

The signs are down now, but they were there for ten years and I for one was happy to know that Vancouver was not going to launch missiles at anyone (though we could perhaps have made an exception in the case of Ottawa).

Sorry, no more political commentary.

But every night—except when it was stolen by UBC students and when city workers went on strike and during World War II and a few times when the firing pin fizzled—the cannon has been fired. This is very exciting in a country that frowns on gun ownership.

The cannon was made back in my old homeland in 1816. We know that because it is engraved on the barrel. That was when George III was king. Poor fellow, he was insane, but that did not stop him from being king. Indeed, it was a solid precedent for other leaders.

Anyway there is no record of the cannon for the next seventy years. There was no long-gun registry back then. The RCMP did not insist that the captain of a ship have a criminal record check and register the serial number before he went out to sea.

For all we know it could have been in many sea battles. The only thing that puts that idea in doubt is that if it was in a battle or two it probably would not be around now. Not much on the gun decks of the old British man-of-war ships survived after a battle. They painted the entire insides of the deck—under the feet, above the heads and on the walls—bright red. That was so that when blood was splattered around during a battle the sight of it on the walls and floor and ceiling would not upset the men doing the bleeding.

The cannons would occasionally get hit by an incoming sixteen-pound ball of iron, which would unbalance their delicate machinery. Sometimes the cannons would simply blow up in the faces of the sailors—not good for the cannons or the sailors. Or the ship would sink after someone else's cannonball put a hole in the hull.

The odds are that the cannon in Stanley Park lived a peaceful life until it wound up here. And it came here because no one else knew what to do with it.

"We're trying to clean out some of this old junk," said the politicians in Victoria. "Would anyone like this cannon?"

The people in the growing village of Vancouver would take anything. Houses were going up everywhere, especially around the harbour. Families were moving in with the men either cutting down trees, slicing them up, or working in the newest fast-growing industry: fishing.

Opposite page: The Nine O'Clock Gun is loaded, ready for firing. This is one of the great traditions. If you have never been there, buy some sushi, sit on the grass and have the soy sauce squirt in your eyes at nine o'clock.
Photo by Don Coltman and Steffens Colmer, City of Vancouver Archives AM1545-S3-: CVA 586-1188

"Hey, did you know there are more salmon here than trees?" someone said to his friend. "Fishing is fun and we could get paid for it."

"Any drawbacks?" asked his friend.

"We might get cold and wet and maybe drown but that is better than cutting down trees and getting cold and wet and crushed to death."

With benefits like that, salmon fishing boomed. Soon canneries opened near Gastown and there was a market for all the fish a man could bring in. This was fishing the way it was meant to be. You hung a line over the side of a rowboat and tried to hook a salmon. Then you pulled it in and did it again. In that way there were enough salmon to last forever. You just ran out of fishermen a lot sooner.

But while they were fishing in Burrard Inlet and even past the First Narrows they needed to know the time. Not one of them had a watch on because you cannot wear a watch while fishing or it would get full of salt water and stop ticking. Anyway, it's unlikely that any of them owned a watch, and many of them wouldn't have known how to tell the time even if they did have one.

They were just like many kids today who cannot tell what it means when Mickey's big hand is on the 12 and his little hand is on the 3.

"Mommy, why does Mickey Mouse have one big hand and one little hand? Was he born that way and can't the doctors help him? Also why can't I have an iPhone so I can tell what time it is and play video games? Why, Mommy?"

The railroad executives had gold watches because they wanted to know what time dinner was served. And the railroad engineers had watches because they had to get their trains in on time or they would not have dinner.

But no timepieces for the fishermen. Most of them started before sunrise and worked all day and they enjoyed fishing so much that they would stay out all night if no one told them it was quitting time.

Along came a good guy, Bill Jones. He was the first lighthouse keeper at Brockton Point when the lighthouse was just a shack with a candle in front of a mirror inside a large glass jar. That would keep wooden ships from grounding on the point when they went in to pick up lumber at the mill.

"I have an idea how to help those poor fishermen who give me all the salmon I can eat," he told me one day. "I want to return the favour."

He showed me how he tied a stick of dynamite to the end of a fishing line, picked up the fishing pole and with one hand held a flame against the fuse. It was then that I started backing off.

"You're going to kill yourself," I shouted.

The fuse ignited. "I don't think that's approved by WorkSafeBC," I said, but mostly I turned around and ran for a tree, which was a mistake because they had all been cut down by Edward Stamp's men.

I fell on the ground because I was not sure that my stretch of longevity would survive a stick of dynamite.

But lighthouse keepers are a brave bunch. He held up the rod and cast out the stick of dynamite with the sizzling fuse. It was over the water when it exploded.

BANG! I buried my face in the mud.

"That was fun," I said. "But next time let's play checkers instead."

"I'm doing this every night at 6:00 p.m. to tell them it is time for dinner," said Bill the lighthouse keeper, who was also the city's first official alarm clock.

Then came the cannon and Bill and some others thought of a good use for it. It was really loud and would save many future lighthouse keepers.

I was at the first firing. October 15, 1898. Six o'clock precisely.

It was really loud, a lot louder than a stick of dynamite. When you put a flame

Cycling through Stanley Park in the 1890s was trendy. More than a century later the bicycle is IN again, this time elbowing cars off many roads.
Photo by Philip Timms, City of Vancouver Archives AM336-S3-2-: CVA 677-277

to half a pound of gunpowder it makes a lot of noise. We all jumped half out of our skin and it was so much fun that the city fathers who gathered around wanted to do it again.

"Wait 'til tomorrow," said Bill the lighthouse keeper.

The next night at 6:00 p.m., BANG! "We will call it the Six O'Clock Gun," said an official.

And the next night at six, BANG! And the next and the next and then on the next night came the mothers from the town across the water.

"You are ruining our dinnertime," they said. "We can't sit down for a peaceful meal with that darn cannon going off all the time."

It was the first women's movement in the city's history—the city officials, all men, facing the protesters, all women.

"Stop playing with guns," said the women.

"It is our civic duty," the officials said.

"It's our dinnertime," said the women.

"How about a compromise?" I suggested.

Seven o'clock was homework time. Eight was too close to seven for the slow learners.

They settled on 9:00 p.m.

"But don't be late because after that the little dears go to bed," said the women.

So the Six O'Clock Gun became the Nine O'Clock Gun and it has never since been late. The children from Port Moody to North Vancouver and Burnaby and Vancouver used it as their clock for bedtime until television was invented.

"What about us?" asked the fishermen.

The city fathers conferred. This was a problem. Keep the kids happy or keep the fishermen happy. The fishermen were voters now. The kids would be voting in the future when the politicians would be old but still running for office.

There was no answer. They turned to me.

"I heard," I said, "that in the future there will come a new food to the western world. It will need many fishermen. It will need many fish farms."

"What is a fish farm?" asked the politicians.

"I have heard it will be a place where you will grow salmon instead of corn but there will be much controversy."

"We like controversy," said the politicians. "Controversy keeps us employed. But does it help us solve the problem now?"

"Yes," said I, not knowing what I was talking about, which was perfect for a newspaper man. No wonder some journalists become politicians. It is an easy transition from not knowing what you are writing about to not knowing what you are talking about.

"There will come a time when something called sushi will be everywhere and so much salmon will be eaten that the rivers and streams and oceans will run out of salmon."

"Impossible," they said.

"Just you wait," I said. "And the salmon will be eaten raw."

"No."

"Yes."

The politicians, being wise, went to the fishermen and said, "The three extra hours will give you time to catch more fish, which will someday open a whole new industry in Vancouver that will change the way we all eat."

"But we are tired at six o'clock," said the fishermen.

The city fathers told them that they should complain to their union.

"What's a union?" they asked.

"Something you will have to pay dues to so you can belong so that they can tell you that you should be getting more money," said one of the officials who was getting a municipal paycheque now and later would get a large pension paid for by the fishermen.

Now most of the salmon are gone, the sushi is made from farmed fish, the fishermen are out of work and the politicians are still getting their pensions. The big bang of the Nine O'Clock Gun is drowned out by the noise of the city and blocked by the big buildings. But it is good for tourists.

However, there was one great moment in the gun's modern life. It was a funeral.

I wish I had been there. Being there is so much better than hearing or reading about it. And much better than seeing it on television, because television is clinical. I mean television is not just a glass window, which would be fine. It's a window with unreality behind it.

If you watch a car race, like the Indy 500, in person you know those cars are going nearly two hundred miles per hour and they are two inches apart and if someone breathes wrong they will crash and then the flying debris might kill you. Pretty exciting.

If you are watching it on television the cars look like they are going twenty miles per hour and the bumper-to-bumper driving looks as safe as riding on a train. Boring. The train is better.

Seeing the Nine O'Clock Gun on a news program on TV is the same. Bang. Boring. Commercial.

In reality it is as exciting as the city fathers felt the first time it went off. BANG! Jump out of your shoes, or skin, and say, "Wow! That was LOUD!"

That is the way life should be lived: in reality, not through images on the screen.

Anyway, as I was saying, I heard about this great moment and I just had to imagine it.

The custodian of the cannon was drinking, as usual. It is always exciting to have an intoxicated man in charge of a gun. When I was in basic training in the air force there was a drill instructor who was drinking, heavily, with another sergeant. It was late at night and they were screaming for me to leave my post and come to them.

I could not leave my post. I also could not disobey orders.

The hollow tree in Stanley Park was large enough for you to fit your entire carriage inside. The tree is now a thin skeleton of its former glory. Someday it may be left to die. Until then tourists come and go and forget about it, not like in the old days.

Photo by Richard Trueman, City of Vancouver Archives AM1589-: CVA 2-141

I stayed at my post. They screamed for me to come. I stayed. In a short while and, thank god, in time, they passed out. Drunks are scary.

When I saw them in the morning they were lying next to a rocket launcher on the base that was supposed to be used in case of attacks by the enemy.

The drunk in charge of the Nine O'Clock Gun was less threatening.

The way the story was told to me by two of the old gardeners, the drunk was drinking while sitting on a bench. Along came a sad man carrying a black plastic container.

"What is the trouble, good fellow?" asked the drunk with the cannon.

"My wife died and I am here to spread her ashes," said the sad man.

"That is illegal, especially around Lost Lagoon," said the drunk.

He was tripping over some of his words like all drunks do, but he got the message across and the man with the plastic container was happy to find anyone to share his grief. It is always good to listen to others when they are sad; then you become an angel, even if you have whisky on your breath.

The man in charge of the cannon offered the man with the burden in his arms and his heart a swig from his bottle, which he hid inside his jacket because it is illegal to drink intoxicants in the park, especially if you are going to fire a sixteen-pound cannon.

One drink always leads to another and another. That is the way it is with the alcohol, which causes much pain, after it takes away much pain. It is like love. You must treat it with respect.

And when the bottle was getting empty an idea was born. Many ideas come to life with whisky and most of them are as solid as the liquid.

"Would you like to send off your wife in grand style?" asked the drunk with the cannon.

"What do you mean?" asked the man with the plastic container, who was now tipsy.

"How about that?" asked the drunk pointing to the cannon.

"We couldn't," said the tipsy man with the container who was wishing they could.

"We could."

And out of such innocence came the greatest Nine O'Clock moment in the long life of the cannon. The drunk with the cannon slipped the container with the ashes into the muzzle of the weapon. He had already loaded it with the gunpowder.

If the cannon had any thought at all it would have been a happy thought. It had been firing blanks for decades. Now it was loaded. Now it could act like a cannon. Now it had something to shoot.

The firing timer was set automatically. All they had to do was wait, and it was just a few minutes before Mickey's big hand would touch the 12 and his little hand would be on the 9.

The evening strollers gathered around. They had no idea the most unforgettable moment in the last century and a half of the cannon's life was about to happen.

The two men did what men drinking whisky always do at great moments like this. They walked up the little hill behind the cannon, slipped into the shadows of the forest and drank some more.

BANG! Actually it was KERBOOM and BANG together. The flame came out of the tip, the tourists jumped and the man with the heavy heart just looked for something he could not see. Through the smoke at the end of the barrel went his wife off into eternal bliss.

He saw the symbolism. He saw the hard, long barrel. He saw the explosion. He felt himself jump. It was like the first time, only better. And like the first time, he put his head back, only this time on the grass, and he fell asleep.

And so the Nine O'Clock Gun goes off at nine o'clock every night. Now it is in a cage because those engineering student rascals at UBC stole the gun once and another time vandals put rocks in the barrel so they would pepper the floating gas stations. All but one of the gas stations are gone but the cage remains.

Can you imagine a cannon that fired iron balls weighing more than many kids can now pick up, a cannon that was born to face down the enemy and kill or be killed, is now protected by a cage?

But you should go there on a summer night, get your takeout sushi and wait for the blast. Nine o'clock precisely. You will jump out of your skin. Promise.

In the beginning it had a lovely home, cosy and dry for an old cannon. Since then the Nine O'Clock Gun has not only been stolen but it has been loaded with rocks that bombarded the inlet. It has also fired off the ashes of one departed woman, much against the rules. Now it is housed in a cage. The old days were better.
City of Vancouver Archives
AM54-S4-: St Pk P121

PS: I forgot to mention the squirrels.

A little over ten years after the cannon had its first shot in the night something else appeared in the park. It was the beginning of a change that changed everything, and nothing.

In one word: immigration.

"Oh, they are so cute. Let's give them some peanuts," someone with a soft heart said.

The little grey squirrels sniffed around, took the peanuts and ran up a tree.

"I've never seen any of those before," said the soft-hearted person.

Explanation: Some officials in New York heard about the relatively new Stanley Park at the other end of the continent. "We would like to share something from our Central Park with your Stanley Park," they said.

So they packed up about ten grey squirrels. No one is really sure if it was six, nine, ten or twelve because they were squirming so fast and they were hard to get into a box. Then they shipped them to Vancouver.

"What a nice gift," said some officials in Vancouver. "We will now have a world-class park. In fact we can start calling it one of the world's great parks because we have squirrels from New York."

Then they opened the box.

The black squirrels watching from the branches of trees shook their heads. No one consulted them about the new immigrants.

The first thing that happened was the grey squirrels had sex. That is what new immigrants are always accused of doing. Then they have babies and before you know it they are everywhere.

And then they did the unspeakable immigrant thing and moved out of their neighbourhood. They took up lodging in the next tree and the next and, since the food and the weather were good and opportunities were everywhere, they spread out until they were everywhere.

The good thing was the black squirrels did not mind. Their children played with the grey squirrel children and they all grew up happily together.

And they did it without any multicultural committees.

In 1914 the good people of New York wanted to share their grey squirrels with Vancouver and sent a box full of them. Before the box arrived there were only black squirrels here, like the one this young boy is watching run up a tree in Stanley Park. Now there are too many greys to count.

Photo by Philip Timms, City of Vancouver Archives AM336-S3-3-: CVA 677-664

THE SKINNIEST BUILDING IN THE WORLD

he good folks of Vancouver took a long time to learn the lessons of the squirrels. That of course proves what Charles Darwin really wanted to write: Squirrels are smarter than people. But he said no one would believe that so he stuck with the theory of evolution, which was easier.

I was having soup in a restaurant in Chinatown when I heard some men at the next table plotting against Chang Toy. This I had to see, because Chang would wipe the floor with them and then charge them to clean it up.

This was 1912, five years after one of the most despicable, disgusting days in Vancouver's history. That was September 7, 1907, when thousands of white men crowded onto Main and Hastings outside city hall. They were demanding that the Chinese be sent back to China, or at least be made to suffer if they stayed here.

They were crazy. They were angry. They were scary.

"Keep Canada white," the mob screamed.

The crowd grew. Now there were almost ten thousand of them. "Kill the Chinks. Kill the yellow people."

As I said, they were scary. They were blaming the Chinese for everything. The Chinese took their jobs, the Chinese lived in filth, the Chinese were spreading drugs through the city, but most of all the Chinese were not white so therefore they were the cause of everything bad.

Of course the Chinese were enticed to come here with the promise of jobs building the railroad. Then they were given the worst jobs, the ones the white men would not take, like dealing with dynamite or tying the timbers together at the top of the wooden trestles that went over the raging rivers. If someone was going to be killed then it was a job for a Chinese worker.

And then they were paid only half of what the white men got. And they had to supply their own food. And they had to pay back the cost of shipping them to Canada. And when it was all done they had almost no money to send back to China, which was the reason they had come in the first place.

And so they slept in small rooms, five or six together, because they could not afford a large room. And the white people said, "Look at how they live, like animals."

And some of them spent what little money they had on opium to dull the pain and loneliness. That was the same drug that had been introduced into China by Britain a century earlier.

"Rule Britannia," the white thugs sang as they marched to Pender Street. "Kill them," they shouted.

You probably saw the mob at the Stanley Cup riot. A mob is a fearless lot, and vicious and thrilled by hurting others, especially defenceless others.

The Chinatown mob was the same, except much worse. I watched them start smashing windows of the Chinese stores. The sight of the broken glass gave them a thrill so they broke more windows. Then they smashed more and more.

The Nazis did the same thing a few decades later in a cowardly attack they proudly called *Kristallnacht*. That means Crystal Night. It was also called the Night of Broken Glass. Nazis and Hitler Youth members went through Jewish neighbourhoods smashing the windows of synagogues and shops and homes.

And something similar happened in the American South, only sometimes there they threw bombs when they went past the churches. That is a part of a religion that says we may have the same god but he made you a different colour so I have to kill you. They had to read between the lines to get that commandment.

What are you going to do if you are inside the store when a mob is smashing the outside? What do you tell your children when you know you cannot protect them?

If you were one of those poor Chinese in 1907 with your windows getting smashed you could not call the police. You couldn't call them because some of them were outside with the rioters smashing your windows with their nightsticks.

Almost a century later it was still disappointing to call the police during a riot. By the time of the Stanley Cup insanity a few years ago the police department had changed completely. Many of the men and women carrying badges and guns were Chinese and South Asian. The department was clean of corruption and bias. I knew some of those cops. They were good. But could they handle a riot? No.

When they were faced with massive numbers of drunken nutcases there was little they could do. They could not shoot them, which is what would happen in Egypt or Syria. The Vancouver police were faced with mass insanity given massive power by massive numbers.

Smashing the windows of London Drugs or the Bay and burning cars is the work of a crazed mind. As much as the police wanted to, and were trained and sworn to do, they could not control that mob.

Enough modern history—just imagine what it was like in Chinatown and Japantown in 1907 when the police were on the side of the rioters. After things calmed down, as they always do, the Chinese and Japanese began fixing their windows with no insurance to help and went about their lives quietly trying to keep out of the way of the white man.

Walking down Pender Street the next day was heartbreaking. So many Chinese men with tears. They did not understand what they had done to deserve this. There were few Chinese women and no children outside. The mothers were keeping their children inside. They were still shaking.

I was thinking about that night five years later while I was eating my soup and listening to the men plotting to get even with Chang Toy.

"He is so rich," one said. "I would like to take his money-grabbing hands and cut them off."

The others nodded their heads.

"You see what happens when you let the Chinese have a business? They just keep making it bigger."

I couldn't stand it any longer. I got up and said to them, "Didn't you learn anything from five years ago? Why don't you leave the poor man alone? He is helping the city grow."

They stared at me. "You're that reporter, aren't you?"

"It doesn't matter what I am," I said. "What you are doing is wrong."

I realized then that two of the four men at that table were city aldermen.

This building, at 130 Powell Street, was damaged during the Vancouver race riots of 1907. If those rioters could only go to a university now and see the future of those they tried to destroy.

Rare Books and Special Collections, University of British Columbia Libraries JCPC 36.025

"Don't you tell us what is right. You are nothing but a left-wing fanatic. And don't think you are going to put this in your newspaper. You know they will never print it."

Then they got up and left. I did not see them pay for their meals.

The sad thing was, they were right, at least about the news. The newspapers in Vancouver would not print a story about white men plotting against a Chinese man. During the riots they had downplayed the stories until you thought almost nothing had happened. The newspapers were all run, of course, by white men, most of whom shared the views of the window smashers.

Chinese newspapers overseas and newspapers in the US and Europe had stories about the riot, but those newspapers took a long time to get to Vancouver and by then the white people were saying, "Look how they exaggerate and sensationalize the news. It was not nearly as bad as they say it was."

Luckily, I did not have to write a story about what I had heard. Chang Toy, who was close to illiterate, wrote his own story. Actually, he composed his own life story.

Chang Toy was fascinating. He was born in China. His father died when he was three and that should have meant that he was destined for a life of harvesting rice and dying young.

Instead his mother pushed him into school. He went for three years, which was a miracle, and he learned enough to know that he would not harvest rice. He heard about Canada and saw a chance to help his mother if he could get there.

Then he heard about an offer—come to Canada and work in a cannery for just three months. Make big money. He couldn't afford the passage but he heard the cannery would pay for it in exchange for some time spent working to pay them back.

Others had gone this way and Chang signed up, but the ship's departure was delayed and when he arrived there was only a month of canning left. He was already in debt.

He worked in the cannery, a brutal twelve hours a day that made his hands hurt, cutting and packing and cutting and packing and his hands soggy and his legs aching and then sleeping in a crowded room and back to the cutting and packing.

He got a job in the Hastings Mill. Everything there was cutting and noise and danger and he worked hard. He was, like Joe Fortes, mocked for being different and he was pushed around.

Chang Toy never learned English. Instead he spoke the universal language of determination and courage. He wound up with an empire despite the prejudice and discrimination.

City of Vancouver Archives
AM571-S4-: CVA 287-21

And like Joe he had one response. He had, as had all his brothers and sisters and friends, learned kung fu as a child. Bend, weave, duck and attack. He annihilated his main attacker.

In all my years, actually centuries, of doing this I have seen the same thing over and over. There is only one way to stop a bully. Hit him. It is a sad truth. It is not the Christian way, it may not be the sociologist's or the psychologist's way, but it really is the only way.

And you must hit him hard. It doesn't matter if he hits you back and you get hurt, it only matters that you hit him, and hit with all your might.

In 100 percent of the cases I have seen, it works. The bullying stops. It does not matter if you lose the fight, or if you get a broken nose. From that moment on you are no longer picked on. There are two reasons for that that I have found: the bully is deflated, even if he wins; and you stop being the picture of someone who can be pushed around.

Of course you have to have the courage to do it. If you do, it will change your life. If you don't, nothing will change.

Chang did have the courage. He was not bothered any longer, at least not by those who would confront him to his face. Behind his back was a different matter.

He worked in a Chinese grocery store for a while and then opened one of his own. He bought property. He hired new Chinese arrivals to work for the white man and paid them most of the money he was making for supplying them to the jobs. He was a middleman. He bought more property. He imported rice from China. He exported canned salmon. He never stopped working. He became rich. He formed a company that covered all his enterprises. It was called Sam Kee, half-English, half-Chinese, in the hope of appealing to all.

Among other back-breaking jobs Chang Toy worked in a cannery, some of the most monotonous, messy, mind-numbing work you can imagine.
City of Vancouver Archives
AM54-S4-: SGN 1466

Opposite page: The World Building was designed so everyone who read the World *newspaper in Vancouver could see it. It was the tallest building in the British Commonwealth, which annoyed the British.*

City of Vancouver Archives AM1477-1-S2-: CVA 1477-5

The white men hated him.

"Who does he think he is with all that easy money?"

I heard that in the coffee shops and on the streets and in the churches.

Then came a chance to get back at Chang for all the supposed wrong he had done to the white folks. He had a piece of property on Pender Street. A few blocks away was the new tallest building in the Commonwealth. It was tall and brash and had an instant green roof that was done to make it look old and dignified. It would later be called the Sun Tower but back then it was called the World Tower. "A building that we want everyone to see," said the city officials.

"But look at what could be in the way of the new skyscraper," said one of the officials who was pointing at one of Chang Toy's lots. "If he builds something on that property we would have to step around his building to see the new glory in our city. It's not right."

The city officials and the others who had been inside the restaurant were now just outside the door, plotting. They didn't care if I heard; they knew I could do nothing.

"They are all moving here. Just because it's Chinatown they think they own the streets," said one.

I thought, well if they buy the land they do own it.

"You notice all those Chinese have to live together. They can't be like us, living everywhere," said the first official.

You bet, I thought. If they moved next to you, you would shoot them, or at the very least smash their windows. Better to live in Chinatown where your windows may still get smashed but at least the smashers will have to travel to do it.

I was eating wonton soup and roasted pork. The Chinese had barbecued the meat but the name wasn't yet in use here. You could not get a meal as good as this anywhere else. The few eateries in Vancouver all had boiled vegetables and boiled potatoes and boiled meat. "If it's good enough for the Queen it's good enough for us," they said. "This is the British way of cooking and we are British." Poor folks, they missed out on immigrant cooking.

"But you never know what you are eating with the Chinese," the white folks said. "They eat cats," I heard.

Actually, the cats and dogs were much too valuable eating the mice and rats to be eaten themselves, and pork and chicken tasted better. If I had only known at the time, I would have loved to tell the white folks of 1912 Vancouver that someday horsemeat might be sneaked into their chopped meat in a supermarket.

The whites also, of course, made fun of the Chinese eating with sticks. If only they had known that their descendants would be lining up for raw fish that they would eat with chopsticks for lunch with their Chinese friends. In fact, many of their descendants would be married to Chinese. Oh, great-great-grandpa, clawing at his coffin, shouting, "No. You can't do this to me!"

Back to 1912 and the politicians.

"It will be a civic insult if Chang builds something on that spot. It would block some of the view of the new tower, which has those lovely statues on the sides that our wives think we don't look at. What can we do?"

"Expropriate his land," someone said.

"How can we do that? We can't just expropriate property for a view."

"No, but we can if we widen the street."

"Great idea," said the other politician. "But it would cost a lot to widen all of Pender. And besides, why would we widen the street when the Chinese would get the benefit?"

"We will widen it starting here, just where Chang has his property and then go the other way, away from Chinatown."

"Brilliant," said his friends.

But there was another problem, they said. "We will have to pay Chang for his property."

They huddled. I ate. This was exciting, watching a plot developing just past my soup.

"I know," said one of them, so excited that he was giddy. "Chang has twenty-nine feet of frontage. We will take twenty-four feet of it. Then we don't have to pay him for his entire lot and he will be left with a useless five feet of land. He can't do anything with that. He will just have to leave it empty and we will have the whole thing but only pay him for part of it."

I had to admit that when it came to devious, evil and downright nasty ideas this was a good one.

I would write a story about it. No one would print it and poor Chang would be cheated, but I would keep the story until later when I would write about it in a book. Meanwhile, I had my soup.

One of the aldermen looked up and saw me.

"China lover," they shouted to me from outside.

I did not know how close that came to another kind of lover that would happen in the 1960s in the South of the US. Then it was N lovers instead of C lovers, but it always seems the haters turn out to be on the bottom rung a couple of decades later.

Anyway, the aldermen and the others left. I paid for my meal and walked across the street to visit Chang and give him the news.

As always, Chang was working. He was getting older but he worked from before the sun rose until after the sun set, and that was in the summer. In the winter he never saw the sun. He just worked.

One of his children translated. Chang always said he would learn English when he had a free moment. He never had that moment.

He listened to his daughter's interpretation of the plot. Then he snickered. He said something in Chinese and his daughter said, "He wants to thank you for your friendship. And he wishes you a prosperous and long life."

The Sam Kee Building of 8 West Pender Street survived in the face of anti-Asian prejudice and still stands proudly today, all five feet of it.

Photo by Major J.S. Matthews, City of Vancouver Archives AM54-S4-: Bu P255.7

One out of two is not bad, but most of all it was intriguing to see that he did not turn to anger. He seemed to accept the news as a challenge. He said, "Goodbye" in English—that was more than I could say in Chinese—and I left.

The next time I saw Chang he was standing in front of his new office, the official Sam Kee Building, the headquarters of his Sam Kee enterprise and a public slap in the face for the politicians who had plotted to undermine and humiliate him by leaving him only five feet of property.

He used the money he got for his expropriated land to build his new office on the shallow plot he was left with. It was four feet eleven inches wide. People came from everywhere at first to laugh at it, then admire it and then stay long enough to do business in it. Chang got richer. His building was famous. His life grew better.

And everyone knew the story, because even the newspapers could not miss this. No one could. It was the skinniest building in the world two blocks away from the tallest building in the Commonwealth, and the world is bigger than the Commonwealth.

People could empathize with the David building next to the Goliath building (there I go with a cliché again) but most of all the good citizens of Vancouver knew that the politicians had been beaten by a lowly man from China. Not only that but he had more money than the whole city council put together.

The white folks of Vancouver may not have liked the Chinese but they disliked the politicians even more.

The skinny little building went on to be included in the *Guinness Book of World Records* while the World Tower, which became the Bekins Building, which became the Sun Tower, went on to become just another old building in the city.

You should go to the skinny building. It is on Pender and Carrall. You will see Pender is wider right there, wider than anywhere else on Pender Street. The city council's plan of widening the street lasted one block. After that the street goes back to narrow.

And speaking of narrow, you can stretch out your arms and hold both sides of the world-famous skinny building in your fingertips. It makes a good picture. There is still a thriving business inside.

There is one other thing. The Sun building is no longer visible from this corner. A new multi-screen movie theatre blocks it. The theatre is part of a Chinese shopping complex.

YOU ARE NOT WELCOME

 was writing a story about them. Everyone was writing stories about them. The public could not get enough.

It didn't matter if we wrote in the newspapers that they were hungry and living in misery and had no clean water. A few of us wrote that in sympathy, but when it was read it was seen as what they deserved.

I was on the crowded deck of the SS *Komagata Maru*. It was a chartered ship from Japan whose name has become a symbol of hatred and stupidity. Hundreds of men stood near me, staring at me, hoping I would be able to help them in some way. I could not. No one could. They were condemned by men with no hearts, but with brains that were sharp and devious and cunning.

Every man on the deck had put on his best suit with a clean shirt. Most had ties. The problem was they all had turbans and brown skin.

Circling the ship were dozens of small boats with men singing "White Canada Forever," a hit song at the top of the charts that year—and the year before and the year before. The men on the small boats liked to taunt those on the ship. They were also there to make sure no one would be so foolish as to jump off the ship and try to swim for shore.

The men in the boats said they would assist anyone trying to swim by holding them under water until they stopped swimming. "Oh, did we say 'assist'? We meant *resist*, silly us."

They thought they were funny, but so did the majority of those who lived in Vancouver. "So what if they don't have food or water. If that's the way they like to live, let them."

It was not only the Chinese who were hated because they were not white but those from India also. It was non-discriminatory discrimination. "We hate everyone who is not white" was a big joke at the time.

The problem with the Chinese was that they had been urged to come here to help build the railroad, but now that it was built what do we do with them? Well, smash their store windows and pull their pigtails and hit them in the head. Then they might leave. That was one solution. Also put a tax on their heads if they still wanted to come.

"How much should that tax be? What do you think is fair, Mr. Tax Collector?"

"How about one year's salary? That would be one year's salary of a white man, which the yellow man will never be able to pay."

"Perfect," said just about everyone who was not Chinese.

"Also, they don't belong here anyway. They're foreigners," said just about everyone who was not from India or China.

"But the country lets in foreigners every day," I said. "Tons of them. In fact tons and tons."

"That's different and they are different," they said. "And again, who are you?"

"A reporter."

"A twister of the truth is more like it."

They were right, in a way. Boatloads of foreigners were pouring into Canada every day. In fact, the year before this was happening to the men in turbans, four hundred thousand other foreigners were allowed into Canada, but the people who did not like me were right. Those four hundred thousand were different. Almost all of them were from Europe and did not wear turbans and you can't get more different than that.

There were 376 passengers on the ship that was ordered to anchor in Burrard Inlet, and to make sure it stayed anchored a Royal Navy gun ship was anchored nearby. Occasionally, just for the sport of it, the sailors would aim their cannons at the ship carrying the men with turbans.

But there was a problem that these white loyal subjects of the British Empire had to face, and it was a tricky one. All the passengers on this ship were also loyal subjects of the British Empire and had a legal right to live anywhere in that empire.

And just as a side note, because I was a soldier, I have to tell you that at one time the Sikh Regiment that fought for King and Country was one of the most highly decorated units in the entire British Empire.

"*Hummm,*" thought the politicians and the Attorney General. "This could

The passengers aboard the **Komagata Maru** *waited without fresh food or water for two months in Burrard Inlet. Nothing came until they agreed to leave.*
Photo by James Luke Quiney, City of Vancouver Archives AM1584-: CVA 7-123

have been quite a problem if we hadn't been smart enough to hire that brilliant lawyer a few years ago."

Actually it was six years earlier that a conniving legal mind had come up with a simple solution to a complicated problem. He had suggested that the only way you could legally get off a ship in Canada was if that ship had come directly from its starting point without stopping. For someone coming from India that was impossible.

Of course stopping somewhere has nothing to do with immigrating, but just think. There is no ship or boat or magic carpet that carries enough coal to get from India to Vancouver. They all have to stop to fuel up along the way. That is why lawyers get paid so well. The politicians made it into a law.

The ship with the men with turbans had stopped for coal on the way.

"Can't come in," said the politicians in Vancouver. "It's against the law."

It went on for two months. No food or water was allowed to be brought to the ship in hopes they would get so miserable they would leave on their own. There were many negotiations, and many reporters, and many sad faces on the deck.

In the end the men in turbans gave in and said they would leave. The government turned generous. Food and water were allowed to be brought on board.

The ship sailed away with the guns of the Royal Navy ship pointed at the tired passengers and the singing of "White Canada Forever" in their ears.

When they got back to Calcutta the world was at war, again. This was the First World War and war changes things. Many of the passengers were seen as terrorists and traitors to Britain. Many were arrested and some were lined up and shot. I never found out how many, no one was counting, but there were many.

The stories of the past are not all good or all bad but some are just plain hard even to listen to.

The good thing is that now men with turbans are doing most of the house building, most of the truck driving, most of the taxi driving, much of the computing, much of the law-making, much of the law enforcing, much of the reporting, and just a smidge of the underworld drug dealing in the province.

Also, in the army, they make good Sappers, and you can't get better than that.

OLD BUILDINGS

This is the home of George Smith, located on Campbell Avenue in Strathcona. For this photo, taken in 1909, he wore his derby and the only white shirt he had. His neighbourhood was made up of burned stumps and smoke. Now it is trendy, with stumps being installed in gardens.
Photo by Walter M. Draycott, North Vancouver Museum and Archives

We have just been talking about the Sun Tower, and I'm going to tell you more about it, but that is only one of the two most interesting buildings in the city. The other is the Dominion Building, which few talk about or even know about any longer.

The Dominion Building and the Sun Tower: one has ghosts, the other naked women. Which do you want to hear about first?

You pig. Okay, we'll start with the naked women and the Sun Tower.

An American was involved. Of course. It concerned sex and money, two things Americans are famous for.

L.D. Taylor came from Chicago. You know all those images of bawdy, bold Chicago? That was L.D.

His name was Louis Denison Taylor, but call him L.D. Everyone did. They also called him corrupt and crooked and devious and smart—and loved. Almost everyone loved him, everyone except his enemies who said he was turning Vancouver into a city of SIN.

L.D. said he never liked Sunday School anyway. And what was wrong with a little sin, even on Sunday? You don't have many characters around now like this. That is either a good thing or a bad thing, depending on whether you like a clean, gentle city or exciting characters that make good newspaper stories.

L.D. made good stories. You like naked women? L.D. put them right in the middle of the city for everyone to see. Police corruption bother you? Not L.D., not so long as the police only overlooked crimes of vice, which L.D. of course loved.

First, L.D. was born the year after I got to New Westminster. That is, he came into the world in 1857. He grew up liking newspapers, bless him. Newspaper people have imagination, even if their pens sometimes inflate what their brains imagine.

Louis Denison Taylor was a fan of corruption and loose morals. That would make him a good politician. A smart man, he was mayor of Vancouver seven times.
Photo by George T. Wadds, City of Vancouver Archives AM54-S4-: Port D149.1

And what he imagined was a little crookedness. Okay, a lot of crookedness. He defrauded a bank in Chicago in which he had a business interest. He liked banks and newspapers; both provided good cash flow.

He was briefly married to two women at the same time, and at the age of thirty-nine he was arrested and charged with embezzlement. We don't know if he was actually guilty because he never went to trial. He was charged in August 1896, a summer in which Chicago was sweltering. By September he was in Vancouver where the weather was much better.

If he applied for immigration to Canada now, what do you think his chances would be?

"What a beautiful place," he told me. "I knew I could mix politics and sex and newspapers here and have a wonderful life." He was right.

Politics? Yes, no more banking for him; newspapers and politics go together much better, and naked women fit in with both.

But he started out humbly. He got a job with the *Province* in the circulation department and here is where, once again, someone proves that if you want something, basically anything, you put your sights on it and follow your vision.

He saved what money he could and though he did no better than most of us he did scrape together enough to buy a tiny weekly newspaper. It was run by a couple who had started it but the husband had died and now his widow found being editor, reporter and floor sweeper left no time for breathing.

I worked for them for a while and they told me to meet the incoming ships and talk to the passengers and find some exciting stories from far away. The farther away the story came from, the more outlandish it could be.

"Can you imagine that they do things like *that* way over there?" was the best reaction I could hope for. And then I waited for the readers to say either, "I *wish* I was *there*," or "I'm *glad* I'm *here*."

Those are the kind of stories foreign correspondents still try for, and I had my pick of them only a short walk from Gastown. Anyway, this sweet couple naturally called their newspaper the *World*.

You see, newspaper people have few inhibitions.

But L.D. was not really interested in news. He wanted sales. And Vancouver was going through a building boom. It was always going through building booms—and occasional busts. People were moving here by the boatload and the trainload. The old-timers were saying, "What's happening with our town? There are streets and houses where there were bears and forests only a year ago. When will it all stop?"

But it did not stop. Only twenty years earlier there had been about a thousand people, mostly men, living in shacks near Gassy Jack's saloon. By 1900 there were twenty thousand people raising families in houses on streets in downtown Vancouver. By 1910 there were a hundred thousand and some were moving out to the suburbs.

So I was forever bumping into newcomers saying they had come a long way and there was nowhere else to go. Therefore they were staying but the government should think about not letting too many more people in, especially if they were from China or India.

Vancouver was a very popular place despite the thick smoke in the air from the burning mountains of scrap wood and the mud and the lack of any living trees nearby. Yes, I hate to tell you, but by 1910 if you lived in Vancouver you had to leave town to see any trees. And they said that would never happen.

George Smith was one of those escaping to the suburbs. He was a newcomer from England and he bought a plot of land on Campbell Avenue, which was

considered then to be way out of town to the east. It was a half-hour walk from Gassy's saloon. He couldn't afford land in the desirable heart of the city around Main and Hastings.

He built his small shack with a storage shed alongside it and an outhouse in the back. Then he put a fence around the whole thing and his wife planted a garden.

All around him were stumps, many of them twenty or thirty feet high and most of them looking like totem poles of charcoal, remnants of the fires that had been started to clear the land. The air was almost always thick with biting, choking smoke from these fires.

No one called it Beautiful British Columbia then. This was more like ugly, barren, chopped-up, coal-coloured, "I can't hang the clothes out to dry or they get covered with soot" Vancouver.

Someone came by and asked George if he could take a photograph of his new home to document the growth of the city.

George had never had a photograph taken and he said yes. Then he got on his cleanest shirt and one of his treasures from the old country, his derby.

He posed in front of his home with one foot resting on a low board of his fence and *click*. His home, his outhouse, his garden, his derby, along with the crowded, tall, burned stumps and smoke-filled air, became a moment in time travel.

That was 1909. More than a century later you can see the photo. A large blow-up of it is on a wall in the Lynn Valley Library. I like that library. It was named after me. But more important than that, when you look at the picture you can say, "George, that's a fine-looking derby, but if you were alive now the government would require you to wear a hard hat and steel-toed boots if you walked out of your front yard."

When George had been looking for a place to build his home, he had read the ad for his piece of paradise in the *World*. It was one of hundreds of tiny ads saying Land for Sale.

Statues of naked women still adorn the Sun Tower. Today no one notices them but in 1912 they were the triple X movies of the day.
Photo by Lee Ann Cafferata

That was L.D.'s gold mine. He printed all the ads for all the plots of land and in a short time he had the fattest newspaper west of Chicago and north of San Francisco. I no longer had a job at the paper because he didn't care about news, only ads. News cost him money; ads made it for him.

He also had this towering obsession. He wanted to have the tallest building in the British Commonwealth in which to put his newspaper. And he wanted the tower to have a phallic look, even though he never said that, but I mean, just go look at it. Sure there are other towers like, for instance, maybe, let me think about it…. Well, there must be some.

No. That is the only building in the city that looks like what we are not going to say it looks like. And then L.D. said he would like naked women hanging around the place where he works. Who wouldn't?

So he commissioned nine statues, all naked, unclothed, breasts showing, towering goddesses of beauty, to stand on a ledge seven storeys up, all of them rubbing elbows or shoulders or something with his erect tower.

I didn't just say that, did I?

Okay, no more. We did not have *Playboy* then. We did not have the internet. We did not have those theatres with XXX on their marquees.

But we did have L.D.'s tower, the top of which—painted green so it would look old or green with someone else's envy—looked a little like it was circumcised.

Stop. That is enough factual description.

L.D. often told me and everyone else, "I want everyone who is reading the *World* to look up and see where it came from." And at the top were the words *The World*, just in case you did not know.

That was brilliant marketing, especially when you got a bonus peep show built into your looking.

Men stopped by his tower on their way to and from work, even if they were working in the opposite direction. Women threatened their husbands not to look up or they would sleep on the couch, which would be difficult in most homes because there were no couches.

"So the floor is good enough for you, you rotten man who can't keep your eyes down."

His building is seventeen storeys high, which officially did make it the tallest in the Commonwealth in 1912. By that time Vancouver folks had stopped calling him an American, so the Brits did not have to swallow a foreign insult.

Foreigner? How could he be a foreigner? Even before he finished his building he ran for mayor, and won. Over the next twenty-five years every time he needed some more money or got bored he ran again. Seven times he was elected.

And why did the folks love him? He said keep out the Chinese, keep out big business, except newspapers, and let the women have their houses down on Alexander Street where they wore as little clothing as his statues.

He was a good friend and frequent visitor to Alexander Street. For five blocks there was nothing but rooming houses where women would comfort poor, tired men so long as their wallets were not empty when they arrived.

Women's groups in the city did not like this at all, but then women could not vote so it did not matter what they liked, at least according to L.D. The women did complain to the police, but the police were having problems fighting off corruption charges of their own. At the same time, L.D. was being accused of having close ties with the vice lords in the city, and that was while he was mayor.

And you think now that there is conflict in city hall over bicycle paths?

But L.D.'s fortune died one day. Suddenly there was a bust in the building boom. It happened back then just like it happens now. His paper died and his World Tower was mostly empty. So he sold his tall and proud symbol and having nothing better to do he ran for mayor again—and he got elected. When you reach a certain age getting elected to something is as exciting as having a tall and proud symbol of something.

The Bekins Moving Company of Seattle bought his tower and put their name in a giant sign at the top. There was nothing sexy about this. For more than a decade the World Building became the Bekins Building. Talk about having difficulty in rebranding.

Later the *Vancouver Sun*, which was across the street, had a big fire in their building. Their presses and city room were gone. Someone looked out the window and said, "That's a newspaper office waiting for a newspaper."

The *Sun* bought the building and moved in and for more than thirty years had their name at the top. Everyone, literally everyone in the city, forgot about the *World* and the building became the Sun Tower. It still is, even though the *Sun* has moved twice since then.

Poor L.D. His world vanished. The brothels that he loved closed down. The police that he loved for their bending of the rules got rid of their corruption. And the naked women surrounding his seventh floor have grown boring. No one, literally no one, looks up at them any longer. And if they did they would shrug. In fact, his tallest building in the English world is now swallowed up by buildings that make his tower look tiny and quaint. He would be embarrassed, and that is a terrible thing for someone who thought he had the biggest tower in town.

Luckily he died before most of this happened. Rest in peace, L.D. You were like a hot sauce in the city. But like most spices, shortly after the meal they are forgotten.

THE DOMINION BUILDING

 ow I want to tell you the sad story of the big building that went up right before L.D.'s tall, erect tower fawned over by naked women.

Sorry to put it that way, but that is the way he always liked to view it.

The wrought-iron stairs in the Dominion Building are a work of art. Go into the lobby and look for yourself. You can even climb them—but beware of the ghost.
Photo by James Inglis

The other big one was just a few blocks away and it was put up by a banker named William Arnold. Now here is a guy I did not like. He was greedy and if there is anything that turns off most of us good folks it is someone who is never satisfied and wants more and more. He was like the government when it comes to taxes on wine.

Anyway, I met Mr. Arnold—that is what he told me I should call him—when he was running a small money-lending company called Dominion Trust. He told me I should treat him with respect because he was going to be rich someday and have the biggest office in the world.

Okay, if that's what you want, I thought. But the people I liked were happy just having a roof over their heads and a beer with dinner. But most of them had to borrow the money to build their homes and Mr. Arnold was right there, ready with the cash.

"Where are you getting the money to lend them?" I asked.

Mr. Arnold looked at me very sternly. "It is none of your business and I would suggest you do not go into that subject any further."

Well, now. You know what happens when you tell a Sapper to bugger off, even if the Sapper has been dead for decades? The Sapper takes out his shovel and starts digging.

The first thing I learned is that Mr. Arnold's pretty daughter was meeting secretly with a young German man. And the second thing I learned was that Mr. Arnold could not be happier about that.

The reason for the secrecy was that Germany and England were not getting along very well. There was talk of war and after all this was British, not Berlin, Columbia. Most of the wealthier people in town who were not American were British. And most of the poorer people in town who were not hating the Chinese were hating the Germans. In fact, most of them were hating both, along with hating the richer people who had all the money.

That is basically the same way it is now among the poorer folks. They still hate the rich because they are rich, which is a sin, unless you are rich. The good thing is poorer folks no longer hate the Chinese or the Germans or the blacks or the Irish or the Natives or the Albanians, because some of their relatives are at least one of those.

But back a little more than century ago hating Germans was the way to go.

Then I heard this conversation on a park bench outside the new courthouse on East Hastings near Hamilton. I was feeding squirrels and not far from me were the backs of a man and a young woman. It is not that I was eavesdropping; it is just that as a reporter it was my duty to gather information. Besides, I thought the man was Mr. Arnold.

"Daddy, I don't know if I love him."

"Darling daughter, of course you love him. He is so handsome."

How could I resist listening to a conversation like that?

"Daddy, he is touching me in places where he should not touch me."

"Daughter dear, I'm sure his hand just slipped."

Now tell me one person who would walk away from that? That would be the same person who would turn off a late-night, steamy soap opera just when they are coming to the subject of the meaning of life, accentuated with touching.

"Daddy, he is German. What will people say?"

"Don't worry, daughter dear, I have always believed all people are equal. And besides, if he doesn't open his mouth no one will know."

Then the man got up. It *was* Mr. Arnold. Whoops. I did not want him to think I was playing reporter when I was just feeding squirrels. I tossed a peanut

Court House, Vancouver, B.C.

The first courthouse was used for only fourteen years before it was found to be too small. It stood across the street from the Dominion Building and was demolished in 1913. A new courthouse was built on Georgia Street to replace it, but it was almost immediately found to be too small and was turned into an art gallery. In the old days Judge Begbie used a stump for his bench and the courthouse was always the right size.
City of Vancouver Archives
AM54-S4-: Bu N13

far away and walked after it. I ask you, have you ever seen a guilty-looking squirrel feeder?

Mr. Arnold then excused himself from his daughter and I could just barely hear him say he had to use the Men's Comfort Room.

That was one of the great things about this corner that had become the centre of the city. There were toilets underground for both men and women. They were put there because the giant, impressive, stone courthouse that dispensed justice and sentenced murderers to hang had no indoor plumbing.

Sometimes you could hear inside a courtroom: "For your dastardly deed I sentence you to hang by the neck until dead." Bang. That was the hammer coming down as the judge stood up and started to leave.

"But Your Honour," the defendant started to say as the judge left the room, "I am only here for parking my horse on the wrong side of the street."

Too late. The judge was out the front door, down the stone steps, across the lawn, down the next flight of steps, under the sidewalk and in front of the trough. *Ahhh.* "I didn't think I was going to make it," I'd hear him say.

Meanwhile the defendant was taken away saying, "I didn't do it."

"They always say that," said the judge.

If you go to that corner now you can still use the bathroom, but the toilet and three of the stone steps that led up to the courthouse are all that remain. Government officials in their extreme wisdom decided after only fourteen years that one of the most beautiful buildings in the city was too small to use for a courthouse any longer. So they knocked it down.

That created an empty lot that became Victory Square. Once a year, on November 11, it is used for a solemn ceremony and the rest of the year it's taken over by drug dealers who now don't go to court or jail or anywhere except to their money-laundering friends.

But let us get back to when there was justice and a courthouse and Mr. Arnold and his daughter. I saw him come back up from the toilet and he looked across the street. It was the empty corner of Cambie and East Hastings.

"That will be the home of my empire," he said to himself while I and my bag of peanuts were listening.

"If I can just keep The Count happy that corner will be the most famous place in the city. Heck. It will be the most famous corner in Canada. No, in the British Empire."

Mr. Arnold was a man of ambition.

When the courthouse was torn down the land was used for army recruitment and church revival meetings. Later it became a sacred plot for one day a year.

Photo by Stuart Thomson, City of Vancouver Archives AM1535-: CVA 99-1477

Then he added, "And it will be all mine."

That's why I didn't like him.

Later, through a little bit of Sapper-like digging and reporter-like finger-crossing, I learned that the German fellow was a real German count. On the other hand, what young handsome German fellow with an expensive suit and polished shoes was not a count? And he had a count-like name: Gustav Konstantin von Alvensleben, a.k.a. Alvo von Alvensleben, a.k.a. The Count. And he had one other thing: money, which he was handing over to Mr. Arnold.

Investing, he said.

Actually, he had arrived in Vancouver about 1905 with nothing. By 1906 he had received many packages from Germany. He opened them in his hotel room. Each was filled with money. He had instructions to make more of it.

The best way was in a trust company that would not ask him where the money was coming from. This happened about the same time as he met the pretty young woman and discovered her father was the vice-president of a trust company.

It is wonderful how things turn out when you are young and good-looking and have packages of money.

What I learned through talking with the captains of incoming ships, mostly from Germany, was that the Kaiser was ripping off the people of his country. He was putting large taxes on things such as wine and beer and donkeys and sausages and castles. And he was not doing anything in return with the money except building up an army in case they went to war with those rotten Englishmen.

The Kaiser's problem was that he was getting so much money that he did not know what to do with it. So he enlisted the help of young, good-looking German counts and asked them to do some travelling. He would send them money to invest and they would keep track of it and make it grow and everyone would get rich, except for the poor Germans who were paying the taxes.

In a way the poor have a good reason for hating the rich.

Anyway, in the language we use now, the Kaiser was laundering his ill-gotten gains the same as the Hell's Angels do now with their money by putting it into legitimate wholesome businesses, like tattoo parlours that specialize in pictures of motorcycles.

Within two years of arriving in Vancouver, Count von Alvensleben had put several million dollars into the hands of Mr. Arnold. Mr. Arnold was very happy. Mr. Arnold told his daughter that she and the count were a beautiful couple and not to worry about his roaming fingers.

Mr. Arnold loaned out the count's money to people who wanted to build little houses for themselves as places to keep out of the rain and raise families and help build a new country. He charged a goodly interest, which made more money for the count and much more money for himself.

Then came that moment after Mr. Arnold emptied his bladder and anointed himself king of the money-lending world. All he needed was a castle.

It would be the biggest building in the world, or at least in the British world, which really was the only one anyone cared about.

So right at the corner of Cambie and Hastings, which was then the centre of town, he commissioned a skyscraper.

Up went the Dominion Building, thirteen storeys high, the highest office building under any Union Jack anywhere on the planet.

Mr. Arnold was happy and, after all, that was what was really important. The only thing he did not like was the thirteenth floor, which was unlucky, so he had

it changed to the fourteenth floor and moved his office into it.

Actually, there was something else he did not like, and that was family dinners when he had to listen to that incessant German accent from his son-in-law.

If you have never been into the building, I ask, what's stopping you? You are not going to get an invitation, because bad things happened to Mr. Arnold and he was not in the mood to have company—I'll tell you about that in a minute—but truly, his building is beautiful. He had a good architect.

You can walk in. The doors are not locked. The lobby has inlaid tile and a curved ceiling and there is a spiralling wrought-iron stairway that goes to the tenth floor and you can pretend you are in an Alfred Hitchcock movie while climbing it.

That became Mr. Arnold's story, too. While he was climbing to the top of his world of money a funny thing happened to the housing market, the thing no one thinks will ever happen but always does. The boom busted.

Coincidentally, his son-in-law was in the Fatherland gathering up packages of investments that could have saved his father-in-law.

I said "could have" because, darn, one other little thing happened while the count and his packages were on a ship heading back to Vancouver.

World War I. Germany versus Britain.

No German ships were allowed to dock in Vancouver. The count's ship was detoured to Seattle. All his money in Vancouver was confiscated by the government as enemy property. When the US also went to war with Germany the poor count was arrested as a spy and he spent the rest of the war in an internment camp at Fort Douglas, Utah.

Back in Vancouver Mr. Arnold did the only thing he could that let him deal with a few bumps in the road.

Now before I tell you what he did, although I bet you have already guessed it, I have to tell you how the media get so many things wrong.

There was a balding, pot-bellied television reporter I met once who did a story about the Dominion Building and the ghost who lives in it.

This reporter talked to the tenants in the building, who are now mostly artists and movie producers, people with good imaginations. They all said they knew about the ghost and it was William Arnold, the man who had the building put up and then lost it.

See? That reporter used Mr. Arnold's whole name but I'm not jealous. Not me.

This reporter said William Arnold went into his office on the top floor and shot himself in the head with a pistol.

Wrong, wrong, wrong.

You must get your facts right.

On October 12, 1914, William Arnold, the vice-president and general manager of the Dominion Trust, went into his Shaughnessy Heights garage and shot himself in the head with a shotgun.

There. That sets the record right.

But he was right about the ghost.

CARNEGIE LIBRARY

ome with me for a walk. Just a few blocks. It's quite safe.

Okay, it does not look safe. In fact it looks like one of the world's ugliest stretches of wasted humanity. No, that is not an exaggeration. I have done some travelling and nowhere in Moscow, Paris, London, Detroit, Chicago, Los Angeles, New York or Kamloops is there anything like East Hastings.

The Carnegie Public Library at Main and Hastings was a gift to the city from Andrew Carnegie, who wanted everyone to have a chance to read. When the city wanted to tear down the building the Carnegie Foundation said, "Don't you dare." The City Hall building next to the library had a different fate.
Photo by Philip Timms, City of Vancouver Archives AM336-S3-3-: CVA 677-655

But it is mostly safe, unless you open a restaurant there or try to improve things. Then the local citizens will picket you, steal your signs and try to make your life miserable because you are trying to make theirs better.

"You are gentrifying our neighbourhood," they yell. "Get out. This is our home."

That is like the ten-year-old saying, "Don't tell me to wash my hands before eating. These are my hands."

And then he tears two pieces of pizza apart with his fingers, which are covered with dirt from the ground and grease from his bicycle, and puts one of the pieces back on the plate for someone else.

"Leave me alone. This is my dinner."

With the ten-year-old you send him to the bathroom to wash or to bed without pizza.

With the self-righteous, pampered and catered-to drug addicts you give them more government money. Then you let them harass the owners of the new restaurants because it is their right. Then you wait for them to go away for their free lunches and dinners at the nice places that give it to them.

"They are having chicken at Harbour Light tonight," I heard someone say.

"I just had chicken for lunch at Union Gospel," I heard someone else say. "And besides, they make you pray at Harbour."

"Let's check the Carnegie. They have good food."

The Carnegie. That is where we are heading. Just walk past the upstanding citizens of East Hastings, at least the few who are standing up, and head to the Carnegie.

This building is a living testimony to the strength of a legal form. "Why?" you ask.

Let me introduce you to Andrew Carnegie, the most brilliant man of modern history, or at least the one every entrepreneur should learn about. And at the same time let me introduce you to the dumbest civic leaders of modern history.

They were the Vancouver aldermen who voted to destroy the beautiful train station at the north end of Granville Street and the courthouse in Victory Square and the train station at the north foot of Main Street and the original city hall. In fact, almost all the beautiful buildings in the city were either knocked down by the politicians or allowed by them to be knocked down.

One of the non-government buildings was owned by the CPR. Surprise. The CPR built an elegant hotel at the north end of Granville Street, about where the

SeaBus terminal is now. But then for good reasons, at least good to them, they wanted people to stay a little to the south where Georgia Street crosses Granville so they built a new hotel there. They called it the Hotel Vancouver. It was where Eaton's, which became Sears, which became Nordstrom, was built later.

To make sure upscale visitors would stay at the new hotel they wanted the older one knocked down.

They went to the aldermen and said, "You know what to do." They did not have to add, "Or you won't have anything to do if you don't do what we want you to do."

So the aldermen did what the lobby group said they should do. Permits were issued and it was knocked down. Believe me, it was an elegant building. I had coffee in there once while talking to a beautiful woman and I was not sure which was prettier, the building or the woman. In the end both went away.

The new hotel, the first Hotel Vancouver, was more modern but in time the CPR executives got tired of it. Changing styles made them want to change hotels, so they built a second Hotel Vancouver half a block away where the TD Tower is now.

Time passed and the big brass wanted a new hotel again. Some people buy new shoes or cars; the CPR big shots built new hotels.

This third Hotel Vancouver is the one you now see but the executives were worried that their second Hotel Vancouver might compete against it, so it too was demolished.

Simple: You don't like something so down it comes.

And then the city decided it would get on the demolition bandwagon and it knocked down its own city hall.

That was also a beautiful building. It was near the corner of Main and Hastings when that was the centre of everything. It had gaslights in the offices and folks would stand outside after dark in the winter just to see this ultramodern easing of the burdens of the politicians and bureaucrats. No more candles for them.

The building was brick with a two-storey tower on each side. I used to wonder if there was a connection between the mayor being called "Your Worship" and his office looking sort of like a cathedral.

But before I tell you how city hall disappeared I have to tell you about what was built next door to it and the man who could still change your life.

Andrew Carnegie was born poor, dirt poor, hungry and poor. His birth, like that of so many of his neighbours, was an accident and unwanted. He was the son of a weaver in Scotland, which was a country of weavers. The Carnegies lived in one room with a dirt floor. His mother and father wove yarn into cloth and tried to sell it on streets that were lined with others trying to sell cloth.

You get the picture. It was not a good beginning.

With no future where they were, they sailed for America. They travelled steerage. We cannot imagine how terrible that was. The slaves had it worse— much worse—but steerage was only one step up.

The poor, huddled masses were locked in the bowels of the ship. The only thing below them was the ballast and the rats, and the rats did not stay down in the bottom.

Andrew and his family were jammed in so tightly that six of them would be on one wooden slab, with other slabs above them and below. They could sit up only by bending over. There was no room to stretch their arms or legs.

Again, you get the idea. It was bad. And in the crowded space between the bunks they cooked, or tried to cook, on a stove fed by charcoal that filled the air with poisonous, choking fumes. And the food that they cooked was what they had brought and after a few weeks it was not in good shape.

Add to that bodily fluids, including those that come up when the ship rolls, and you have ghosts who don't understand why people now go on ocean cruises for vacations.

They were allowed to climb to the open air on deck for an hour a day, but not on all days. For many, the last time they got to be on that deck was when they were buried at sea.

By the time I met Andrew Carnegie he was sailing to Europe first class on the most luxurious ships.

"How did you do that?" I asked.

"Simple," he told me. "I believed I would, and so I did."

I thought, come on, please. I have heard that positive thinking stuff before, but really, it's luck, isn't it, or a rich ancestor dying?

"I know what you are thinking," Andrew Carnegie said to me. "That's what everyone thinks, but no, it is belief and work and then you make your luck and *you* become the rich one who dies." Then he winked at me and said, "Sometimes there is a little luck, but you have to use that luck or it will blow away."

He told me that when they got to America he got a job as a bobbin boy in a spinning mill. His Scottish friends were still in the cloth-making business and his job was hopping barefoot over the moving machines changing spools of thread twelve hours a day, six days a week. He was paid enough to feed himself for three days. He was thirteen years old.

His next job was as a telegraph messenger. You know those old pictures of the boy riding on a bicycle delivering telegraphs? He did it without the bike. And he gave all his money to his mother.

Then came that little bit of luck. A rich and kindly man in his town had a library. He had four hundred books, which is not very many by modern standards. They could fit in about twenty cardboard boxes. On the other hand that is four times more than most people now read in a lifetime. With so much texting going on, who has time for reading?

Anyway, this nice man opened his library to the poor kids in his town for two hours every Saturday. They could read anything they wanted.

Andrew had learned to read in his few years in school but his family was too poor to have any books. There were no libraries in town and there was no more schooling waiting for him.

Instead, he read in this man's home. He could not wait for Saturdays and he read. He read every book that was on the shelves. He read Shakespeare and history and math. He read every book on science, geography and economics. Whether he understood or not, he kept reading. And then as he read more he did understand. He read books on business.

When you were fourteen what kind of stories did you read? I am not knocking you. I was still trying to work out the simple sentences in the police gazette. I am just telling you how Andrew Carnegie did not waste his lucky chance.

His mother had faith in him. When he was twenty his mother gave him five hundred dollars raised by mortgaging their home. Many people get money from their parents but Andrew took it and invested—successfully—in a delivery company.

He later received shares in a sleeping car company that merged with the Pullman Coach Company, which went on to be an extremely profitable enterprise.

And then he put his profits into a small oil company. Who would put their money into oil when people were still heating their homes with wood and coal?

The answer? Smart people.

This was not the stock market of the Ponzi schemes or day trading or margin buying. He was putting into practice what he had read. Work at finding something small that could grow into something big and put your heart and wallet into it.

"So what does positive thinking have to do with any of this?" I asked him.

"Everything," he said. "I believed things would work out for the best. I believed that so much that I started to fool myself into seeing that things were working out for the best. And after a while I wasn't fooling any longer. Things were working out just the way I had hoped they would."

And then came talk of a terrible war, a war that would pit people in the same family against each other. A civil war.

It sounds crass, but a war must be won if you believe in your side. And it seemed obvious that investing in steel at the beginning of a war would be not only a smart thing to do but patriotic, too. No war before had used steel for anything but swords. This one would be different.

He put his money into steel just as the US was heading into its crushing Civil War. The war was terrible but if the US were to remain a nation the north had to win. It needed steel to do that. The new rifles were made of steel. The bayonets were made of steel. The Gatling guns, a brand name for the first machine guns, were made of steel. The only things not steel were the cotton shirts of the soldiers.

The Battle of Antietam, September 17, 1862; more than twenty thousand men blown apart in one day. And then the Battle of Gettysburg; more than fifty thousand wounded or killed in three days of shooting and stabbing from July 1 to July 3, 1863.

Those were just two battles. Death by someone else's rifle is bad no matter when, but steel in the Civil War was forged into a destructive power no one had imagined. It became the nuclear weapon of the nineteenth century.

But because of steel and good generals and a bunch of other things, the US survived, slavery was abolished and Andrew Carnegie became richer than anyone could imagine.

Funny how all that goes together—pain and death (which are wrong), freedom (which is good) and a nation that is still trying to unify itself (which is crazy). And out of that came wealth for some. As awful as it sounds and is, war always makes some people rich.

And then Andrew Carnegie, who had warehouses full of money, said something that would stick in the throats of most rich people. He whispered it into my ear.

"Nothing is worse than worshipping of money."

"Are you kidding?" I said.

"No, I mean it. Money is evil. The amassing of wealth is one of the worst forms of idolatry."

"Yes, that is nice of you to say now that you are rich, but rich people can afford to say things like that."

That was me, who had about two hundred dollars in the bank and no government pension, trying to mock one of the richest people in the history of the world.

"Sure, you can say money means nothing to you now that you have money," I went on. "But that doesn't mean anything to us folks who buy coffee instead of whisky because it's cheaper, not because it is healthier."

I wonder, now that fancy coffee can cost more than whisky, what Andrew's reaction would be to the price of a low fat, no foam, extra hot, double shot grande latte?

I imagine that when he stopped laughing he would say there is nothing wrong with plain tea.

Then he told me something that is still the most shocking thing I have ever heard in my life. And remember, my life is no trivial matter.

"I am going to give away my money."

"You're kidding?"

"No, Jock, I'm not. Money is bad. Collecting bottle caps is more fun."

What? The world's richest man calling me by my first name and telling me that he is going to be just like me, worried about making the next rent payment?

"That's nice," I said. "But how, and where?"

I did not ask if I could have some. Okay, I was hoping it but I would not say it. That is what all street beggars ask. "Can I have some of your money because you have more than me?"

Well, no. Why don't you work for it? Why don't you get a job hopping barefoot over cloth-making machines and changing the bobbins? You are wasting your time standing on a corner asking for money when you could be delivering newspapers or cutting grass and then reading books on how to improve your life.

So, no. No asking.

But Andrew Carnegie had a plan. He gave his money to hospitals and charities. He gave to cultural organizations. He built Carnegie Hall in New York so musicians would have a grand place to perform. But most of all, he built libraries. He wanted others to have the same chance he had had.

As far as his money went, he had mountains of it. In the end he gave away everything except a shoebox full of cash that he could live on. "Now I am happy," he told me.

I told him about Mr. Arnold in the previous story. I told him how Mr. Arnold lost his money and so he blew his brains out.

"Shame," said Mr. Carnegie. "He could have used the time to do some reading, for free, in the library."

Andrew Carnegie built more than twenty-five hundred libraries around the world, most of them in the US, but also many in Britain and Ireland. He built some in Australia and Fiji. Almost any city or town that wrote a letter to him asking for a library got a library.

"What about Vancouver?" I asked.

Work began on the new library as soon as Carnegie had given his approval for the project and the contract had been signed. Perched atop the columns of its classical portico in 1902, workmen construct the floor of the dome that will complete the impressive entrance.

City of Vancouver Archives AM1376-: CVA 1376-27

"Do they have poor kids there who would like to learn and improve their lives?" he asked.

"Yes, of course," I said. The video game had not yet been invented. There was hope for those kids if they were given a chance.

"You will have a library. Just follow the rules."

And he sent a legally binding contract to the city of Vancouver. Yes, a free library. Super. Wonderful. What do we have to do?

Nothing, said Carnegie and his people. They would supply the building and the books. All Vancouver had to do was maintain it—you know, wash the windows and buy new books, especially, they said, local writers.

Okay, okay, okay. The words came out of the Vancouver city people faster than their mouths could shape them. They were in actual unanimous agreement. Imagine, something for nothing. Just supply a janitor and a librarian.

The city officials signed on the dotted line, and the building went up right next to city hall, because Main and Hastings was still the centre of town. The building was, and still is, beautiful. You can still see it. Thanks to that blessed legal document I mentioned earlier, the building has not gone away. Go inside. Don't be frightened by the drug dealers out front. They stay away from anyone with combed hair and a clean shirt.

Once inside, gaze at the marble stairs and the stained glass windows. Visit the reading room. It really has books, and in that room you feel good. You are in a place of quiet and learning. You could turn into another Andrew Carnegie. Tons of kids in the 1910s and through the twenties, thirties, forties and fifties did their homework in there. Lots of young minds grew strong in there and old minds travelled in peace between hard covers.

Now go back a half century to 1958. Time travel again. The city fathers had moved to a new city hall and they knocked down the old beautiful city hall that was next door to the library. They could have turned it into a museum or an office building or a care home for aging, demented politicians, but no, they knocked it down. There is now a strip mall with a dollar store where the red brick city hall once stood.

And again time passed and Main and Hastings was no longer the centre of town. In fact, as you know, it is an outpost of human misery. It is ugly. It is miserable. And it is an embarrassment.

And the city officials said, "Why are we keeping this old library here when no one around here can read?"

So they passed the order to demolish it.

Mistake.

The people in the Carnegie Foundation heard about it and before the Vancouver politicians could congratulate themselves for getting rid of that old-fashioned, out-of-place ugly thing that was taking up space that could be turned into more dollar stores they put a STOP order on it.

"Stop what?" said the Vancouver politicians to the Carnegie people.

"Stop the demolition."

"You are not even from this city," the politicians said. "What right do you have to tell us what to do with *our* library?"

The Carnegie people held up the original contract. "Read it," they said.

"This is gibberish," the politicians said. "This building has been here for more than fifty years. You gave it to us. It's ours. And now we want to get rid of it."

"Read it," the Carnegie people said.

"Mumble, mumble, mumble." That's the way politicians read when they really don't understand what they are reading.

"It says you will maintain the building," the Carnegie people told them, helping them a bit with the reading.

"So?"

"So, maintaining it does not mean demolishing it."

"You're kidding?"

The Carnegie people were not kidding. The politicians were peeved, but I was willing to bet that the city lawyers would be no match for the Carnegie Foundation lawyers.

In short, that is why the Carnegie Library is still there. One piece of paper, and that is the only reason it is still there. And although most of the building has been taken over by social programs for the poor of the neighbourhood there is still a reading room with about four hundred books in it.

The opportunity is still there.

FALSE CREEK

eorge Vancouver was impressed.

"If there were ever to be any civilization in this remote part of the world those people would have a wonderful inland sea. They could go fishing from their backyards."

I'm not sure if he actually said that, but as he sailed partway into the creek all he could see was water in the middle and trees on the sides. He had oysters for dinner taken from right near the shoreline.

This is how False Creek looked when half of it had been filled in during the construction of the Great Northern Railway terminal. At one time the water went another kilometre inland to the hills of Clark Drive.
City of Vancouver Archives
AM54-S4-: Bu N540.004

Later another Englishman, Captain George Henry Richards, sailed farther inland and got stuck in the mud.

"Darn. This is not a creek," he said. "It is a false creek." That was in 1859 and that was all it took. He wrote the name on a map and you know if you start renaming places no one will know where they are. For instance, SoMa. "I live in SoMa," someone told me. That was someone very trendy.

"Is that near NoMa?" I asked, trying to be cute.

"Of course not," he said. "No one lives in NoMa. NoMa has not yet been discovered and so it's not *In* and if it's not *In* no one would live there."

"So where is SoMa?" I asked.

He looked at me with pity and astonishment. "SoMa is South Main, which is now *In* so everyone lives there. NoMa is North Main and no one lives there because that is not yet *In*."

I have been wandering up and down Main Street for 125 years, since it was called Westminster Avenue. And it was called that because it was built to go from Gastown to connect with Kingsway, which took you to New Westminster. Very simple. You could not get lost.

Now I did not know where I was.

In the 1880s the road that was to become Main Street was called Westminster Avenue. Chinatown was on the far side and a bridge was needed to cross False Creek. The bridge could be raised to allow boats through.
Photo by Philip Timms, City of Vancouver Archives AM336-S3-2-: CVA 677-988

Anyway, the name was changed to Main Street to make it sound more American. That was back in 1910 when the town was growing and Americans were heading north to take advantage of low housing prices. They did not know you had to build your own.

But the city council changed the name to make them want to buy on a street that sounded more American than British because every American town had a Main Street. Yes. That is true. I don't know why you doubt me. I was there.

Anyway, back in those days Main Street turned into a bridge when you got to the area about where Science World is now.

That was because of the topic we are talking about: False Creek. In case you did not know, False Creek used to go all the way to where Clark Drive is now.

Don't worry if you live in Surrey and have no idea what I am talking about. Just close your eyes and picture this: a massive stretch of land now all covered with weeds and railroad tracks that is more than two kilometres long and in places almost a kilometre wide was once a calm, clean inland ocean. If you do ever get downtown, go over to Main Street and stand near the big ball that is Science World. Now look to the east. You see that rise in the land, that hill, far in the distance?

Good. You are doing well. That is Clark Drive. When your great-grandparents came up here from Seattle to tour around, that stretch was all water. When they took a ride on a False Creek ferry they had to pack a lunch *and* a dinner.

What happened? Glad you asked. Someone wanted to make some money and then someone went broke. The usual story.

As you know, the Canadian Pacific Railway had been in town for years. They came in the easy way, along the flat coast of Burrard Inlet. Granted, they had killed a lot of Chinese workers going over the Rockies but the final approach in railroad terms was a piece of cake.

Later another railroad wanted in. It was the Great Northern Railway. The city said fine, come, but there was a catch. There was no way to get into the city. They were coming from the east and between their locomotives and the city was all this water.

"If we could find a way to get into the city we could take advantage of all the wealth, all the trees and salmon that they have," said the Great Northern officials.

There was a steep incline from about where Nanaimo Street is now up to where Clark Drive is now. Clark Drive was the top of a long, sloping hill. Down below, on the western side of it was the water of False Creek.

Two problems: trains don't do inclines and trains don't swim.

The solution: dig a trench from the bottom of the incline right through the hill that held back the water. That way the trains would not have to go uphill. That was about three kilometres of digging. At its deepest the trench would have walls eighty feet high.

You'll have to excuse me. For a hundred years I used English measurements and then Canada switched to metric. I am sometimes lost between the two.

Now all this digging was going to be hard, so the first thing they did was— you guessed it—hire a lot of Chinese. They were good at hard work.

The job, done with steam shovels and fingernails, took about two years.

There was one other thing, and this was the brilliance of the plan. All the dirt that they took out of the trench dug from Nanaimo Street to Clark Drive they dumped into the waters of False Creek. With each shovelful of dirt more water disappeared and the tracks were getting closer. And with each shovelful more of the beauty of Vancouver disappeared. And with each shovelful the smiles on the faces of the railroad officials grew broader. The smell of money did the trick.

Not only would the Great Northern get into Vancouver but it would have a place to park its trains. Sure it cost a bit but you have to spend money to make money.

I watched them spend more and more. They hired more Chinese workers. Of course they were being underpaid, but what did you expect? There were more of them and so they were costing more. And they built tracks through the ditch, which was given a new name. It was called the Cut, because would you rather have your trains go through a cut or a ditch? You can change the feel of almost anything by changing its name.

Did you know that one of the world's best-selling cooking oils used to be one of the worst-selling oils? And it comes from Canada.

It was rapeseed oil. Now who is going to sprinkle *that* over lettuce? Not you, not me. It was used to lubricate machinery.

How did it get that name? The grass it comes from is related to the turnip. The Latin name for turnip is *Rapum*. Hence: rapeseed. That was like naming a boy Sue. It made a good song for Johnny Cash but the boy named Sue grew up tough and unloved.

What's more, rapeseed oil had a bitter, acid taste. Bad name, bad taste, pour it on that rusty hinge. That works.

Then some bright farmers found a way of growing it with low acid. Tasted good, but still no one would buy rapeseed oil.

And then some bright person had a brilliant idea. The world's main producer of rapeseed is Canada. Change the name to Canola oil. Everyone loves Canada, but why the "ola"? CANadian Oil, Low Acid. You get it? *Can-o-la.*

It is now the world's third most popular oil, after soybean and palm oil, and it's healthier than either of them.

Excuse me. Detours are fun but they don't get you where you are going.

Anyway, the Great Northern Railway was digging its ditch and planning its future and spending a lot of money to do it, and here is another thing you should always do: Listen to your accountants.

But the managers of the Great Northern could only hear the chugging of their steam engines getting closer to their new home, an endless field of hard-packed dirt where the water used to be. Onto the dirt went the steel tracks and at the end of the tracks, just off Main Street, they built a mammoth station to handle all the passengers they would attract.

And alongside the tracks on the land that once was water they built a road that went from the end of the Cut at Clark Drive to the door of their new station. They called it Great Northern Way.

"This time we will really see men walking on water," they joked.

Then they went bankrupt.

Whoops. As I say, listen to your accountants.

The Canadian government took over the company and changed its name to Canadian National. The only thing left is the road, which is still called Great Northern Way. It's where traffic police often set up a speed trap. Men and women now get tickets for driving too fast on asphalt, which once was water. That is just nature getting back at us.

A funny thing happened about ten years ago when Vancouver wanted to put a SkyTrain line through the Cut. Environmental groups picketed it saying no one should disturb this natural environment.

WARREN G. HARDING. THAT WOULD BE MR. PRESIDENT TO YOU

American President Warren Harding waves to the Vancouver crowd during a parade on July 26, 1923, shortly before his mysterious demise. His morals were so loose they fell down as fast as his pants.
City of Vancouver Archives
AM54-S4-: Port P853.1

t was a bad trip. When you go on vacation you want things to turn out well. When you end up dead it is not the best experience.

Such was the final postcard from Mr. Harding after his visit to Vancouver. "Having a miserable time. Wish you—or anyone—were here instead of me."

160

And not just dead, but there was a strong suspicion of murder.

That would make it a presidential assassination. Yes. True. If it was murder, and many think it was, he would be the first and only US president killed in Canada.

First of all there are a few things you should know about Warren G. Harding.

I slipped down to Washington DC to check this out myself, because I could not believe all I was hearing. If it was true, at least he would demonstrate that inept, crooked, immoral politicians are nothing new. But the depth of his idiocy was head-scratchingly profound.

First there was his adultery. No one could count the number of one-night stands he had. Yes, he was married, but every week or so his eyes would see some new beauty and that was it. He would have her in bed before the week was out.

Or he would have her in a closet in the Oval Office, in which his wife at one time caught him—and her.

He also had at least five mistresses over his thirty-two years of marriage, including one for fifteen years, but most of his wild nights and afternoons and mornings came during his two and a half years as president. He made Kennedy and Clinton look almost saintly.

I would watch Harding go out for a night on the town and an FBI agent would follow. His one job was to keep a record of whom the president was sharing presidential closeness with.

Actually, he had two jobs. The other was to pay the blackmail demands of the women to whom Harding wrote gushy love letters—and there were many. He fell in love frequently and he loved to express his love.

The women would then call the White House and demand money or they would go to the press, and the payments would follow.

Of course, that was not all the press. The famous *Washington Post*, the paper that helped bring down Richard Nixon when he was accused of corruption, would print nothing bad about Harding. That was because the publisher was a poker buddy of the most powerful man in the world. He was also a pimp for the president. He also supplied the whisky for the poker games, which went on all night and included members of the president's cabinet and other officials who would stagger into meetings in the morning trying to figure out how to run the country, or how to make their heads stop hurting.

In case you were wondering, this was during Prohibition, when alcohol was illegal for the rest of the country.

Canada did okay because all the whisky in the White House came from here. At least with all the thieving and philandering they helped the economy of Canadian distillers.

Let me tell you two other things about President Harding: one I didn't see, the other I heard about from everyone, including the president's wife who spoke in a moment of frustration.

Firstly, one of the president's confidence men who had been ripping off the veterans' hospitals took too much extra for himself, and President Harding, in an executive decision, tried to choke him to death. Yes, literally, the president of the United States tried to choke one of his advisers to death. A security guard in the White House broke up the fight and pried Harding's fingers off his adviser's throat.

The problem nowadays is that so many people try to hold back their emotions and choose to go through the courts. That's why the courts are so crowded. If we had more Hardings we would spend less waiting time for justice.

By the way, two of his advisers committed suicide. At least that is the official version. Oddly, one of them passionately hated guns and yet was found next to a pistol with a bullet hole through his head. Some people who are natural doubters think he was murdered. People like that give politicians a bad name.

The second big news would have been on the front of the *National Enquirer*, had there been an *Enquirer* then.

The headline? "I'm His Wife but Not the Mother of His Children."

Okay, yuck. This is not a guy you want playing Santa Claus on Christmas morning but it's okay for him to be head of the most powerful nation on earth.

He had at least two children with his lovers. He had no children with his wife. You might think she could not have children.

Wrong. She had a son from a brief marriage before she met the man who would be king, or president, or the man with the greased zipper.

So it was not her biology that prevented her conceiving. I suspect Mr. President was too busy with external relations to deal with domestic tranquility.

Anyway, we are back to why all this interest in BC with the twenty-ninth president of those United States.

He was coming to Vancouver, the first US president to do so. It was just going to be the tail end of an Alaskan cruise with a brief stopover in Vancouver for a round of golf, a little speech and lunch. Also he had heard the women here were very pretty.

First thing, the speech. July 26, 1923. Forget the date—it was summer and the president of the US was speaking in Stanley Park.

People thought this must be important. He had nothing to say, but he was a very important person so the folks came out. There was no hockey game on that night.

Fifty thousand eager Vancouver residents crowded into the area where Theatre Under the Stars is now. They spilled over into where the rose garden is now and they spread out to where the children's zoo is no longer.

Did you know that the anti-zoo people were so strong that when they got rid of the zoo—I am not going to argue about that: cages are bad for animals but animals are good for kids—anyway, when they got rid of the zoo they also talked the park's officials into cutting the metal ball off the metal nose of the metal seal statue because "It gave a bad image of seals."

So now if you go to the pool at Second Beach you can see a metal seal with its nose pointed up in the air. Nothing is on it but it is politically correct.

Back to the Prez. He spoke. Only those in the first couple of rows could hear him. He had practised speaking in the grand Roman style, which had become the English style and the Canadian parliamentary style of oratory, making sweeping statements and sweeping gestures and saying nothing.

"Canada and America are great friends. We should remain thus."

"What did he say?" someone in the future rose garden asked me.

"Not much," I said. "But I know you will treasure this moment because you were in a crowd where you could not see and could not hear the president, but you will always be able to say 'I was there.'"

And then the president of the United States asked: "When is lunch?"

They went to the fanciest hotel in the city. The major hotel. The place you went when you wanted to impress someone, especially the US president.

The hotel has since tried to separate itself from the lunch. I will not mention its name out of fear of their lawyers. I will only say it was the kind of hotel that the president would dine at, the most luxurious and famous hotel, the one the city's name was connected with, and outside of the minor point of possibly contributing to his death it was a perfect setting.

The reason something might have gone nasty and criminal here was this was a foreign country. The secret service might have turned its back for a moment. The president's wife might have slipped into the kitchen. One of the president's enemies might have sprinkled something on his salmon and crab.

Or maybe the plate given to the president might have been left out in the warm summer air a moment too long and some bacteria might have had a happy hour on his fish and crab. That might have happened, except that his was the only plate that something went wrong with.

In any case, the president ate and burped and after lunch he went for a round at the Shaughnessy Heights Golf Course. He was playing with the famous dignitaries of the day, not that he cared about who was who, because his tummy was hurting. It hurt really badly. He was sweating and his head was foggy.

To cover up his illness, because a president should not look weak, he moved from the sixth hole to the seventeenth, but his stomach hurt more. He finished the game in great pain.

His personal doctor, whom other doctors called a quack, said it might be his heart or his head.

"It is my stomach that hurts," said the president.

"Then it is definitely food poisoning," said the bright doctor.

He gave the head of the western world some herbal cures. President Harding's personally chosen doctor believed all things could be cured with herbs.

The presidential party went straight to the harbour and got back on the US Navy ship that had carried them to Alaska and now headed for Seattle. They would have made better time if the ship had not crashed into another ship in Seattle's harbour.

It happens, you know.

The president gathered his strength to give a speech at the University of Washington, but he cut it short and left halfway through it. By the time the audience had realized the speech was over and started to applaud he was gone. His stomach hurt badly.

Then he was on a train heading for San Francisco where there were top-notch hospitals. Or if he was feeling better he could just change trains for one going back to Washington DC.

He was in a presidential hotel suite in San Francisco. His doctor gave him some caffeine pills and the president said he felt better. Of course he did. A cup of coffee, even in a pill, always makes you feel better. It is God's best gift to us, a drug that gives you a high with no side effects and is legal.

So his personal doctor and two other doctors said so long, as he was feeling better they could leave and have dinner.

That left Warren G. Harding, the head of the army and navy and one nation under God, alone with his wife.

Her account was that she was reading a newspaper article to him about him and telling him the good things that were said in the article.

Her account further stated that he said, "That's nice," and then died.

By the time the doctors got back to his bedside he was absolutely, totally, without question, dead.

The cause of his death could have been easily determined by an autopsy. Except his wife said there would not be an autopsy.

Within two hours of his demise his wife ordered that the body be embalmed. He was drained of blood and refilled with formaldehyde, which meant there could be no chemical analysis of what caused his parting from this life, along with his separation from his office and wife.

And then she had someone put some makeup on him to make him look the picture of health, perfumed his body to make him smell sweet and then put him into a coffin for the long ride back.

The Warren Harding memorial in Stanley Park features his face flanked by two lovely stone maidens. In his lifetime he was flanked by many maidens.
Photo by J.W. Moore, City of Vancouver Archives AM54-S4-: Mon N40.1

No autopsy, no answers, but lots of questions.

Did his wife murder him? Did his enemies murder him? Did he commit suicide? Or did he simply wish he had ordered the vegetarian plate in Vancouver?

Whatever the answer the questions always go back to his visit to a foreign country and what, if anything, happened to his lunch. One thing is for sure: If he was murdered then Vancouver was the crime scene.

Two years later a memorial to Harding was unveiled in Stanley Park at the spot where he spoke. It shows a small head of the president flanked by two large women. I could never figure out if the symbolism was intentional or not.

If you go to Theatre Under the Stars, and you should because it is one of the best summer entertainments in Vancouver, just look to your left. Harding's head is still there, with his women.

Like the performances on the stage, the Harding show was quite a comedy too, as well as a tragedy and a mystery.

THE LIONS GATE BRIDGE

The impressive Lions Gate Bridge frames one of the "Empress" liners as it passes the tip of Stanley Park in 1939. The truth is the bridge was built just so the land in the British Properties could be sold.

City of Vancouver Archives
AM54-S4-: Br P35

ow would you feel if you did all the work but then got none of the credit? That would make you like a television cameraman working with a reporter. The cameraman does everything but the reporter is the one who gets seen.

Suppose there was a party celebrating all you had done but you were not invited. The King and Queen were there, but not you.

Bummer. We did not use that word then. We said this was a terrible miscarriage of justice. *Bummer* is better.

It was your idea, your persistence, your ingenuity, your sweat, your baby, but then when it was presented to the public you were left back in the crowd, totally ignored.

Serious bummer.

I was standing next to Alfred James Towle Taylor, who liked the name James better. It was the official opening of the bridge, six months after it actually opened because they had to wait for King George VI and Queen Elizabeth to get there.

We were way back on the road that had been cut through the forest. We could just barely hear the speakers who were standing near the new concrete lions.

Many people were mentioned but not James. He tried to hide his hurt but it was hard after putting almost twenty years of his life into this bridge.

The ceremony ended with the ribbon cutting. A line of cars following the royal caravan went over it, squeezing between the crowds who were unable to stay on the walkways. The toll was not charged that day.

James turned around and walked the other way, away from the bridge, back to the city. I went with him. We had been friends since the early 1920s when we had stood together at the lookout spot at Prospect Point in Stanley Park. That is where a restaurant now has the famous sign: EAT. Tourists get the basic Canadian philosophy there.

But long before the restaurant existed James was pointing across the water to the forest-covered hills of West Vancouver.

"That could be a small city," he said, "if we could just get people there."

West Vancouver was then a remote, rural municipality of a few thousand beachcombers, almost all of them living in waterfront shacks.

"Nice idea, but impossible," I said.

"I will build a bridge," he said.

"People don't build bridges," I said. "Railroads build bridges."

The mighty Canadian Pacific had built countless spans across British Columbia and already had one going to the north shore. It was the Second Narrows. No, not the Second Narrows that now takes an armada of cars and trucks back and forth to North Vancouver. It was the first Second Narrows, which was a railroad as well as a car and pedestrian bridge.

It was just where the rail bridge is now. If you are going north on the Second

Narrows and you are in the right-hand lane, look down. That is the second Second Narrows you see, which replaced the first Second after a barge hit it and almost knocked it down.

Historians of Vancouver's bridges have a joke. "Where was the first bridge?" "Do you mean the first Second Narrows or the first First Narrows?"

That's where Abbott and Costello got the idea for "Who's on First?"

If you don't know what I am talking about I have great sympathy for you. Go to YouTube and look up "Who's on First?" Stop reading. Do it now. And then thank the bridge builders of Vancouver for having a first Second Narrows followed by a first First Narrows followed by a second Second Narrows followed by a third Second Narrows, which is now called the Ironworkers Memorial.

Anyway, I said to James that no one could get the money together to build a bridge and no one could get the licence from the city to build it and most of all it would be impossible to build a road through Stanley Park to get to the bridge.

The Sappers could do the work, but the people of Vancouver would come down with sticks and stones and kill us, and except for me that would be bad.

James was an engineer who was born in Victoria but lived in Nanaimo and, as you know, people from Nanaimo don't take no for an answer. Perhaps you didn't know that but it is true. I know some people who ride motorcycles, Harley-Davidson motorcycles, in Nanaimo. Go ask them.

James went to city hall and got the licence.

But then he was up against another problem. The CPR. It did not want a second bridge built because it was collecting tolls on its first bridge. Without getting confusing, that was the bridge over the Second Narrows, the one that took people and cars and trains and charged a toll. Another bridge closer to downtown would cut into its profits so it did not want that.

Also, and more importantly, the CPR owned the most prized and expensive property in downtown Vancouver and Shaughnessy, and it did not want competition from land it did not own. That would be land in West Vancouver. So it fought the idea of a bridge that would move potential customers in a different direction.

The CPR of that day was much like the NRA of today. Its lobby was all muscle. What it wanted it got. And what it did not want, as with the NRA and gun control today, did not happen.

A vote was taken of the good citizens of Vancouver on whether they would want a bridge that went to West Vancouver.

"Vote No," said the CPR. "It is a dumb idea. A road would have to be cut through Stanley Park to get to a bridge that would go somewhere no one wants to go."

The vote was overwhelmingly NO.

James took his family and moved to England. He would work on selling his idea over there. But he knew there was a large problem facing him. The people in England would not want to help build a bridge on the other side of the world.

On the other hand they might be interested in buying land with a view of the ocean in a beautiful country where they could continue to be rich and look down on everyone else. West Vancouver would be a perfect setting for an Englishman who wanted to start a new life in that quaint land where they still unbelievably had High Tea, a tradition that was starting to fade in England.

There was just one other little matter. They could not get to this England away from England without a bridge.

James went straight to the wisest and richest family he could find, the beer-making Guinness clan.

You know about Guinness, don't you? It is that black and white stout that Canadians save for meals in an Irish pub and the Irish have for breakfast.

Go back a bit. Another detour. What is stout? What is Guinness?

History lesson: no notes required but a glass of Guinness would be good.

One hundred years before I landed in New Westminster, ancient history to me, a fellow in Dublin took a chance. I love guys like that.

Arthur Guinness said he would open a brewery but he was not going to make one of the fancy new beers that were flooding the market. He would turn out not only traditional old stuff but the bottom-of-the-barrel, old-time swill.

The workmen in England and Ireland who had few extra pennies would always buy this beer. It was dark and bitter. It also took its name from those who drank it. It was called porter, because the porters, those who carried the things no one else would carry, drank it so that they could have the strength to carry more.

It was a strong beer, which they called *stout*, which means strong.

Arthur Guinness wanted to open a brewery to make porter. Those who were in the business of leasing land laughed at him.

"No maker of porter could ever succeed. He would fail in a short time. Ha ha."

So they offered him a good deal. Cheap rent on a spot on the edge of Dublin for low rent, but one stipulation. The lease would be for nine thousand years. Ha, ha. Big joke.

They were sure he would fail in nine months and have to pay them forever.

Ha, ha. Arthur Guinness made fine porter. Very fine. It caught on not only with the porters, but with the rest of the world. It became the most famous beer on earth, in fact in the history of the earth.

Arthur asked his employees for suggestions to improve things. He was already employing a third of Ireland with many farmers growing hops and others making and shipping and hauling beer. And he was making his employees happy by paying them not only in wages but in Guinness for breakfast and Guinness for lunch and Guinness for dinner. For a long, long time every employee got a free quart of Guinness a day. In fact there was so much Guinness being consumed that there was a slowdown in the production of Guinness, so the practice of giving it away to employees was ended in the 1980s.

But long before that the Guinness family kept many of the people of Ireland from starving during the worldwide depression and the beer became a symbol of national pride.

The employees, always eager to help, put some thought into the making and selling of this black beer, and after a few more pints of Guinness said, "This is a very stout porter." They suggested that the word *porter* be dropped, because not many people in the new world knew what a porter was, and that it be replaced by the word *stout*. That was a well-known word because they had all been through a world war in which there was a famous song that said: "Give me some men who are stout-hearted men… And I'll soon give you ten thousand more."

The Guinness family changed their label to say: Guinness Stout. It dropped *Porter*.

Now when you order a stout you get a Guinness.

The makers of stout, which as I say means strong, grew unbelievably rich, and the Guinness people came up with an advertising slogan: Guinness Is Good for You.

Who could doubt something like that? In truth, if you take out the alcohol it *is* good for you. In some West Indian countries Guinness was added to condensed milk to give hungry and skinny children a chance to grow up.

By the way, since I have your attention because we are talking about something you can still buy and drink, Guinness Is Good for You was once judged by the advertising people of Madison Avenue to be the world's second best slogan, after Drink Coca-Cola.

Drink Coca-Cola simply tells you what to do and what to do it with, which is good advice if you want to know the secret for selling something or getting ahead in life. Just tell yourself what to do and then figure out what to do it with. It's guaranteed to work.

Guinness Is Good for You is fuzzy and warm. I like that better. Besides, not one Sapper I ever served with drank Coke but they all hungered for Guinness.

Back to the story:

James Taylor was working on his project. He went to the Guinness company and when he saw the original nine-thousand-year lease on the land hung on a wall behind a thick piece of glass he knew he was dealing with people who would take a gamble.

He asked them to lend him money to buy land in Canada. That was a big gamble. One bonus, he said: If Englishmen move there they will drink Guinness along with Labatt's.

They loaned him seventy-five hundred dollars. At the same time the tiny town of West Vancouver was suffering. It was deep in the Depression. The municipality needed money. It sold Taylor forty-seven hundred acres on a hillside that it was happy to get rid of. No one would live up there anyway. It was

Without the Lions Gate Bridge there was no easy way to get to the British Properties, and therefore the land beneath what is now a community of multi-million-dollar homes sold for less than $20 an acre. Photo by Leonard Frank, City of Vancouver Archives AM54-S4-: Van Sc P116

far from the water, which was the only reason anyone would ever want to live in this remote wilderness. He got it for less than twenty dollars per acre.

James formed a company called British Pacific Properties. If you drop the middle word you have, well, you know what you have.

Much later, after many families from England moved there, Guinness built a shopping mall for them. What to name it?

Just outside of London the brewery that made Guinness was called Park Royal.

Hence. Make the folks in their new homes in Canada feel right at home.

Back to James again. Now that he had the property there was a reason for building a bridge to get to it.

Things had changed in Vancouver because of the Depression. So many men were out of work there were breadlines in the city. Women were not out of work because women were not expected or allowed to work. They just went without and hoped the men would bring some bread home to them.

You can look at pictures of the soup lines of the 1930s. Lines of men getting handouts of soup and bread. But they were still trying to keep their dignity.

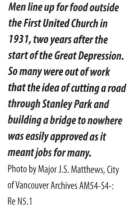

Men line up for food outside the First United Church in 1931, two years after the start of the Great Depression. So many were out of work that the idea of cutting a road through Stanley Park and building a bridge to nowhere was easily approved as it meant jobs for many.
Photo by Major J.S. Matthews, City of Vancouver Archives AM54-S4-: Re N5.1

They were still wearing suits, even though they were tattered. Dressing down to sloppy levels had not yet entered the world.

James made a proposal to Vancouver again. He would build a bridge that would mean cutting a road through the middle of Stanley Park, which would be unthinkable were it not for the fact that it would create jobs.

He promised to hire virtually all local labour to do the cutting and the bridge building. Thousands of men would be working.

The vote on the bridge passed overwhelmingly. The CPR tried to stop it but was pushed aside by voters who would be getting a paycheque for the first time in years.

James had done it all.

The bridge was constructed by the Dominion Bridge company in a large factory at Boundary and Broadway, which would become Boundary and Lougheed after another politician. If you go there now you will see Bridge Studios, makers of motion pictures and television movies. It is the same building.

The steel and wires went up. It took incredible amounts of work and planning and it gave jobs to many. And the people of Vancouver watched the construction as an open-air play of form and physics and balance over open space, sort of a continuing saga of the possible over the impossible.

And Charles Marega, after several years without work, got a job. He was an Italian sculptor and James Albert Taylor commissioned him to make a pair of lions for the bridge. The only disappointment to Marega was that he would have liked to make them out of bronze or marble. He had to settle for concrete as there was not enough money for anything else.

But he wrote to friends that he was thrilled just to be working. It was a good ending to his life. He died two months after his works of art were installed on the bridge.

Also one worker, Lester Thorstad, was killed when some soft ground collapsed below him at the footing on the south side of the bridge. Work stopped for that day. Despite there being no safety harnesses or hard hats or steel-toed boots, no one else lost his life.

And then, when the bridge was almost complete, a toll booth was built—twenty-five cents per car—and a huge area on the side of a hill in West Vancouver was prepared for housing, expensive housing.

Charles Marega was a sculptor with no work when he was hired to create the lions for the bridge. The budget only allowed for concrete, not bronze or marble, but it was his last crowning glory, he said. He died two months after finishing the work.
Photo by A.C. Kelly, City of Vancouver Archives AM1399-S3-: CVA 1399-399

Alfred James Towle Taylor, the creator of it all, was exhausted but happy. His dream had come true.

But then some younger men in his company thought they could do a better job. They elbowed and shoved and manoeuvred themselves up higher and higher in the company. If you have ever been in an organization where the old-timers have been pushed out as the newcomers come in you know what was happening to him.

Taylor was squeezed out. I don't know how it happened. He did not know. It just happened.

"The day the bridge is finished I'm quitting," he told me.

"You can't," I said. "This is all because of you. It's yours. You can't walk away."

But he did. The day the bridge was finished, Alfred James Towle Taylor quit the company he had formed to build it. When the official opening was announced he was not invited.

We walked back to Vancouver on the new road through the park and heard the celebrations going on behind us. He did not turn around.

"You know," he said, "if this idea catches on and West Vancouver fills up with people that bridge won't be wide enough."

We walked a little farther and he added, "But that's their problem now."

He later died in New York during a business trip. His last wishes were that his ashes be scattered from the bridge. His wish was carried out.

One man was killed during the construction of the Lions Gate Bridge, in 1938, but for thousands of others it was a lifeline through the Great Depression.
Photo by Major J.S. Matthews, City of Vancouver Archives AM54-S4-: Br P81.22

And years later when a road was cut through the bush next to the new shopping mall to connect the bridge to the Trans-Canada Highway it needed a name. Someone proposed Taylor.

Today you get stuck in traffic on Taylor Way heading to the bridge, which is still too narrow. He would almost smile about that.

DEADMAN'S ISLAND

 ou can't go there. You can walk around Stanley Park and there it is, right in front of you, a lovely island between the park and the city. It is now attached to the park by a narrow strip of land but it has a large gate, which is closed, and a gatekeeper who will say to you, "No. You can't enter the island."

Not fair, you say.

Good thing, I say, because they are finally getting some rest.

Despite being connected to the mainland by a causeway, Deadman's Island today is off limits and out of bounds, a naval installation manned officially by sailors and unofficially by ghosts.
Photo by Henry Loo

"They" are the dead Natives, First Nations, aboriginal young men in the flowering of their lives, call them whatever is politically correct this week, whatever. They were brave beyond belief.

Once upon a time—that is where stories begin—nice, friendly people lived around what is now Stanley Park and along the shores of what are now False Creek and Kits Beach. They were nice and friendly partly because they had it all. They had oysters and salmon and deer and salmonberries and blackberries and there was no reason to go off fighting and conquering because, well, why leave home?

But up north, that would be around Squamish today, there was a band of Natives who had different ideas. They wanted more. Those folks are always around; think of Europe, think of the Middle East, think of England and North America and South America and Africa and Asia.

The aboriginal young men from the area around Squamish took the trail that became the Sea to Sky Highway and in what would become West Vancouver they rowed across the water and stepped off in what would become Stanley Park.

"Nice place," they said. "And look at the chicks."

Always when men go to a foreign port the women look good. That is because the men have been at sea for a while. In this case they'd been in their boats about an hour.

The women were all over the beach and nothing drives a sailor more mad than women on a beach. So they captured a bunch of them. This has been going on since before the Bible was written. Men from somewhere capture women and then take them back home and the next generation of people look different.

"How did that happen?" they ask.

The new people are inferior until one day one of the different-looking people becomes the leader of the people of wherever. Then they do the same thing again.

Anyway, back to the capturing of the women on what would become Third Beach.

The men of the village of Stanley Park went to rescue their women, but it was too late. The bad guys were loading them onto their boats for the ride back. And besides, the men from up north had spears with pointy ends, which they knew how to use. The men from the park only used spears for hunting.

The nice guys had a meeting. This was a meeting where they actually had to

As these Sḵwx̱wú7mesh longhouses, located in Coal Harbour and photographed in 1886, attest, Stanley Park was a village for centuries before the white man came and put up signs saying "Don't Pick The Flowers."
Royal BC Museum, BC Archives
D-04723

decide something important: the future. Politicians now say they have to make hard decisions. Nope. Not like this.

They faced the enemy.

"We could fight, but you outnumber us. If we fight we will all die, but some of you will die also."

The enemy agreed.

"We will give ourselves to you, to kill, in return for the women to go free."

Holy unbelievable. We are talking about a group of eighty men. Look around your neighbourhood and count eighty, all men, and can you see them offering themselves to be killed to spare their wives? I don't mean to downplay men now. Maybe many would do it but most would say, "Wait just a minute. Let's talk this over."

There is no way to express the courage of the men from the park.

The bad guys had a brief meeting. Fight them and some of us will die. One of those might be our leader, their leader said. Let us think about this.

Was it better to have notches on their spears or women in their boats?

Notches win out every time. That is where pride and bravado come into play. Captured women are exciting only until they start demanding that you do the dishes. Notches are forever.

The bad guys chose the killing. The good guys lined up, or whatever they did, but they stood still while one after another was killed with a sharpened wooden spear. Ten, twenty, forty, sixty, eighty. No screams, no begging. All pain, all misery, all strength, all dead. It happened near Siwash Rock. If you go by there you can feel the ghosts.

It was near Siwash Rock, off Stanley Park, that a band of very brave men sacrificed their lives for the sake of their women.
Photo by Bailey and Neelands, City of Vancouver Archives AM336-S3-2-: CVA 677-116

The bad guys let the women go free. At least they were good to their word. The bad guys then went home and showed off the notches on their spears. Their wives were happy they did not come back with perky young somethings that would be a big distraction before dinner.

The men had bragging rights. They had killed an entire tribe and lost none of their own. The fact that the tribe did not fight back was not mentioned. Remember, the victor always writes the history.

Then the women of the area that would become Stanley Park carried their dead braves back to the other end of their peaceful land and prepared them for burial. Their burial was not underground. Their hope was to be close to the goodness of the sky.

The dead men were placed in wooden boxes made from cedar trees by the old men of the village. Then they were hoisted into the arms of the trees to be above the earth.

This was done on a tiny sacred island that they could only get to at low tide.

There were no newspapers, no televisions, no totem poles telling the story of the braves.

Time passed. Much time. Generations came and died. The Sappers arrived in New Westminster, far from this tiny island, and white men came for the yellow stones that were under the ground and in the rivers. One of them was John

Morton, from England. He met two other Englishmen and they headed out to find gold in the Cariboo. They, like many others, walked almost fifteen hundred miles from what would become Vancouver to the end of the gold trail without finding any gold.

Tough. Come all that way and nothing to show for it. Can you imagine walking halfway across Canada and not finding even a postcard?

John made some money selling nails to blacksmiths along the way. The smithies used the nails to keep shoes on horses. The smithies made a good living out of the gold.

John and his friends returned to what would become Vancouver basically broke, hungry and miserable and all those things that happen when all your dreams have gone to pot and it's raining on your head.

He tried to make bricks, because that was his business in England, but how do you sell bricks when the woods are everywhere?

Then he was offered a real-estate dream deal. He could get 180 acres—at the time that was the most you could buy in one plot—for only $550.75. Not only that but, "Look at this map," said the agent, who had laid claim to the land from the colonial government.

Once the forest came down to the water. Then came a sawmill and then came a city. Now the city is planting trees on the sidewalks that run alongside the water, right where that boat was beached. The building in the background is the Hastings Mill, one hundred years before the fireworks of Expo 86 filled the sky.

Photo by Edouard Gaston Deville, Royal BC Museum, BC Archives D-04729

In the crudely drawn map there was a plot of land between two bodies of water. One was the Pacific Ocean, the other Burrard Inlet.

"There are 540 acres in total in there. If you have two friends you could get the whole thing."

Tempting. Except he was in New Westminster and this land was way up there, somewhere in the forest in a place without a road or a cabin or a white man. Probably there were no Natives there either because it was so far away.

It would be like you being offered some land… actually there is no place left on earth that is so remote, so it would be like you being offered a good deal on a piece of the moon.

"I'll take it," said John Morton.

Who could blame him? In real estate, like in hunting for gold, you take chances. He did not freeze to death while hunting for gold so he doubted that he would be burned in real estate. On the other hand he had made nothing in gold. Real estate would be different. We are all dreamers.

And he had two friends. They scratched and borrowed and begged and put their money together and bought the entire plot.

I won't keep you in suspense. Their plot became the West End, everything from English Bay to the Burrard Inlet or to put it another way from the Sylvia Hotel to the Bayshore Hotel and from Stanley Park to Burrard Street.

Of course none of that existed and it was a three-day journey through the woods to get there and who, unless they were totally crazy, would buy that anyway?

Robert Burnaby, for whom Burnaby was named, had his faults. For one, he tried to swindle West End property away from someone he thought was a naïve greenhorn.
Royal BC Museum, BC Archives
A-01134

This was before a sawmill started cutting logs on the edge of the inlet. This was before Gassy Jack opened his saloon. This was a crazy notion.

The few people who learned about it mocked John Morton and his friends. They called them the Three Greenhorns, a very insulting title to carry.

John built a cabin on his property. It was a beautiful place overlooking the water. Many people who get a view lot do that. His cabin was in the spot where the Marine Building now stands. Pity he did not hold on to it.

Even though the property was remote there were some who tried to swindle the land away from Morton and his friends. One of them was the man for whom the city of Burnaby is named. The city loves him now but he was a bit mischievous back then, at least according to a judge.

Robert Burnaby sailed from England to BC a few months after I arrived with the Sappers. He was a businessman. He thought there was money to be made in a new world.

He briefly got a job as the secretary for my boss, Colonel Richard Moody, which gave him great credentials, but he quickly moved on. Who wants a government job when there is real estate waiting?

Burnaby told John Morton that he, Burnaby, actually owned all this land that he, Morton, had just bought and he, Morton, would have to vacate the premises. Burnaby showed Morton the official paper that said just that. He, Burnaby, had a prior claim. "Goodbye, go away, leave," he said to Morton.

Morton took the matter to court. The judge looked at the document and said it was a blatant forgery, "obviously written by a liar or a knave."

With those credentials Burnaby went to Victoria and was elected as a member of the legislative assembly.

Back to John Morton. There were a lot of business deals that came and went and a lot of dirty dealing that happened, and in the end poor John Morton was reduced to digging ditches. Later he owned a farm in Mission, where he was happy and died many years later, far, far from the West End, which became one of the most densely packed places on earth and made fortunes for those who bought in early.

The point of telling you all this is that shortly after Morton bought his part of the West End a friend of his was offered another piece of land. It was a small island nearby that was up for sale for five dollars and Morton wanted to row over and take a look. He asked me to go along because he had heard that there was something spooky about the island.

Besides the fact that my entire life is spooky and that I live in an unbelievable world that mixes make-believe and reality, there was actually nothing I could do to help him with spooks.

We left Coal Harbour, which is one of those names that sounds ugly but sticks. Everyone, from old Captain Vancouver to John Morton, had seen coal there but it was useless coal. It would hardly burn. Nonetheless, the spot became Coal Harbour and it still is today.

Anyway, we left Coal Harbour and I rowed. I hate to admit that, but I, a working journalist, actually worked. It was one of the rare times.

"Where are we going?" asked I.

"To that island over yonder," said John.

"I heard it's haunted," I said.

"That's why I invited you. You have a way with ghosts."

"Does it show?" I asked.

He did not answer because we were at the island. We climbed out of the rowboat and walked around. I had never been there before.

Almost immediately John saw boxes up in some of the trees. He poked his walking stick into one of them and, OMG, bones fell out.

Okay, we did not say OMG, but if you were walking in the woods and poked a stick into a box and bones fell out you would not *say*, you would *shriek*, OMG.

That is what he did. Me too. I am not ashamed to admit that bones falling from a box over your head can make your skin shrink.

After our trip John's friend said no and John said no. His excuse was he had enough land already that he had no idea what to do with but the real reason was the bones.

Later, when we heard the story of the braves, John was even happier that he had said no. That is the end of the story with John but not the end of the story of the island.

A rotten guy named Theodore Ludgate got control of the island thirty years later. He wanted to build a sawmill on it.

The mayor said, "No." The mayor said it was part of Stanley Park. Ludgate said it was not.

The mayor said, "You cut down a tree and I will arrest you."

Ludgate said he had the deed and would cut. The mayor sent the police to the island and Ludgate sent his loggers.

Ludgate started chopping and the police started arresting.

Theodore Ludgate logged the whole of Deadman's Island with no respect for the dead who rested there or for the trees, the past or the future. The mayor of Vancouver read him the riot act, but it did not help.

City of Vancouver Archives
AM54-S4-: Port P532-2

The short version of the story is that the matter went to the court, but the court then, in 1909, was not much quicker than the court now.

For two years a contingent of thirty police was assigned permanently to the island to prevent Ludgate's loggers from cutting. Yes, I know that sounds crazy, but the police loved it.

"Your duty tonight, guard the island."

The police had two years of camping with no crime and no bad guys to chase.

In the end the court said that Ludgate had the right to the island. He cut down every tree that grew there. It was noisy and miserable and the island was

stripped and there is no record of what happened to the boxes with the bones.

The only thing that can make you smile is that Ludgate went bankrupt. How? Why? Don't know. It must have been the ghosts.

Later the island was turned into an isolation ward for those with smallpox. That was a deadly disease and those who had it were thrown out of their homes. They ended up on Deadman's Island where they either survived or did not and were buried. Those who survived were ostracized because of the marks on their faces.

Life is not fair.

Then the island was used as a burial ground until the big city cemetery was built at Fraser View.

Around World War I the federal government took control of the island because it was a good site from which to shoot anyone coming into the harbour to attack Vancouver.

That is the best thing that could happen to the ghosts of the warriors; soldiers and sailors guarding their resting place. Perfect.

And so it has remained. The entire island is now called the HMCS *Discovery*, a ship in the Canadian Navy that does not float and never moves but is guarded day and night.

To you braves of once upon a time, rest, finally, in peace.

This is how Deadman's Island looked before it was logged and the resting places of brave young men were cut down from the trees and demolished.
Photo by Philip Timms, City of Vancouver Archives AM336-S3-3-: CVA 677-564

THE UTTERLY UNBELIEVABLY STUPID, REPEAT STUPID, PIG WAR

ar is the best invention humankind has ever made. It gives us great music, great stories and, for the last century, great movies.

Were it not for wars men would have to sit through endless romance films instead of *Rambo* or *Saving Private Ryan*.

You would not have those manly pictures if we did not take the time to blow up each other's cities and kill men with different uniforms along with large numbers of women and children. We call those last two collateral damage and we are sincerely sorry about that.

But on the other hand if there were no wars then men, and many women now, would not get to wear medals.

The Pig War was sort of like that, but there were no movies made because it looked so stupid it was embarrassing to both sides.

On one side was the United States of America. On the other was the British Empire.

The reason for the war? One pig. Actually, one dead pig.

The year was 1859 and the battlefield was San Juan Island, a beautiful place that you can see from Victoria. You could row a boat to it from Vancouver Island. In fact, it was so close to Vancouver Island and so far from the US mainland that most people in British Columbia thought it was naturally part of Canada.

SAN JUAN WATER BOUNDARY

Scale, 1: 750,000 or 11·84 miles to 1 Inch

LEGEND
— Boundary contended for by Great Britain
— Boundary contended for by United States
— Boundary awarded by Arbitrator, Oct 21st, 1872
— Compromise offered by British Commissioner

Opposite page: Wars are fought for many reasons— land, oil and human rights are big on the list—but Canada and the US once fought over a pig. They had ships and cannons and marines, and the pig was not even turned into bacon. There's only one additional ingredient you need for a pig to start a war, and that's pigheadedness.
iStockphoto

Left: The boundary line between the United States and Canada was contentious for many years in the San Juan Islands. The solution? Let's have a war about it!
David Rumsey Map Collection

Unfortunately the Americans did not think so and were trying to tax the Hudson's Bay Company for being there.

The HBC was the only business on the island and had a regular supply ship coming and going each week, mostly picking up lamb chops that the company got from its sheep ranch.

185

There were about one hundred British subjects living happily there with perfect weather and days of peace and tranquility.

There were fewer than twenty Americans living on the island, also enjoying the same peace and tranquility and getting along fine with their British neighbours, but all it takes is one stupid, pigheaded, arrogant demand to ruin everything.

Enter the pig. It was owned by one of the employees of the Bay who allowed it to wander free and in its freedom it dug up and ate some potatoes planted by one of the Americans. The American got really mad. He tried shouting; he tried pushing the pig away; he tried hitting it.

Have you ever tried to stop a pig from eating?

In the end he shot it.

Okay, that was wrong, but the pig was trespassing. Nonetheless the American offered the pig's owner ten dollars, which was much more than any pig was worth.

"Ten dollars for a pig! I will teach those Americans what happens when they kill a British pig. I want a hundred dollars!" said the pig's owner.

That was the pay for three months of work.

The American refused to hand over the money. He was threatened with arrest by officials of the Hudson's Bay Company.

Dumb.

The other Americans on the island sent word to the government on the mainland of the US where officials said this was an international travesty of justice and sent sixty-six soldiers to protect the American settlers.

Dumb.

The British said that was an invasion of their island and sent three warships.

Dumb.

The Americans sent more soldiers, 461 in all with fourteen cannons. That was enough to blow up the entire island.

Dumb.

The British sent the Royal Marines and more sailors, 2,140 in all, on five warships with seventy cannons. If war had broken out there would have been a hole where the island was and the ocean would have poured in.

This was common practice in the nuclear arms race of the 1950s and '60s. Russia and America: we have more missiles; no, we have more missiles. No, we do. No, we do.

If anyone had pulled the trigger then there would have been no planet.

Do we have to say it again? Dumb. But that is what we do.

The Americans sent a general from Washington DC to meet with James Douglas, the man who had saved British Columbia from the Americans just one year earlier. Remember, he got the Queen to claim it as a colony because there were so many Americans here looking for gold.

Douglas was still in a protective, anti-American mood.

The American general took a ship down the east coast, through the Panama Canal and up to Victoria. Meanwhile the British and American troops were still facing each other, each with orders not to shoot first, so they did the only thing mature men could do. They taunted and insulted each other's armies and underwear over the quiet and tranquil no man's land that separated them. Occasionally some sheep walked between the armies, which can cause premature ejaculation for a soldier itching to fire a cannon.

Each side was hoping the other would shoot first so they could have some good stories to tell and get medals.

Finally the general and Mr. Douglas met.

"This is about sovereignty."

"This is about national pride."

"This is about military superiority."

Then they both agreed, "This is about a pig that was overvalued by some stupid farmer."

They both said they would pull back their armies and navies, but keep a force of a hundred men on both sides, with guns, just in case either side tried to do something sneaky.

For twelve years the British and American soldiers faced each other. Eventually they started talking and drinking and making friends and having parties and celebrating Queen Victoria's birthday and the Fourth of July all together with barbecues of roasted pig.

Can you imagine spending a war here? These were the officers' quarters on San Juan Island during the twelve-year war in which no shots were fired. "Shall we spend the afternoon swimming or sunbathing? We'll have pork chops for dinner. Please invite the enemy as usual."
City of Vancouver Archives
AM54-S4-: Out P168

187

It was a good place to spend a military career.

But bad things were happening in the hands of politicians; that is, bad things for Canada. Both Britain and America said they would ask a neutral power to decide who owned the island and, believe it or not, they chose Germany.

It is almost absurd how absurd is the world. Fifty years later Britain and America would be at war with Germany but then Britain and America were asking Germany to help prevent a war between them.

It is like Americans now going to Vietnam for vacations and young Germans with their children building sandcastles on the beach at Normandy. Why do we bother with wars in the first place?

Anyway, the Kaiser in Germany was asked to decide who owns San Juan, an island of whose location he had only the vaguest idea.

The problem for Canada and Britain was that during this period many Germans were leaving Germany for a better life somewhere else. Three million moved to America. In fact, by 1870 there were more German-language newspapers in New York than English.

Only a trickle came to Canada.

The Kaiser thought and thought. For twelve years, during which time he was overtaxing his people and forcing them to leave, he thought.

Sure San Juan was close to Canada but his people were living in America. Maybe if he gave San Juan to America his people would love him and happily pay more taxes. It makes no sense but neither do the expense accounts of Canadian senators, and they still hope they are loved.

"San Juan is in America," said the Kaiser.

"Darn," said James Douglas and the people of Victoria who could take a ferry there today without a passport if only one pig owner had not been so pigheaded.

If the ten dollars had been accepted the pig could have been eaten, the armies would not have shown up, there would have been no international incident, the Hudson's Bay Company would have had a sale on sheepskin slippers and the island would have slipped into Canadian hands.

Dumb. Stupid. Dumb.

 utcase. The first time I met her I knew I was not dealing with an ordinary, boring woman. She was a nutcase.

When I walked into her home she was pulling a rope attached to a pulley in the ceiling with the other end of the rope going down to the back of a chair and the chair was rising.

"I don't like reporters," she said.

There was nothing, absolutely nothing, in the life of Emily Carr that would fit inside a framework of normalcy, including her pet monkey Woo.
Royal BC Museum, BC Archives I-61505

I have met many people like that. I don't blame them. After knowing reporters all my life, actually all my lifetimes, do you think I would trust them? You tell them something and you have to put your faith in someone you don't know to tell the story back as you told it.

Come to think of it, I don't know how I have ever found anyone to talk to me. "May I sit down and talk?" I asked.

"Only if you can fly. Can you fly, Mr. Linn?"

"What do you mean?"

She pointed to the chair now hung near the ceiling. "There is your chair."

Okay, at that moment I was in love. I must clarify that. It was not the kind of love that I had for Pauline Johnson with whom I wanted to snuggle. Pauline was beautiful and in the way boys and girls have been behaving since we were creatures in the sea I was attracted to Pauline. Then we could make more little Paulines.

Emily was different. I loved her mind. I hate to say that but it explains it all. I did not want to snuggle with her mind but, for goodness' sake, her furniture was hanging near the ceiling and I loved the mind and the woman who would do that.

I also liked her paintings, though they all looked the same to me. One tree, two trees, one totem pole, two, etc.

"I see you looking at my paintings. You don't like them, right?" she said to me.

I said I liked them.

"You are full of crap," she said. "I can tell a liar when I see one."

Then she took a long drag on her cigarette.

"They did not like this when I taught school," she said.

"I heard that was your problem."

"What was my problem?"

"You smoked in school when you were teaching."

"So what? And I cursed the bad attitudes. I cursed them with curse words. You have a problem with that?"

If you want to be an artist, study the life of Emily Carr—rejected, lonely, despairing, and then "discovered" at the very end. Take up running a boarding house instead. She did.

Royal BC Museum, BC Archives D-06009

"No, ma'am."

You see, that is why I liked her, in a Platonic sort of way. Poor Emily. By the time I met her she was a washed-up artist. Those were her words.

"No one is ever going to buy my work."

"Maybe," I said. "There will come a time when people see the original inhabitants in a different way. They might even like them."

She shook her head, which was covered with a skull cap that she wore all the time.

"Are you crazy? They see them as savages and they will always see them like that."

This was true. The government was snatching the Native children from their parents, which really was kidnapping, and forbidding the potlatch, which was like forbidding Christmas and Easter to a Christian, and not allowing the children to learn their own languages. In a word, the government would erase the savage from the savages, though they did not say it that way.

When I'd thought about that I said, "You're right. So why are you painting totem poles?"

"I like them."

That is the problem with artists. They are out of step with government edicts.

Then she reached out for her monkey, which was her pet, and it climbed on her arm and sat on her shoulder.

You can see why I said she was a nutcase. But she also lowered the chair so I could sit on it.

"You are not so bad," she said. "Not good, mind you, but your face looks like one of those on the totem poles so you can sit."

Her life in short: She was raised by a Victorian father who transplanted Victorian life to Victoria—high ceilings, pictures of Queen Victoria on numerous walls, slipcovers on the chairs and the couch that covered the legs of the furniture because it would be obscene to see exposed legs, even those of a couch.

Emily did not like that. That upset her father so Emily disliked it even more. Her father went out of his mind. Emily did the only thing she could. She became an artist.

Now being an artist in those days meant that she would paint landscapes and her father agreed. It was called dabbling in the arts and a daughter should be allowed to do that.

Then her father died. It happens. Her guardian, chosen by her father, said she could go to California to study art, so long as it was landscapes.

She went, but then she got on a freighter going to France. Sometimes kids do the craziest things and you want to kill them. It is a good thing they are faster than you.

She learned amazing ways of painting things, close up and personal and far away and still attached. It had nothing to do with Victorian painting.

Emily came back to British Columbia and painted totem poles far up the coast, in the Queen Charlottes before the name was changed to an aboriginal name. No one wanted her work.

She was broke—that happens to artists—so she quit painting. If she could not make a living off art she would run a boarding house. That was her way of saying "Screw you" to the world and to herself.

But there was income in renting rooms to folks who did not want to be homeless so she did that for twenty years.

Can you imagine giving up everything you love and want to do for two decades?

This is where the historian and the journalist fail. They say she gave up art for twenty years and ran a boarding house but it was not twenty years, not in the beginning. As with all of us it was one month that became six and became

Emily Carr grew up in a staid Victorian home. When she left that she travelled with her friends and animals in her caravan named "Elephant." Her life was as much her art as her art was her life.

Photo by Mrs. S.F. Morley, Royal BC Museum, BC Archives B-09610

twelve and is it Christmas already? And then two years became six and those became ten.

"I can't believe I have been doing this for ten years. Once upon a time I painted pictures. That's a joke."

We all say that.

And then ten years more and thoughts of a brush and canvas and paint were a distant memory. "I once thought I could paint trees. Now I use the sawdust to keep a fire going so the guests won't complain."

She said that to a mirror.

And then what happens? She becomes famous overnight. The Group of

Seven—that was Canada's artists to the world and they all lived in Ontario—got to see Emily's paintings of trees.

"Magnificent. Wonderful. Just what we are trying to do," they said.

Just as an aside, every time a reporter writes "they said" I wonder if they said it all at once. Imagine the Group of Seven together in a room looking at Emily's trees. "Okay, the official word is, now, all together, 'Magnificent. Wonderful. Just what we are trying to do.'"

"Oh, come on. Someone didn't say it. Let's try again."

Anyway, Emily was made an honorary member of the Group and she was suddenly famous, while she was still running a boarding house.

How the heck did this happen? Out of the blue the famous men with brushes decided that a woman on the West Coast who lives with a monkey was pretty good. Why did it not happen sooner? You only get angry when you think about it, or disappointed, or disillusioned. No, life is not fair.

Anyway, she was closing in on sixty when her fame came. But of course fame at home does not naturally follow. She was closing in on seventy when the Vancouver Art Gallery had a one-woman show of her paintings. The gallery was then a small building on Georgia next to a movie house.

"Totem poles? Trees? Why are we looking at these?" some patrons of the art of Victorian landscapes said.

Three years later she was too sick to paint any longer, and four years after that she died.

The Vancouver Art Gallery now has a permanent display of her trees and totem poles. When it moves to a new and larger building it will have an even larger permanent display. And the Emily Carr College of Art has graduated thousands of students, most of whom look at things in strange and challenging ways.

The only difference is none of them are allowed to smoke in class. Emily would have probably lit up anyway.

GRANVILLE ISLAND

here is one thing that is true. Actually, there
are many things that are true, but anyone who
wants to make a statement that is supposed
to be profound starts with "There is *one* thing
that is true," or "I know *one* thing is true."

I have written many stories about politicians
and educators that begin with them saying
that.

That means any three-year-old is smarter because they know many true things.

But one thing that is true is: Anything can be fixed, unless it can't. There are some things that cannot be fixed, like someone young being killed. No matter what, it cannot be fixed.

But just about anything short of that can be. Granville Island is one of my places for proving that anything can be fixed.

Let me take you back to 1943. It was a dark and stormy day, even though the sun was shining; that poor old sun just could not get through the muck of air that hung over Granville Island.

"If I don't burn to death I'm going to choke to death," joked Jack McFarland.

He was working one of furnaces that roared with searing hot flames out of its open mouth. The fire was so fierce it yelled and so hot it was burning the skin behind what had been his eyebrows before they were burned off.

Jack was pulling another glowing bar of steel out of the fire and as soon as he did his helper shovelled another mouthful of coal into the fire. Then the helper dropped another steel bar onto a grating in the furnace and pumped the bellows to make the fire hotter. They worked like this all day. One glowing bar out, one shovel of coal in, followed by one grey bar that would quickly turn red.

Jack used tongs and threaded the soft steel through a link in a chain. Then he slid the unbelievably hot steel into a press. He closed it by pushing down on a lever with his foot, then he pulled a lever on top with his arm and the power fed by a steam compressor next to the press slammed the two sides together, bending the link into an oval, and presto, another link in a chain was finished.

"It is better than the old days when men had to beat them into links with their hammers," said Jack.

A hundred more and he would have about forty feet of chain done for the day. Four other furnaces in the same foundry were turning out the same links, one by one. On the island ten other foundries were doing the same.

They were all making chains for the Royal Navy, which was on the high seas fighting a war and going through chains like spaghetti sliding off a plate.

The air was so thick with coal smoke that when men left for the day they would walk off the island in single file with a hand on the shoulder of the man in front of him so that if the first man started falling in the water the one behind could grab him or at least fish him out.

Without exaggeration, if you stretched your hand out in front of your face you could not tell how many fingers you were holding up unless you cheated and counted them with your other hand.

I was going there to do a story on the state of the island. I hadn't been there for donkey's years, since long before the First World War. There hadn't been much reason to go there because there was no island. It was a sandbar that the indigenous folks had used forever to collect oysters. Then a few sawmills opened on the banks of False Creek and the railroad filled in half of it and the water got a little dirtier and more mills opened and the water got worse and the oysters were fewer.

However, no one except the Natives noticed and no one paid any attention to them. Then came World War I and the federal government thought the spot would be perfect for building foundries and making chains for the Royal Navy. It was well protected from the enemy and had easy access to the sea.

So great sheets of galvanized steel were driven into the ground around the bar and the entire area was filled in with sand dredged up from under the waters of False Creek. Then asphalt, that brilliant creation of man that puts an end to all that nuance of soil and seeds and birth and growth and life, was poured over the island. Rail tracks for trains that connected up with barges carrying railcars were dug into the asphalt and the air got darker and the government was happy and the oysters were gone.

Now it was well into World War II and time to go back and update the story. I walked halfway across the little wooden bridge that crossed over the muck that still made it officially an island. I could not even see the edge and there was the problem. Where I thought I was going this way my next step took me that way and the bottom of my foot slipped on something and, *owww*. I can't believe this but I have just fallen off the bridge and I am going straight down. I was so shocked I didn't even have time to say a bad word.

Then *schmack*! Or maybe it was *smochk*! That sounds more like it. *Plop* is too gentle. It was the weight of one human hurtling through space and hitting the primordial ooze that we came from, except in this case the ooze was contaminated.

It was low tide, which was lucky because if I had fallen in the water I would probably have swallowed some and gotten typhoid. The water was filled with the floating, bloated carcasses of dogs and horses and things that were no longer identifiable as anything. And even though I could not have died, even immortals get sick.

I had trouble standing up in the muck. When I forced my feet down I was up to my crotch in stuff that I did not want to have touching my crotch. Many years later I met reporters who would hate to go out in the rain. Wimps. Anyway, I yelled "Help" many times. Someone yelling help in the muck around Granville Island was not a terrible cause for alarm so it took a while before a worker leaned over the edge of the bridge.

"What are you doing down there?"

I could barely see his outline.

"Can you help me get out?"

He said nothing. He left and came back with a ladder, lowered it over the side and left again. I struggled through the muck, climbed up the ladder and was alone. My saviour was gone, no one else was there and I was wearing gook from my hair all the way down. My mother would not have approved.

I tell this story in great length because I came out of the ooze being born again. That happens every time I find something new to believe in. This time my religion was that things could be fixed. Anything. Almost anything. The only problem was, and continues to be, that I did not know how or who or when. I just knew it could be.

Can you imagine one of the established religions being based on anything that flimsy?

I walked home. Not many people noticed because the smog was so bad. I took a bath with my clothes on and went back to the island to visit Jack.

"This place is the son of Hell and should be buried next to its father." So said Jack McFarland. "Bury it."

I was thinking no, it could be good. Just give it a chance. I left his sweatshop and walked toward what I thought was another factory but I could not be sure. It was foggy with red and grey and orange air impossible for seeing and unfit for breathing.

Then I heard a scream. It was blood-curdling and scary and it came from the

The Vulcan Iron Works' neighbour on Granville Island was the Wallace Foundry, which belched out smoke day and night. The main product was chains for the Canadian Navy.
Photo by Dominion Photo Co., Vancouver Public Library 20429

foundry I had just left. I ran back and found Jack on the floor gripping one of his hands with the other and screaming even louder.

I wrapped my arms around him trying to soothe him.

"My finger, my finger," he screamed.

He held up a bloody mass of a hand and I could see that the index finger on his left hand was missing. In its place was a stub squirting blood.

"It got caught in the machine."

Like so many others he had failed to pull his hand back from the steel jaws before they closed over the steel bones they were being fed. In less than a second, chomp. Finger gone, and the wide-open, horrified eyes seeing what was happening before the pain shot up to the head and down to the groin.

After the screaming there was the huddling of men shouting things like, "Does it hurt?" and "Bite on it, that helps."

The screaming was only muffled now because of pride. So many others had lost fingers, and even hands, that it was embarrassing to go on about it even if the pain was overwhelming.

"Here's some iodine," someone said.

And the medic with dirty hands holding the bottle poured the red liquid over the throbbing, raw stump and the pain shot through Jack's arm and out to eternity.

"Here's a bandage," someone else said. "Now rest for a little bit and we'll take over your shift."

That was it. Jack did not go home. He did not go to the hospital. He did not do anything except take a drink of whisky that someone offered him and squeeze his injured hand with his good hand trying not to scream.

In an hour he was back at work. I know that sounds impossible, but he was, just as all the others who lost fingers had been. If they went home they would lose a half-day's pay. I don't know how they managed to still grab the ingots with their tongs and put them into the presses, but they did.

Forty years later I was at the official opening of the Granville Island Market. It was still owned by the federal government but now there was a farmers' market and there were theatres and boutiques and restaurants. One of the restaurants was called The Sandbar after the original spot in the creek surrounded with oysters.

The new island was the work of a few politicians who had some good ideas. That happens sometimes, thankfully. And they were helped because the government already owned the land. Had that not been the case the fight would still be going on over how it should be developed and how it should be zoned and how to get rid of the street people like the ones who beg in front of shops downtown.

One amazing thing now is that there are no young beggars with their dogs and signs saying, " No Job, No Ambition, No Pride, No Care, Please Give," anywhere on the island. The commissionaires who enforce parking rules simply say to the beggars that they can't be there, it's against the rules. And they leave.

If they tried that downtown it might work.

There was no magic to the turnaround. There was no hero that made the transformation. A small group wanted to do it, they talked another group into it and the government did something good and presto, it is now the biggest tourist attraction in the city and the most popular spot for locals to spend a Saturday.

I went back for another story. It is now impossible to fall off the bridge. There are railings.

The water is clean, the air is clean, the kumquats are overpriced and the Improv Centre theatre is the best entertainment deal in town.

I once wrote a story about the last foundry on the island. It is still there because the rules say there must be at least one example of the old industry that still functions. I also wrote about a woman who does wonderful weavings. That is an old industry, too, but new to the island.

And I met a young woman playing the violin and collecting money for her talent. There are many street performers who audition and work on the island. They are all good. She said she had been told a relative of hers once worked on the island. "That was during the war," she said. She wasn't sure which war. She was not even sure there was more than one. She had heard he was hurt while working here but that was all she knew. Her name was not the same as Jack's.

But maybe. Who knows? In some way we are all connected.

The moral: Don't despair. Main and Hastings will someday be the trendiest corner in town.

I know. Trust me. I've been there.

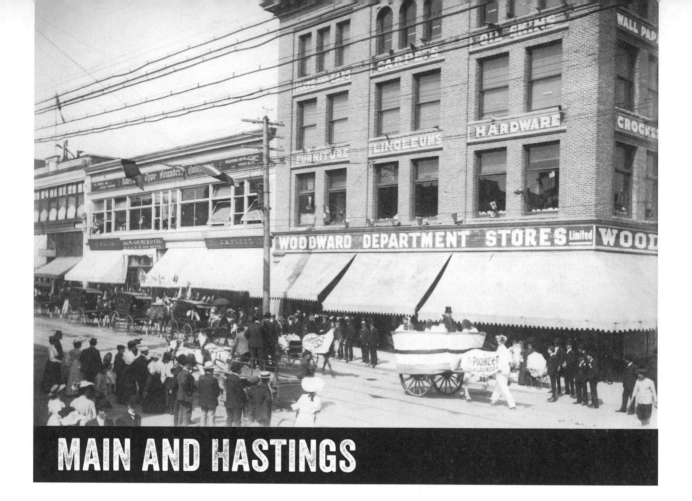

MAIN AND HASTINGS

It was once the trendiest area of town, Hastings heading toward Main Street. Parades and pedestrians and shops and shows gave it life. It is now, so very slowly, coming back to life.
Photo by Philip Timms, City of Vancouver Archives AM336-S3-3-: CVA 677-524

ometimes the folks in government get it right: Granville Island.

Sometimes they screw up with mind-numbing stupidity that defies any hint of intelligence higher than a glob of chewed gum stuck on the bottom of a shoe: East Hastings.

I spent some time there drinking beer with the teamsters when they were pulling logs out of the forest. Actually, that is wrong. The poor oxen were doing the pulling. The teamsters were doing the drinking and taking the credit for the pulling.

Later I spent some time in a shack along the skid road when rent in town was getting too high. The shacks were sort of early laneway houses; small, humble abodes that kept the rain out—except for the holes in the roof and the lack of glass in the windows, but we could walk to Gassy's saloon and stumble home.

"They live on Skid Road," people would say, explaining the pedigree of those of us who could not afford a room above the bar. They looked down on us but we had quiet nights with clean air and fresh water from pots put under the holes in the roof.

Those who lived in dry, expensive rooms over the bars had noise all night and cigar smoke rising up through the floorboards. Have you ever smelled cigar smoke when you were hungover? Skid Road was the place to be.

I moved back about fifty years later and got a room at Carrall and Hastings. That was now the place to be. It was throbbing with life, exciting all night long and since I had given up drinking I could enjoy it.

You don't have to know where I am talking about but just picture a street crowded with people coming and going and shopping and eating and meeting and drinking. It was alive. That was because on the corner across from my apartment was the BC Electric Railway Company building, which was the Grand Central Station of Vancouver.

All the streetcars of the city would pull into the building, which had great arched entrances and exits. Folks would change there for Burnaby or South Vancouver or Mount Pleasant, which really was pleasant.

They could even get a streetcar that would take them to Chilliwack, which was so far out in the country you might as well be going to another country. Those streetcars on thin rails hit seventy miles an hour, which was against the law, but when the chasing police cars could not catch them it was fun. The streetcars made the trip in less time than cars do now. That is one of those facts, not embellished.

For a long while the CPR ran a steam engine from Burrard Inlet to False Creek with tracks on Carrall Street right across East Hastings. All the buildings were set at an angle so the train could pass by. You should go down there and look. The angled buildings and the tracks are still there.

Then they built a tunnel and ran the train underground. It was a short trip so the train crew did not die from the smoke but up above there was room for a civic improvement where the train had gone. The city built a tiny park and called it Pioneer Square.

It was the meeting place for loggers and for businessmen. Ladies with baby carriages came to chat. It was a true civic spot where people could feel proud of being there.

You know it now as Pigeon Park, a cesspool of broken shopping carts and broken people where drug dealers stand selling their crack while addicts with no money crawl on their hands and knees searching the ground for any drugs that may have fallen from the hands of the dealers.

By the way, you know what crack is, don't you? It has destroyed many cities and neighbourhoods and you should know. It is powder cocaine that has been heated with water and ordinary baking soda to produce an oily form of the drug that can be rolled into lumps or "rocks" when it cools.

This form of cocaine can be smoked, and it makes a cracking sound as it burns; hence crack cocaine. Taken like this the drug hits the brain like a giant explosion on fireworks night. The high is instant. So is the addiction. And the compulsion to have more is so strong that a crack addict once told me he would have killed his mother to get more.

Not nice.

But there was no crack when I was living there. There were crowds getting on and off the streetcars. And there were crowds buying clothing and coffee and groceries.

And there was Benjamin Kubelsky walking hand in hand with the very young Sadie Marks, right there, right past Carrall and Hastings after they had been to Woodward's Food Floor to get the makings of matzo ball soup.

You could get anything at Woodward's.

No one noticed them but they were clearly in love, which was a problem because Sadie was more than ten years younger than Benjamin. If you were a mother or father, what would you say?

The same as me.

And Sadie's parents said so too.

But on this night they were going home to the fancy apartment building where Sadie lived. They walked along past all the nice stores on East Hastings. They walked past the Pantages Theatre on East Hastings. Yes, there were marquee lights on Vancouver's Broadway, which was East Hastings.

Benjamin was performing there in burlesque, which was an endless array of song and dance and comedy. He was a young comedian.

Then Sadie and Benjamin walked past the Carnegie Library, they walked to Jackson Street and entered the fancy polished-white apartment building where Sadie lived with her parents.

Her parents had invited Benjamin for the Passover Seder, a traditional Jewish holy meal, as they had done every year that he had returned to Vancouver. They had no idea that little Sadie would fall in love with older Benjamin over the dinner table. She had been only fourteen and he twenty-five at their first meeting.

"No you can't. He's too old. And again, no you can't." That was her parents saying the same as you would have said.

Benjamin went away, came back a year later and played the same theatre. It was still the centre of town. And he knew Sadie would be there. A year later he did the same, and the year after that, and eventually she was old enough.

Sadie and Benjamin stood under the tent that is put up for a Jewish wedding and they drank wine from the same glass, each taking a sip. Then they wrapped the glass in a cloth and stepped on it, smashing it so it could never be used again, signifying there would never be another for either.

Sometimes symbols are beautiful.

Then they went to work and changed their names to Jack Benny and Mary Livingstone, two of the most famous radio comedians in American and Canadian history. Of course they had to change their names. How could a Jewish person on the radio be successful?

I am telling you this because it all happened on East Hastings, which is now the scummiest street in Canada. Sadie and Benjamin would not have walked on it. He would have been afraid for her. She would have been plain afraid for herself. She would have been embarrassed to live there. The drug dealers would have been menacing. The closed and boarded-up windows would give no reason to be there.

Mary Livingstone and Jack Benny were two of the biggest radio stars of their day. Here the pair, along with Benny's comedy partner Eddie "Rochester" Anderson, have their luggage checked by a customs officer in 1944. If a hotel said it would not allow blacks in, Jack Benny and his entire crew would move out.
Photo by Jack Lindsay, City of Vancouver Archives AM1184-S3-: CVA 1184-524

What happened?

The stupid city government listened to the lobby group and drank their free liquor. The rubber tire makers were trying to expand after World War II. Again, I am not making this up. They hired spokespeople who would go to government people and repeat the mantra: The future is with tires, not rails.

That was all. The lobbyist for rubber tire makers went across North America and sold the politicians on the idea that buses and cars were the way of the future. Streetcars were dinosaurs. The city aldermen, all of whom were visionaries, could see the benefit of streets crowded with cars and buses instead of light rail, which for some reason always gets through.

Vancouver got its first taxi in 1910. The city was annoyed, fearing that the taxis would take passengers away from the streetcars.

City of Vancouver Archives
AM54-S4-: Trans P38

They abandoned the streetcar and said, "Look how modern we will be. We will have buses."

They closed the Grand Central Station at Carrall and Hastings. People no longer met there. Buses went up and down the street, but they went up and down every street. There was no reason to go to East Hastings to change for the tram to Chilliwack or Burnaby or Kitsilano. There were buses going everywhere and all you had to do was learn which line connected with which other line, which then would connect you to another line (or was it that other line?) to get you where you hoped to get to.

To put their stamp on how much they wanted to get away from the streetcars the city government ordered the streetcars to be burned, which was done under the Burrard Street Bridge. Made lots of air pollution.

Suddenly, and I mean suddenly, there were no crowds on East Hastings.

"I'm not going there to buy my hat and groceries and have coffee. I can just take a bus and then transfer to another bus, and then wait for that connecting bus to get my tomatoes. No, of course I won't meet Mary as we always did. She is taking another bus somewhere else. In fact, I haven't seen Mary for weeks, or months."

In weeks, or months, the street emptied. And the stores had no customers. The little ones went out of business and the big ones cut back. Save On Meats went from twenty-six full-time butchers to six. Over months and then years Woodward's carpets got frayed and worn. The wonderful Christmas displays in the windows got smaller and then disappeared. Then the store did the same.

And then: This became an unfolding tragedy and I and every other reporter asked, "What are you doing?"

The provincial government closed Riverview, the hospital for those whose ills are demons and things that turn a sunny day into a terrifying run through a dark tunnel. The hospital that cared for the mentally ill was shut down. They did this because new drugs were found that could control schizophrenia. That was good. Suddenly the voices that screamed inside heads at their victims could be quieted.

But that only worked if the drugs were taken. And that only worked if someone reminded them to take their drugs.

The government said it would open housing for the patients who were turned out on the street with their plastic bags filled with bottles of pills. It said they would have care workers who would care for them.

The government lied, plain and simple. That was my interpretation. Or at

The Crease Clinic at Riverview Hospital was a foreboding place, but while open it provided a safe home for many who now wander the streets. Some politicians thought it would be cost effective to close it.
Photo by Doug Brons

least it exaggerated or misspoke or, in the parlance of the newsroom, it was full of caca. Actually, we used a different word.

I met with members of the provincial cabinet.

"Where is the housing for the ex-patients? And where do they go for care?"

"We have both," the cabinet minister said.

"Where?" I asked.

"I don't have my notes with me now, but we have them," the cabinet minister said.

"You should not need notes. Do you have such places?"

"Yes, we have them and you are wrong to say we don't."

"Where are they?"

That was when the aide to the minister butted in and said the interview was over.

Yes, this really happened—and still happens.

I was working nights during the early days of the closure of Riverview, and there was one place they had opened so in their view they were telling the truth. For the hundreds of patients who were initially released from Riverview there was one relief centre.

It was in a basement under a junkyard at Main and Prior. I went down there. It was good that the bare light bulbs hanging from the ceiling were connected to loose wires because heads kept hitting them. If they had been in a socket where they should have been they would have exploded.

The ex-patients wandered from one room stacked with beds to the next stacked with beds, most looking like zombies in a netherworld of dim lights and screams. It was not like the hospital with its clean beds and clean rooms and privacy.

The care workers were saints. They were mostly thin, probably because they worked so hard, and they truly cared for those with devils in their brains. But when I saw one, then two, workers dealing with ten, then twenty, then forty people coming in for the night there was no way this was like an oasis.

And then I went outside and the hundreds of others who could not get into the shelter were wandering the streets. Actually one street. East Hastings. And that is when the drug dealers moved in, because there are no drugs better than heroin and cocaine for treating mental illness. Science may not agree, but the laboratory of the street proves it wrong. Heroin and cocaine and crack chase away the devils. Of course they replace them with hell, but that is later.

The drug dealers found easy prey. And if the buyers were not quick enough to put up the money they were given for food then the dealers helped them by taking out knives and cutting open their pockets to take it. Immediate customer service.

Over the years the government did create more care centres. That is an easy sentence to write—that is what historians do—but think of what happened during those years. Many pockets, many knives, many moments dulled by heroin or thrilled by cocaine and then hours and days afterward of something between hunger and starvation, between screams and drugs. The word to describe it has not yet been invented.

And in time, hey presto, East Hastings.

The rows of drug dealers and addicts crawling on the ground looking for salt-crystal-sized bits of dropped crack, and crime and…oh, come on. Words don't come close.

On the other hand, think of Granville Island or New York City. I met a young reporter from New York. He said it a thousand times worse than Main and Hastings. He would not go into Times Square or Grand Central Station without an open knife in his pocket. The great white way of Times Square was growing dark. Crack had shut it down. And Grand Central was collapsing; the walls were falling in, along with the safety of virtually every neighbourhood in the city. That is why he left and moved to Vancouver.

But New York was like Rocky. It came back. It was down on the canvas and bloody and dizzy, but it crawled back up and put up its fists. It was not the work of a mayor named Giuliani, who took all the credit. It was the work of thousands of people who said they were sick of the crime and the dirt, sick of living in a place that was unlivable, and they started complaining to their politicians and they complained to the newspapers and some of them started sweeping their sidewalks.

Some stood up with signs near the crack dealers. The signs said No Drugs Here. The police came to protect them. The newspapers put them on the front page. Then others joined the protest.

Developers were going to knock down Grand Central but one worker, trying to fix a leak in the ceiling more than a hundred feet above the floor where drug dealers held court, found a painted star under decades of tobacco soot. He cleaned it and the newspapers heard about it and wrote about it and the worker cleaned more and found more stars.

An entire constellation of stars was found that no one alive had ever seen. The people and the newspapers started a campaign to save the train station. It worked.

The drug dealers were driven out by simply enforcing no loitering laws. The walls were repaired and the travellers came back and some of them were hungry so small restaurants opened. Then more came to see the stars in the ceiling and more shops opened.

That was when the mayor said that if it worked on a train station it might work in Times Square. He ordered the area flooded with police. The drug dealers left. The lights came back on. He took the credit. You can't blame a guy for stealing an idea, at least not when it works.

Today Times Square is as safe as Disneyland.

The same will happen on East Hastings. Some day a tour bus will stop there and the driver will tell the tourists that once upon a time this was a slum, unlivable and frightening. The tourists will be looking at one of the cleanest, brightest streets in Vancouver.

It is already starting to happen. Save On Meats has the best hamburgers in town and the Pidgin Restaurant across from Pigeon Square serves a side order of courage with each meal, no extra charge.

And someday a girl and a boy will walk along the street holding hands and see only each other, not only because they are in love but because the drug dealers will have been pushed out by the crowds who are going to the theatres on the street.

It happened in New York. It happened on Granville Island. It will happen at Main and Hastings.

ROGERS SUGAR

enjamin Rogers was a good old boy.

He had the basic attributes of a redneck: He hated anyone who was not white, and even if you were white but you were in a union, he hated you, too.

The BC sugar refinery can still be seen from Powell Street in East Vancouver. Can you imagine getting a loan for a business based on the promise that "only white hands will touch our white sugar"?

City of Vancouver Archives
AM54-S4-1-: M-11-65

Benjamin Tingley Rogers (second from the left) is seen here relaxing with friends aboard his yacht in 1910. He had a big head and lots of smarts but, unofficially, a small heart. Rogers made good sugar but left behind a bitter life.

Photo by H.M. Burwell, City of Vancouver Archives AM54-S4-: Bo

Considering it was 1890, less than forty years after the slaves were freed in the US, which many whites still thought was a very bad idea, and less than twenty years before white brutes smashed windows and heads in Chinatown in Vancouver, Benjamin Rogers fit right in with large parts of the population. Good old boys have small brains or shrunken hearts, sometimes both.

Anti-Chinese, anti-black, anti-turban, anti-anyone who was not like the sophisticated white people who thought they were better because, after all, they were white. What else was there?

What part of that does not make sense?

Benjamin also did not like you if you complained, even if you were white and not in a union. "I don't care about their legs; they work faster if they stand," he said about women in his factory who wanted to sit down during their ten-hour shifts of sewing up bags of sugar. They sew faster standing up.

He said that with a deep Southern accent, which made him sound more like a redneck even though some people with that accent have normal-sized brains, and some people without it don't.

But he did use his brain in a conniving way, which means it was not his head that was lacking. He knew the politicians of Vancouver were much like him, and there is nothing that makes an American redneck from the South happier than meeting a Canadian redneck in the North.

"I'll make you an offer," he said to city council. "You give me forty thousand dollars (that was like forty million dollars now), you don't tax me for fifteen years and you supply me with fresh water at no cost for ten years and I'll build you a sugar refinery."

I was covering city council at the time. I know the quotes are accurate because right after I put them in my notebook I wrote as a note to myself, "Even this city council is not dumb enough to go for that."

Boy, was I wrong. I thought as a reporter I knew everything but I did not know the power of a redneck.

Ten years earlier Ben Rogers had seen what happens when people organize and go on strike. His father was president of a sugar refinery in New Orleans. The working conditions were miserable. The workers walked out.

Ben's father walked out of the factory and yelled at the workers to go back to work. Someone threw a brick at him and hit him in the head and killed him. You can understand Ben's dislike of protests.

He left the South knowing how to run a sugar refinery but with no money to build one and ended up in Vancouver with those same contradicting forces. Many have dreams, few have the money to make the dreams come true. But Ben was smart—not nice, but smart.

Vancouver was only five years old and desperate for any industry other than trees and fish. Rogers said he could give it to them if they supplied the money and resources he needed. He presented his plans to city council: Give me everything and be patient.

"You will have a new industry and eventually you can tax it and charge for the water. Eventually it will profit the city. Eventually everyone will be happy."

They did not look impressed. Ben added, "Meanwhile anyone who wants to invest in it will keep all the profits along with me. Would you like to invest?"

Crazy, I thought. Private profits on a government-financed industry. Nice if you can get it.

Benjamin went on. He was only twenty-three years old.

"One last thing before you decide," he said. "I will never hire anyone who is yellow to work on my white sugar."

Bingo.

"Only white men will be employed?" said the city fathers, who were all white.

"Of course not," said Benjamin. "White women will be hired too, so long as they don't want to sit down on the job."

"Where do we sign?" said the white fathers.

Benjamin built the biggest factory on the West Coast of Canada and then with the profits from it he built the biggest mansion in the West End for himself. It was on Davie Street. Then he petitioned city hall not to allow a streetcar to run near the house. The streetcar would take people from inside the city to the beach and Stanley Park.

When he lost that battle he built the biggest supermansion in Shaughnessy for himself. No streetcars would run there.

He was on the board of the Vancouver Hospital, which was prestigious, but he never participated in a single debate about its care and refused to give a penny to its upkeep. He said public bodies just squander money so he would not give any to them.

And eventually when his workers went on strike to get a raise he hired private detectives and strike breakers to force them back with a cut in pay.

He died at fifty-two of a brain hemorrhage. His obituaries said he was a captain of industry. They did not say he was a nice man, or even a good old boy. His unofficial autopsy said his brain was large. It did not say that about his heart.

THE GEORGIA VIADUCT

 was talking to a woman at Strathcona Community Gardens about her roses. They smelled so sweet. I remembered when this was a city dump that smelled so bad it had to be closed.

Strathcona Park and Gardens are near the Georgia Viaduct. The park runs along Prior Street and the viaduct begins where the street ends. Don't worry if you have no idea where that is.

The first Georgia Street viaduct made part of Vancouver look like a tiny Venice. That was in 1915 when there was water where Beatty Street and Costco are now. It was a viaduct with a purpose. The only bad part was it was built so badly it collapsed under its own weight. Whoops.
Photo by C.P. Dettloff

The one thing about telling a story is if you talk about something someone else knows nothing about you lose that person and the story goes bust, so skip the location. Just think garden with roses that was once a dump that is next to a viaduct, which is a road for cars that goes over something and connects something to something else. It could be anywhere.

From the 1930s to the early 1970s Vancouver's thriving black community was called Hogan's Alley. It was demolished when the city built the Georgia and Dunsmuir viaducts that connected to Prior Street, which was a quiet, barely used street running through Hogan's Alley.
City of Vancouver Archives AM1535-: CVA 99-2458

Outside the garden I heard young, beautiful people with children shouting, "Tear down the viaduct."

That was the kind of rallying call that would bring out the reporter in me. It was not quite like "Stop the War in Vietnam," or "We will smoke pot because it is our god-given right to smoke... [pause, inhale]... What were we talking about?" But "Tear down the viaduct" had a certain kind of civic-minded ring to it.

I left the roses and looked at the protesters. They were young mothers and fathers and children. All were white. All were thin, which is the politically correct way of saying they were all upwardly mobile, white entrepreneurs who were adventurous and smart and had the world in their sights and they ate very little meat but drank expensive coffee.

"Down with the viaduct."

Good for them. It is time to get rid of it, I thought.

The viaduct leads cars into the centre of Vancouver. Actually it is two elevated roads. One leads cars along Prior Street into the city, the other leads cars out of the city onto Prior Street. Again, don't be concerned that you don't know the location of Prior Street. You only need to know that it runs alongside the homes of the protesters.

Now, go back a while ago. Not too long. Do you know the name Jimi Hendrix? Of course. You would hate to admit you did not. He was the black, left-handed guitar Mozart who played the American national anthem at Woodstock.

In fact, those who stuck around to witness Hendrix's mind-blowing rendition of "The Star-Spangled Banner" were awestruck. "The way Jimi Hendrix played the American anthem to a mass crowd of soaking wet rockers turned it from a right-wing conservative song into an anthem of a generation of civil rights crusaders, anti-war protesters and music lovers everywhere."

Another reviewer said that. I wish I had but as Jimi showed there are always better writers around the corner. Nonetheless, I was in the mud and I heard the music and if my mind had been my own that day, which it was not, I would have said even more. Jimi's guitar made the best moment of Woodstock. Period. Everyone said that.

The music of a descendant of a slave celebrated the nation that enslaved him and millions of others with the most beautiful, amazing notes that went with the words "by the dawn's early light."

If you don't know "The Star-Spangled Banner" you should read it. After a night of cannon fire from British ships on an American fort, one of the American prisoners of war on the ship wrote a poem. After a night of bombs bursting, the first light of dawn saw "our flag was still there."

The tune was a rip-off of a famous British beer-drinking song, but the words were goose-pimple raising.

Jimi Hendrix practised that music on Prior Street, before the viaduct was built.

You see, and I apologize for explaining this because I know you know it, Jimi came up from Seattle to visit his grandma. She worked in a chicken shack on Prior right near Main Street.

There were a lot of chicken shacks then, and they were all run by black women. And if you were brave enough you could go to Main and Prior and get the best-tasting chicken in Vancouver. This was in the 1950s and '60s when America was worried about nuclear attack from Russia, and Canada was spending most of its energy trying to stamp out the history of the Natives so they would not have deal with that anymore.

But in Vancouver there was a small community of black people.

"Oh, my god, what are we going to do with them?" asked the people of city hall. "We can't shoot them. We can't tell them to go away. But can you imagine black people, negroes, living here? Unimaginable. First Chinese, then East Indians, and now *black* people?"

Much of Hogan's Alley was bulldozed in the early 1970s to make way for the Georgia Viaduct. Gone were the shacks, the back alleys and the homes that had been there for half a century.
Photo by A.L. Yates, City of Vancouver Archives AM54-S4-: Bu P508.53

The neighbourhood they lived in was called Hogan's Alley. It was one of those black words. It sounded good. Someone named Hogan lived there once.

But on any night you could go there, if you dared, and hear music. Unimaginable. And eat fried chicken. Is it safe? You could get murdered!

There was someone, once, who got murdered there and stuffed in a garbage can.

Of course in the rest of Vancouver there were many who got murdered and stuffed under cars or in parks or just left, but in Hogan's Alley it could happen to you. It could happen to you anywhere, but a reputation is hard to shake, especially for a black neighbourhood that sells fried chicken and has music at night.

City council wanted to get rid of the blacks, who had lived there for several generations and had come from eastern Canada and the US.

"How do we do that?" city aldermen asked.

One had an idea. "We will modernize the city. We will put freeways right into the city like they are doing in Seattle. No traffic jams, ever."

"What does that have to do with those people living in East Vancouver?" asked an alderman who clearly was not as cunning as his friend.

We will start the freeway on Prior Street.

Brilliant.

Wait a minute. Wouldn't it be more sensible to put the freeway on a major street like Hastings or Broadway or Twelfth Avenue?

If we put it on Prior Street, that quiet backwater where no one ever goes except black people, we would have to take over the land, expropriate it, and plow down the houses and chicken shacks and god only knows what other evil places to make the freeway. And the people in the houses that remain would not be a problem. Those people would not want a busy street for their kids to play on. They will move.

Presto. Two problems solved. Get folks into the city quickly and they won't have to see any black people on the way.

There would have been a Hero of Vancouver medal for that alderman, except that his descendants who married outside their ethnic group erased his name from the history books.

Within a couple of years the chicken shacks and the houses of the blacks had been demolished, the music was gone, the culture was gone, the viaducts were built and the city fathers met and said, "This idea of a freeway coming into the city is dumb. We don't want to be like an American city with congestion. We want to be Canadian. No more freeways."

With that the freeway idea died and the houses that remained were occupied by Chinese families who were spilling out of Chinatown. The traffic on Prior Street zoomed by. It was now a quick way to get into the city. Go down formerly quiet Prior and zip over the viaduct and you are downtown.

The only problem was that Prior was now as busy as a two-lane Broadway. However, the only people affected were Chinese and they did not complain. They never complained.

Forty years later the Chinese moved to Richmond and white, upwardly mobile families moved in. They painted the houses, put tons of money into renovations and planted gardens and were thrilled at getting homes so cheap so close to downtown. The only problems were the viaducts. They made the street unsafe for their children.

Protest.

White folks want the viaducts removed. That shouldn't be a problem since developers now also want the viaducts removed so they can build high-rises. The viaducts will be removed.

And now in the neighbourhood there is a tiny memorial to Jimi Hendrix right where the chicken

Jimi Hendrix played his guitar on this sidewalk in front of Vie's Chicken and Steak House on Prior Street near Main. Jimi's grandmother, Nora Hendrix, did most of the cooking. Jimi lived in Seattle but spent his summers here.
Photo by James Inglis

shack that his grandma worked in used to be. It is next to a new condo building. And nearby is a sign that says Hogan's Alley. It is near a trendy coffee shop that plays recorded black soul music for the mostly white patrons who say this is their neighbourhood. The city must make it safe for them and their children. Not only safe, but quiet and peaceful without the traffic that uses the viaducts.

When the city does knock down the viaducts one of the city workers driving a big excavator that will be smashing into the foundations will be black. It's only fitting.

The Ancient & Honorable Hyack Anvil Brigade.

ANVIL BATTERY

By 1906 the Anvil Battery was a tradition of defiance. Not allowed to shoot off a cannon, they fired an anvil with gunpowder and a hot poker. It began at Thomas Owen's Blacksmith and Machinist shop on Eighth Street, a hotbed of civil disobedience!

New Westminster Archives IHP0480

t is Victoria Day 2013. I am in the stands watching the ceremony that I think is one of the best on earth.

No, I am not overstating it.

You want to see independence, self-reliance, defiance, courage? There are more words but in short if you want to see ordinary people standing up against the powers-that-be, or at least were, go to New Westminster on Victoria Day.

It was a long time ago, a very long time ago, when I stood with the other Royal Sappers and fired our rifles into the air for Queen Victoria's birthday. First we fired the cannon. We had only one and we did not have many spare cannonballs, so we shot it just once.

That was not enough for our beloved Queen. So we got our Brunswick rifles and stood in a row, firing twenty-one times. I can't believe I could hold the rifle that long. It weighed almost ten pounds, and each time we had to put it down by our sides, load it with more powder and a ball and then heft it up, wait for the command, and fire.

It was as they had taught us in basic training. Don't worry about aiming, just stand in a row and keep shooting. If you don't hit the enemy someone else will. And if they hit you someone will replace you. That's why I loved the army. It was so compassionate.

But this was different. We were firing for our Queen and we loved her and no rifle was too heavy.

After we disbanded, the New West Fire Department took over. They were really just a bunch of guys who pulled a heavy wagon and enjoyed doing something exciting, like saving lives and homes. They were not paid, which made all of them heroes—or crazy.

Anyway, after the capital of the colony got switched to Victoria things changed.

By the way, do you know how that switch happened? It was pure corruption and stupidity and more corruption and dirty deeds, which means it was your government in action.

Here's what happened: James Douglas was the governor of the colony of British Columbia. It was because of him, as I mentioned, that you are not shopping in Costco in Bellingham without a passport. He saved BC from becoming part of America. He was tall and strong and loyal to his Queen but there was something else about him. He hated New Westminster. It was dirty, with muddy roads and too many saloons.

James Douglas liked the cultivated life of Victoria, which had raised wooden sidewalks and tea shops. That was like the England he had never lived in. Besides, he lived in Victoria and he was governor and he wanted the capital to move from New West across the water to his hometown.

How do you get that done? Largely of course through sleight of hand. You arrange for a vote of the House of Assembly, which was in Nanaimo. That was like the legislature of today.

One speaker from Victoria would give an argument for moving the capital and one speaker from New West would give an argument for keeping it on the mainland.

The speaker supporting New West was Captain William Franklin. He loved New West. He also loved whisky.

The night before the speeches a couple of supporters of Victoria took the good captain out for a few drinks. They had some more. Then they washed it down with some beer, then a nightcap and then more beer to cover the nightcap. The head finally hit the pillow but the head had no memory of hitting anything.

When the captain awoke he tried to look in a mirror but the image was too fuzzy. He grabbed his speech and tried to find the door. His head hurt something awful.

When he got to the assembly a member of the opposition helped him by taking his speech from his shaking hands, but then, whoops, the member of the opposition dropped the speech. The pages were not numbered.

He apologized and put the pages back together in some sort of order, but not quite the order in which they were written.

And then he helped Captain with his glasses.

"Oh, dear, Captain, it seems I have dropped your glasses."

When the glasses were found it was discovered that the lenses were missing.

"Oh dear, Captain, it seems your glasses are broken."

The poor captain, who could not see and whose head was killing him, tried to get the pages of his speech in order but he had no idea which page came first.

"Captain. Would you begin your speech? We are waiting."

That was the speaker of the assembly doing the rush job. He also wanted the capital moved to Victoria which would be easier for him to get to than New West, which was a massive inconvenience.

The captain, with his head hurting and his eyes blurry, began reading, but it did not sound right. It was the middle of his speech.

So he started again, just in case it would sound better the second time. It did not. A third try and he asked for an adjournment, which he was granted.

However, when he returned with the pages in their correct order and a new pair of glasses the speaker told him that the adjournment did not mean that he could have a second chance to give his speech. "Only one opportunity, the same as the other side."

I was there. That is what happened. But it is curious how the people of New

West and those of Victoria tell the story. In New West the pages of the speech were dropped by a foe and the glasses were popped by a foe.

In Victoria the story is that the speech maker was drunk.

Moral: Never trust what you hear from just one side, especially if you agree with that side.

The vote was thirteen to eight against New Westminster. Victoria, on a remote island far from the bulk of the population and just a short ferry ride to the US and more south than Bellingham, became the capital of British Columbia.

And that was the beginning of the trouble with the cannons and the Queen and the birthday wishes.

"No, you cannot fire your cannon for the Queen."

That was the political power seat in Victoria speaking to the former power seat in New West. This was the year Victoria became the capital. It was flexing its political muscle, as most new powerhouses do.

"We will be the only, repeat *only*, city in the colony to salute the Queen."

That was Victoria being really snotty about its power. It has grown up now and is much nicer, or at least it says it is, but it still wants to have the biggest celebration.

"And to ensure that no cannons be fired outside the City of Victoria we will confiscate all other cannons from all other cities."

That would mean the one cannon in New West, that being the only cannon outside of Victoria.

"Screw you."

That would be the people of New West responding to the official edict as they saw their cannon being hauled away.

Actually, they did not say that. That is a modern expletive. What they said was, "That is unacceptable to us and we will not obey your order." But those words have lost some of their oomph over time.

However, the people had plenty of oomph. The mayor of New West was also a blacksmith, a man of considerable oomph, and he had an idea.

They had no cannon, but he had gunpowder and a couple of anvils and you know what happens when you put gunpowder in a confined space and ignite it?

"It goes bang."

That is what a seven-year-old boy said at Queen's Park in New West on this day of the big bangs. He was asked by a reporter who was trying to explain the meaning of why they blew up anvils. The balding, tubby reporter told the boy named Trevor about the government taking away the city's only cannon. It was the kind of history the kid should know about.

In fact, I followed this reporter back to his television studio and was saddened when I learned the editor who was going to put the pictures together and was born in Vancouver and went to school here knew nothing about the celebration.

And then another editor stopped by to chat. He was also born here and he, too, went to schools here and he also knew nothing about it.

I said, "That's crazy. This is important. These are the people who made this place good and strong. How come you don't know about it?"

"They didn't teach us," the two editors said. "And by the way, who are you?"

"A visitor from another world," I said, and then left wishing the schools would wake up before the important stuff was all forgotten.

At least they are still keeping it alive in New West. We Sappers were replaced by the firemen, and they were replaced by ordinary citizens, but two heavy anvils are still pulled out every Victoria Day. The good citizens put gunpowder on the top of one of them, place the other anvil on top of it and then, with a long, very long, pole whose tip has been in a fire and is red hot, one of the ordinary citizens touches off the gunpowder.

Bang. Actually, *BANG*. And the car alarms in the parking lot go off. *BANG* and the folks in the grandstands jump. *BANG* and you feel the percussion in your chest. It hurts. Cannons, even when they are anvils, hurt. Don't stand close enough to let it fall on your foot.

On that first anvil day the ordinary folks in New West fired off their anvils and they were proud. The heads of the government in Victoria shot off their cannons. They were ticked off about New West, but they did nothing.

The Queen, of course, heard neither of them but the people in New West cheered louder than the people in Victoria. Of course they did. The underdog always feels proudest of all.

Over the years the people of New West have turned the firing of anvils into a sacred ceremony. Those in the red jackets—yes, red jackets just like we Sappers wore—have official names: the Shooter Offer, the Left Hand Picker Upper, the Right Hand Picker Upper, and the seriously very important Swabber Offer. If he does not swab off the hot remains of the previous firing the next firing may fire too soon and that would be bad for living organisms in red coats.

More than a century later the Anvil Battery still fires off its hunks of steel in honour of Queen Victoria's birthday. You can watch in Queen's Park in New Westminster every Victoria Day. After the first firing all the car alarms in the parking lot are screaming.
Photo by Paula Aitch

Every Victoria Day in Queen's Park, in the baseball field, the anvils are fired. It is a testament to defiance, independence and imagination. If you could see it you would get a bang out of it. (Sorry.) If you can't get there, watch it on television. That balding reporter has done a story on it for almost twenty consecutive years. I don't know how he gets away with it, but he feels very strongly about the tradition.

The anvils of New West were silent only one year, in 1901, the year their Queen died. She would have appreciated the quiet.

IMPERIAL PALACE. KANADIAN KNIGHTS OF KU KLUX KLAN. VANCOUVER B.C.

CANUCK PLACE

Glen Brae house was built by lumberman William Tait, who named it after his home in Scotland. Local women protested that the domes looked like female breasts.
Photo by Stuart Thomson, City of Vancouver Archives AM1535-: CVA 99-1494

e are God's chosen people. We are white and therefore we are God's people."

I was listening. I had heard about these psychotic nutcases but I had never actually listened to them. Now I was absorbing their words and twisting in my skin.

"We must kill the inferior yellow people and black people and brown people. They are dirt in God's eyes."

"Are you kidding?" I thought. "You look ridiculous wearing bed sheets with pointy tops."

"The coloured people are taking over the world. We must stop them."

"Why?" I asked.

The bed sheets stopped. "Who are you?"

"A reporter trying to get the inside scoop on you people."

"Get out. Get out before we kill you."

They started to rush me, but I'm an old soldier and I dodged and twisted and outmanoeuvred them while they were tripping on their robes. I was out the door and down the stairs. I was running. There were more than a dozen of them but I had enough now for a good story and I was not going to let them erase the words from my head with their rubber heels.

Down the stairs, out the door and over the wrought-iron fence. Whoops, they were still coming.

I got to Granville Street and my feet were flying. Then I met a bunch of Chinese who were walking toward me on Granville. They were going all the way to Richmond to work in the fields. They would be there shortly before the sun came up and they would sleep on the side of the road for an hour and then go to work.

Behind them were some Japanese. They were walking to Steveston to go back on their fishing boats. They were in Vancouver to pay the taxes on the boats. They had little left after that but enough to keep their families fed.

This was before the edict to put all Japanese in jail. If there were not enough jails then put them in the barns at the PNE and shut the doors, for goodness' sake. They are yellow. I mean they are Japanese and you know what that means?

Well, I didn't. But the men in the dirty white sheets did.

"It means they are cursed and we must drive them out," said the sheets.

That is what they said before they started chasing me through Shaughnessy, past the most expensive homes in Vancouver, past the dark-skinned nannies pushing the carriages of the white babies.

"Wait," said the leader of the dirty white sheets. "We must harass the nannies before we kill the reporter."

Then they saw the Chinese and the Japanese. They were outnumbered ten to one.

"Retreat, men. We could beat them but it would be too much trouble."

They turned and ran back to the massive home they called their headquarters.

I had only gotten into the home because I had been a friend of William Lamont Tait. He was from Scotland and had made a pile of money owning a lumber company back when there were trees to cut down.

He used some of the money to build one of the largest homes in the city. However, many people, mostly women, did not like the home because it looked like it had two large breasts sticking up where a normal conservative roof would be. These were women who did not believe women should look like women, at least not in public, and certainly a roof should not look like a woman.

William liked his roof. He called his home Glen Brae, which is Scottish for valley between the mountains, which it certainly looked like. He did not like the people who wanted him to tear down his home so he put a large, black, wrought-iron fence around it. The fence came from Scotland. It looked like a fence that was meant to keep people away from his roof because roofs that look like women need protection from women who act like drunken men.

And then William Tait and his wife died and the house was bought by a group that did not identify itself honestly.

There were sixteen rooms in the house and a couple of secluded back ways in and out. They were useful when the neighbours were out front protesting bumps on the roof. I used one of the back doors to get into the KKK meeting.

Brave behind their robes, the KKK turned the Shaughnessy mansion into their headquarters during the 1920s. Despite their electrically lit burning crosses it was a dark time.
Photo by Stuart Thomson, City of Vancouver Archives AM1535-: CVA 99-1496

"We are not the KKK," someone in white told me once.

He could have fooled me. White pointy sheet over white pointy head with long white robe over pointy display of pointless power.

"We are the KKKKK," he said. "The Kanadian Kouncil of the Ku Klux Klan. And you had better never forget that."

No trouble there. I also remember a really bad stomach ache I had as a child.

Anyway, aside from occasional forays in the dark along Granville Street, mostly in the Shaughnessy area where no one else was out at night, they confined themselves to marching around the house with the bumps. They stayed inside the fence and carried a cross with electric bulbs powered by a large battery.

But their problem was that, then as now, it rains a lot in Vancouver. You just can't put your sheets out in the rain without them sagging and clinging and getting all muddy. It is hard to be scary when the point on your head looks like a bent-over clown's hat.

I've seen a lot of racial hatred in Vancouver, but I've learned it is really hard for even the most mind-warped people to stand up against being laughed at.

The KKKKK just simply vanished. Krazy Kooks Killed by their own Kinky Kowardliness.

Now the home is a sacred place for children with terminal illnesses. For most, the Christmas lights are the last they will see. The house, now called Canuck Place, has a soul.
Photo by Mike Martin Wong

Now the house with the bumps has become the home with the heart. It has a new name: Canuck Place. It is sacred. It is closer to God than any church or synagogue or mosque in the city.

It is where children go to pass their last nights in this world. They are all children with cancer, children who are four and five and six and seven and eight years old. Not old enough. They are children who tell their parents not to worry and not to cry.

Pip was there one Christmas Eve. I was watching her. She was a nurse and there was still one child in the home who could not go to her real home for this special night. She was too sick. All the other children were taken away, almost all by ambulances, all with tubes running into their tiny arms, almost all with no hair, almost all of whom were happy to be home for Christmas Eve, even if it was only for one day.

But there was one who could not take the trip, so Pip stayed.

"Don't you have a family?" I asked her.

She looked around at the bedrooms and said, "These children are my family, and tonight one of them may need some care."

Outside the home there were television cameras and politicians and dignitaries and a children's choir, and all the trees and bushes were covered with lights. It was the one night of the year when the home got public recognition; the one night when it was almost empty.

The little girl who had to stay behind could not get out of her bed to see the lights, so Pip pushed the bed closer to a window.

"It is so pretty," said the girl.

"Your mommy and daddy will be here in a few minutes. They called and were stuck in traffic," Pip said.

"That's okay," said the little girl. "I'll wait for them."

And then she fell asleep.

Her parents did arrive, in a rush, filled with pain and anxiety, and their daughter did wake up and they had presents and some fizzy, sweet pop—just a sip because the little girl could not swallow more. And there were tears and hugs and smiles and more tears and the little girl said, "Don't cry, Mommy. It's Christmas."

Then the television people and the dignitaries left and Pip turned on some music, Christmas music, turned it on in every room, and she leaned against the door jamb watching the little girl and her parents.

"Bless you," I whispered, then tiptoed down the stairs and out into the chilly air of Christmas Eve. I had no power to bless her. That would have to come from someone else. But I believe everyone in that home, whenever they come, despite the reality of what is happening, is blessed. Bad things, good things, they come together, and after ten thousand years we still have not figured out why, but it is true that even a little good can push aside a lot of bad.

I turned around as I went out through the gate. The bad things from the men with the pointy heads were gone. The strength of one little girl had replaced them.

MIRACLE MILE

 t teaches you everything you need to know about how to get ahead in life. No kidding.

You look at one statue and there is the lesson. All you have to do is see it to know what happened, and how you can avoid the same thing happening to you.

This bronze sculpture by Jack Harman, standing at the entrance plaza of the PNE, captures a fateful and unforgettable moment in the lives of two great athletes.
Photo by Angela Huxham

But sadly, while I was standing in front of the statue, I heard: "Another dumb monument to old runners. Why don't they put up something new, like a statue to Lady Gaga?"

Come with me to the corner of Renfrew Street and East Hastings. It is the good part of East Hastings. Don't worry about packing bear spray.

There is a statue of two runners. It used to be a block away in front of the stadium where the two runners ran, but when they tore down the stadium they moved the statue. Makes no sense, but you can't argue with municipal statue movers.

The year was 1954. I only mention the year because the parents of some of you were alive then and they did know about this.

The place was Vancouver, the Empire Stadium, built just for this race. Actually, it was built for the Commonwealth Games, but this race was the one thing that made the games so exciting. This would be the first time the fastest two men in the world would run against each other.

To be honest, there were women in Africa who ran faster just going to the market to get more beans for dinner, but they were not white and they were not men so they were not invited to the race.

Back at the race: John Landy from Australia was the fastest runner on earth, discounting the African housewife. He had run the mile in 3:57.9, which was very fast for someone not from Africa. He was 100 percent an athlete. He did nothing but train and run.

Roger Bannister was from England and he was the second-fastest runner at 3:59.4.

But at one and a half seconds behind Landy, Bannister was by far not the favourite in this race. He was also training to be a doctor and spent most of his time doing that. Running was done in his spare time.

Both of them, with six other runners, were at the starting line in Vancouver. The Queen was watching and a hundred million others were listening on the radio. Millions more were watching on small black and white televisions. The woman in Africa did not know about the race. She was cooking her beans.

Bang. The starter's gun fired and the men took off. By the beginning of the second lap Landy was way out in front. The announcers called him the "fastest miler on earth." Bannister got behind him but was eating Landy's dust. He was at least fifteen strides behind. The crowd was screaming.

Off on the side of the track was a young photographer who was not happy.

Charlie Warner was twenty-five years old and worked for the *Vancouver Sun* and had been told to take the day off. The older, more experienced photographers would handle the big event but Charlie didn't want the day off. He wanted to work because this was exciting and that is what photographers live for. He would work even if he didn't get paid for the day.

He went to the track but did not have credentials. Hurry! He had to have a press pass because security would not let him onto the field without it.

He signed the release forms. You have to do that in case a runner runs into you and kills you. They don't want photographer's families suing. It looks bad.

His heart was racing and he grabbed his press pass and ran with his giant Graphlex 4x5 Speed Graphic camera, which was the press photographer's number one assault weapon on news.

For those of you who grew up with digital you have no idea of what the photogs of old went through. The camera weighed eight pounds. You had to hold it with two hands. You had to set the speed, set the opening of the lens, cock the shutter, then aim at the subject, guess at the focus, and then push the release on the shutter. *Click.*

That was it. One shot. It was like the muzzle-loading rifles of old. One shot, then reload. One picture, then slide a metal plate over the film, pull the case holding the film out of the back of the camera, turn the case over, slide it back in, pull out the metal plate, put the plate into a holder on the back of the camera and then shoot again.

When they got a good picture they earned it.

Charlie went to the finish line but it was packed on both sides of the track. The big-time photographers from around the world had taken up every spot and were protecting their places with elbows.

Poor Charlie. I saw him so dejected. The most he could do was walk up the track about fifty yards. There would be no good pictures at that distance from the final ribbon. The most he could hope was to get them a few seconds before the end. It would be a picture that would be forgotten. In fact, it would probably never be seen, but he was there so he would take a picture anyway. At least it would be a souvenir.

That is where he was standing as the runners came toward him on the fourth and final lap.

Landy was still in front, still leading but only by about five strides now. Bannister was catching up but still so far behind there was no doubt Landy would win. The crowd was getting ever louder. What was happening was what makes racing the best sport. You can see who is winning and who is trying to catch up.

There are no judges sitting behind tables saying that the precision diver had her elbow slightly to the left so that magnificent flight through thirty feet of air was disqualified. Not so with running. The one in front wins.

Then Landy did something strange. He later said he did not know why he did it. It was something you should never do, *never*, no matter what.

He looked back. He looked to see how far in front he still was. He turned his head to the left. It was just for a second.

It is good for your ego to see you are still in the lead, but when you turn your head while you are running you break your pace, you upset the air blowing around your head, you lose your concentration. In short, you do something very dumb.

Bannister saw the head turn to the left and something in him gave his feet wings. He flew by Landy on the right. It was instinct and it all happened in an instant.

And it was at that instant that Charlie Warner pushed his shutter release. He alone in the entire stadium was close enough to record that moment. As the head turned his thumb tapped the release. Most of the people of the world see something like that and then they push the button. Charlie was a fine news photographer. He pushed the shutter as he saw it. It was instinct.

Five steps later and Bannister was in the lead and the finish line was in front of him and Landy was behind him. Bannister did not look back to check.

He crossed the line and collapsed into the arms of someone waiting to help.

Then he struggled up on his own feet and staggered to Landy to hug him. That is a good sport.

There were hundreds of photos of the finish. There were hundreds more of the hugging. Many of them were tremendous still pictures of the moment of triumph and loss. The photographers were all in the right spot for the pictures at the end of the race.

Charlie went back to the darkroom at the newspaper and developed the film. He prayed. I don't know if he really did or not but I'm betting he did. He could have missed it. They were moving so fast they could have been out of the frame before the mechanism of the camera responded. He could have gotten them and missed the head turning.

"Oh, my god. It's there."

The negative had the image of the head turning and Bannister passing Landy. The perfect moment.

The next morning his picture was on page one of the *Times* of London. It was on page one of most Canadian newspapers and in the sports section of virtually every newspaper on earth.

It was chosen as the best sports picture of the year by the National Headliners Club in America, the first Canadian picture to get the honour.

Denny Boyd, who was a friend of mine and everyone's because of his warm column in the *Vancouver Sun*, suggested that a statue be made from the picture.

It was, and the statue is now at Renfrew and Hastings. If you want to know how to get ahead in life, look at the two bronze men. One is looking back, the other is moving ahead.

Don't ever look back. Don't ever regret. Don't ever try to flatter yourself by looking back at those who are not fast as you. Don't. Look at the statue and see why.

The race was called the Miracle Mile. It was the first time in history that two men in one race had run the mile in less than four minutes.

The best part of it was Charlie's picture. He never bragged about it. In fact, he never mentioned it unless someone brought up the subject. He never looked back.

Opposite page: John Landy looks back over his shoulder to check on Roger Bannister. Big mistake. You can learn much about life from this moment. Charlie Warner of the Vancouver Sun *took the picture that became the statue. You can learn much about life from how he took the picture.*
Photo by Charlie Warner

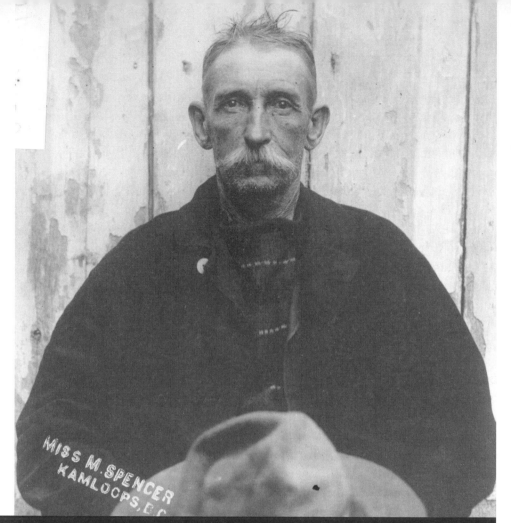

BILLY MINER

ou can order a Billy Miner pie at the Keg or a Billy Miner drink. There's even a Billy Miner Alehouse in Maple Ridge.

I say that is ridiculous, but he would have laughed and laughed and then said, "That is very kind of you, sir. I appreciate your kindness."

That was Bill Miner, always polite and gentle, even if the situation was brutal and deadly.

If you are asking, "Who was Bill Miner?" I say gather around the cracker barrel and let me tell you a story. If you are asking, "What's a cracker barrel?" I say look it up. There are things you should know.

But as for Bill, he was a thief, a robber, a criminal sentenced to life in prison, and he was loved. How many guys do you find like that now?

He was the first train robber in Canada, though some researchers say there was another train robbed before him. So maybe he was the second train robber in Canada. But he was magnificent as a human being.

Early life? Born in Kentucky. Brutal, drunken father, bad for modelling your life after. Robbed stagecoaches as a teenager, caught, sentenced to a term in San Quentin prison in California. Enter hell.

Beatings from guards were commonplace. They were actually sport for the guards, who used thick rubber hoses.

They would tie a prisoner's hands behind his back with a rope and throw the rope over an overhead bar. Then they would pull down on the loose end of the rope and make the hands and arms go up until the pain became unbearable.

Screaming was just part of the fun for the guards. Begging did no good. The usual practice was to leave the prisoner with his shoulders ripping out of their sockets until he passed out from pain, which took quite a while.

Sexual brutality was rampant. When the guards were finished beating the younger prisoners the older ones would have their way with them. Billy Miner was one of the youngest and there was no one to complain to.

He was in and out of prison. There were no education or counselling services. By the time he was fifty he had spent more than thirty years in damp, cold, noisy cells. He had been beaten uncountable times and locked in solitary confinement for uncountable months, perhaps years in total. No one was counting.

That meant no light, no toilet, and a concrete floor to sleep on, which the guards threw water on to make it colder and wet his clothes. Food was bread and water, nothing else, which is not good for your health. Also, there was nothing to do, which is not good for making time pass.

Now what kind of man or even dog would come out of a world like that? A mean and miserable one, right?

Wrong.

When I met Bill he was a perfect gentle man. I separate those words deliberately. He was simply the nicest fellow you could meet. He was polite. He was kind. There is no overestimating the strength of the human spirit when it wants to be strong.

He was generous to those needing help—he especially liked to help old folks—and he loved wearing nice clothing, a suit with tie and polished shoes. Who could not like him? Plus he barely drank. After so many years in prison he was not going to lose his freedom to a bottle.

His only problem was he knew of no other way to make a living than by robbing stagecoaches. Okay, we all have our shortcomings.

I met him after he left America simply to avoid being hunted by American law enforcement. They were looking for him because he had escaped from his last prison, which is something else he excelled at. He moved to Princeton, BC, and changed his name to George Edwards and for seven years lived as a most respected gentleman—now one word—who occasionally had to go away for business.

When he returned to Princeton he usually had enough money to help local folks and buy new clothes for himself. Some of the good citizens suspected what he might be doing but they all liked him too much to say it.

One of his business trips was to Mission where he and two friends boarded the Canadian Pacific's *Imperial Limited*, heading to Vancouver. It was the CPR's prize luxury train. It was always on time. It carried some of the country's most important citizens along with the most valuable of assets.

George Edwards looked like he belonged, but the train had barely gotten up to speed when he tied a bandana around his face and with his gun out ordered the engineer to stop.

"Stop?"

"This is a robbery and I would appreciate your assistance in stopping the train; otherwise I will kill you."

You can't beat him for being polite and still making his point, and besides, neither George Edwards nor Bill Miner ever killed anyone.

The train stopped at Silverdale, just west of Mission. You can still rob the government at that same spot by getting your gas there because it is just outside the high-tax boundary. Every day hundreds of motorists from Maple Ridge drive to within a hundred feet of where the train was stopped to do some legal cross-border gasoline shopping.

Anyway, George had the engineer unhook the passenger cars and then ordered him to drive off with nothing but the big engine, the coal car and the baggage car. Easy.

They stopped less than a mile away in Whonnock, a lovely town in which not much else has ever happened, and emptied the safe of the modern equivalent of six million dollars in gold and securities.

Whether that was the first or the second train robbery in Canada, it was then the largest robbery in the history of the country.

Officials in the CPR head office were furious. Not only were the losses huge but they had no insurance. Why would the CPR need insurance? They owned everything and who would dare try to take it?

Also their reputation was hurt. Rich people would stop shipping gold and bonds on their trains if they could so easily be held up, and without the shipments of gold and bonds they would be reduced to just carrying people. How humiliating.

"Catch him at any cost," said the CPR, and the railroad police, who were more powerful and had more informants and more guns than any police force in Canada, including the Mounties, went forth to catch him.

But who was him?

I met George Edwards in Princeton and I had my suspicions, but I was not about to ruin the life of a good man. Besides, all he, or someone, had done was rob a train. It was not like he'd stuck up a corner store where the owner was actually working for his money.

Everyone, and that was *everyone* who was not working for the CPR, hated the CPR. It overcharged the ranchers for shipping cattle and overcharged the farmers for shipping wheat. It held onto the best land and treated everyone with contempt. It was not unlike government transportation companies now.

The people of the land said the CPR stole from the people while the train robber, whoever he was, only stole from the CPR. He was their Robin Hood.

When the railroad police came into Princeton the people said, "Nope, no one of that description lives around here. No, sir. Never seen such a man."

When the police asked me I said I used to be a policeman myself before I retired, and I know what kind of a man you are looking for, but I have not seen anyone around here except gentle men.

"No one who I thought would or could rob a train."

I was honest.

He got away with it for three years. The trouble, or the good thing depending on which side you are on, is the police never give up. They finally got Bill but they did not get the loot.

His trial was held in Kamloops and although Bill Miner, alias George Edwards, was never conclusively linked to the robbery in Mission, there were other robberies and there were his prison escapes. The sentence was to spend the rest of his life behind bars.

When the train left with Bill Miner on board a band came out to play, not because he was a criminal in shackles surrounded by guards but because he was a hero.

When the train neared New Westminster the authorities learned there were so many people waiting at the station to greet him that they wanted to take him off early and sneak him into the prison. The train slowed at Sapperton but there were hundreds of people also waiting there to wave at Bill. I was among them.

It was so strange for an ex-cop to be waiting to cheer a criminal, but then I looked around and there were other ex-cops waving. When someone has

The old grey walls and thick bars of the BC Pen could not keep Bill Miner inside where it was damp, dark and brutal. Bill would think a modern Canadian prison was like a fancy hotel.

Photo by Bailey and Neelands, City of Vancouver Archives AM54-S4-: Out P10

raised his life to an art form and overcome incredible hardships you can't help admiring him, even if he robs trains.

The crowds at the New West station were overwhelming and loud and cheering. This was not the way to instill humility in a prisoner. By the time I got there I saw the guards puffing up their chests. This would be the high point in their careers. They got to touch Bill Miner.

The BC Pen was an ugly place when it was built and an ugly place when it was torn down. But Bill's reputation was go good and his appearance so suave and gentle that the daughter of the deputy warden took a special interest in him.

No, it was not romance. He was sixty-two and she was in her twenties. But she had found religion and wanted to save Bill Miner's soul.

And possibly because of her influence Bill had many meetings with prison officials. He was way past beatings and rapes and solitary. He was the elder statesman of the prison, by far the most distinguished and polished and gentle man behind the grey walls, including the prison officials.

Now I don't know what was discussed at the meetings but I can have a guess. It did not concern his soul. It was more likely cash that was discussed. To be more precise, the location of the missing gold and securities, most of which had had their face value multiplied by stock splits and interest.

And whatever happened in those meetings the result was that Bill was transferred from the shoe-making shop behind the bars inside the prison to the brick-making yard outside the bars but still behind a fence topped with barbed wire and inside the tall grey walls.

Somehow Bill and three others managed to dig a hole under the fence, slipped through it and then found a ladder to climb over the wall.

How did a ladder get next to a wall inside a prison?

When their escape was discovered there was a half-hour delay in chasing them while the guards were ordered to lock all the other prisoners in their cells.

The three who went with Bill were quickly recaptured but Bill never was.

This time, instead of in the headquarters of the CPR, there was thunder in Parliament in Ottawa.

"I would like to ask the prime minister how such a notorious criminal could escape from the most escape-proof prison without inside help?"

Politicians always make such profoundly obvious observations. The questions went on but the answers never came.

However, in the offices of the CPR there was happiness. They could now stop fussing over the missing securities. The gold was another matter, but the securities were more important.

In answer to the politician's obvious question, obviously a deal had been made. The CPR owned not only the land but the prison system too. Well, it did not actually own the prison but it owned it in the same way as big muscle groups can own politicians. For once, Bill was happy about corruption.

He probably took some of the gold and moved back to the US. In another obvious observation, he could not have taken it all because he could not carry that much. Gold is heavy, he was travelling alone, people were looking for him and he was getting older.

But he would have taken some and the rest of it, most of it, is probably still there, somewhere in sleepy little Whonnock, which is just a little west of Silverdale and a little east of Maple Ridge if you happen to be interested in going for a treasure hunt someday.

Bill went to Georgia where, naturally, he robbed another train. He was caught, imprisoned and escaped again. Aside from being kind and gentle, robbing trains and escaping from prison were his best qualities. It is a pity he did not put his mind and energy and perseverance into running a business or a city or a country. We would have had a better world.

He died behind bars. Usually when a prisoner perishes without family his remains are given to a medical school to practise on or they are buried in a potter's field behind the prison walls, but Bill had already become so popular with the people in the community in Georgia that the citizens paid for his funeral. It was the first and last time that happened.

In New Westminster, just outside the old BC Pen, which is now a comfortable housing subdivision, there is a street named Miner.

It is the first and last time *that* has happened.

CHARLIE'S TREE

o doubt you have seen it. If you have ever driven east after the Port Mann Bridge, you must have seen it. It is a giant stump of a cedar with a large metal Canadian flag nailed to it. There is a sign now that says Charlie's Tree. The sign is fairly new.

If you remember back before the highway was widened the road made a big curve as it went around the stump.

Charlie's Tree is still beside the highway. The bend has been removed from the road just before the 200th Street exit going east but the tree—actually the stump—stands strong and proud.
Photo by Antonio Vendramin

That curve and that tree are testaments to the power and strength in some people that let them win over stupid bureaucracy.

Once upon a time (again) that area in Langley was all farms and forests. A boy named Charlie Perkins lived on one of the farms and he would swim in a pond with four of his friends.

Time passed and Charlie was holding onto a plow behind a horse cutting furrows in that land. More time passed and a war broke out in Europe. England was in the war. The British Empire was in the war. He was a subject of that empire.

Charlie, like many in British Columbia, felt deep in his heart that it was his duty to enlist. He got on his horse and spent a full day riding to the army enlistment centre in Vancouver. His four childhood friends did the same.

At the end of the war only Charlie came back.

Those statistics were not unusual.

Charlie went back to his farm but part of him, like part of anyone who is a good person, was still with his friends. There was a cedar growing near where the old pond was and Charlie planted a vine near it.

Vines, of course, are not good for trees but Charlie wanted to plant something that would touch something that was there and, besides, the tree was big and strong and could carry the extra burden, just as he was doing.

Then he wrote the names of his friends on a plaque and nailed it to the tree.

Monuments sometimes help.

Time passed. Charlie was now growing older while the country he fought for was simply growing. A highway across the entire nation was under construction. It was like building the railroad again but this time everyone would have the freedom to drive in their own cars.

That would be great, except the highway would go right through Charlie's farm. I don't know if he liked that or not, but since he had no choice about it he did not fight it. He was paid whatever the government said it was worth, which of course was not what it was worth, and now he would have to cross a road to tend half his farm. He had seen worse. He would survive.

But one day he saw the surveyors coming. They were heading straight for his tree.

"The road is not coming here, is it?" he asked in that way of asking something that you prayed would not be answered in a way you did not want it to be answered.

"Afraid so," said the surveyors.

"But my tree. That tree. It's in memory of friends who died for this country," said Charlie.

"Sorry. It's in the way," they said.

Charlie said something, probably under his breath, and the battle lines were quietly drawn. He protested in town. He protested to his local politicians. He protested to the local newspaper. Nothing happened.

Then the bulldozers came and Charlie did something. He sat on the ground in front of his tree. He may have done something else, too, though some members of his family say he did not. His nephew of two generations later told me he held a shotgun on his lap just to say he meant business. His grandchildren told me he was a peaceful man who would never do anything like that. We all want to see our ancestors in the light that we like best. None of them was there.

I don't know. I wasn't there either. I was in Kamloops with Phil Gaglardi, Minister of Highways, who was in charge of the road construction through BC. He had gotten the reports from the work crews about this old fellow stopping the highway. This obstruction could not be allowed to go on and what should they do?

Phil was a menace to travel with. He would speed and he would be pulled over by the police and they would give him a ticket, even though he was the minister, and he would get back in his car and speed some more.

Speeding is crazy. A few times I thought we would die.

"Please, slow down," I would shout.

"I love this," he would say, with a giant smile.

I can't defend speeding—it does kill people—but in Phil's defence I can only say he did what he wanted to do without worry about reputation or rebuttal.

In his office I asked what he was going to do about the man blocking the highway.

"Leave me alone for a few minutes," he said. "I have some thinking to do."

I left. I did not want to see this. I knew what he was going to do. When the door closed behind me he took off all his clothing and started to run around his desk. It gave him freedom, he said. I am not kidding. The government minister

Phil Gaglardi saved Charlie's Tree. He also ran around naked in his office. He also got tickets for speeding on the highways he made. Bless him. His life-sized statue stands in Gaglardi Park, Kamloops.
Photo by James Hull

243

stripped almost every day in his office and ran around naked while pondering problems.

It sounds like he was a madman but his mind was tough as nails and he made decisions obviously without caring what colleagues thought.

A few minutes later he opened the door looking fully refreshed, dressed and smiling the same smile he had when he was driving over the speed limit.

He called me and his secretary into the office.

"You know what he does in there?" I whispered to her.

She nodded and shook her head in the way parents or teachers do when they know a little one is strange but so brilliant there must be allowances made.

"Take a memo, please," he said to her.

"To the chief of construction, Number One Highway. In the matter of the tree and the road, curve the road around the tree. Signed, Phil Gaglardi, Minister of Highways."

"That's all?" asked the secretary.

"Okay, add a PS: 'Don't be an idiot. Those men paid with their lives.'"

The secretary did not add the PS.

Phil was a warrior. The road was curved. Charlie lived in peace. What's more, a curve in the road brought attention to the tree and for those who dared stop at the old pullout there was a lesson waiting for them.

Later some teenagers drinking at a party in the woods set fire to the tree and killed it. They should have been made to visit the graves of the men whose names were on the tree but of course nothing was done to them. The top of the tree had to be cut and the only thing left for everyone now alive to see is a stump.

The new wider highway has taken away the curve but the stump is still there and it still has the flag on it, along with the plaque bearing the names. You can't miss it and you shouldn't.

Every year on November 11 members of the local branch of the Royal Canadian Legion place a wreath on the lofty stump and other people leave poppies, flags and flowers. In the battle for his friends' memories Charlie was the winner.

THE PENTHOUSE

kay, this is for family reading. My dear wife, rest her soul, would hunt me down and do terrible things to me if it were anything else.

The Penthouse was the most classic of all the nightclubs in Vancouver, and for one good reason: It had the things my wife would hunt me down and kill me for if I looked. But it also had class.

Joe Philliponi inspects the extensive bar collection at the famous Penthouse nightclub on Seymour Street.

Photo by Dan Scott, *Vancouver Sun*

The Cave and Oil Can Harry's were good nightclubs. They had celebrities and they had music and they had drinks with tiny umbrellas sticking out of them and containing enough sugar to cause diabetes before they hurt your liver.

The Penthouse, on the other hand, basically had whisky and soda. Sometimes Jimmy Durante or Louis Armstrong would play there. That was the class. Sometimes women with even more suggestive names than Tricksy Dixie or Bubbles For You would perform. That was smart.

And all the time Joe would watch and drink coffee.

"I never drink alcohol," he told me. "Bad for your head, bad for your liver, bad for your wallet—but good for mine."

That was very, very smart.

Joe had worked in a coal mine. Then Joe ran a taxi company and a boxing gym but he had younger brothers and a sister to support and the cab and boxing businesses were not enough. What to do?

Very simple, he thought. Men like to watch women undress, women like to watch classy big-name performers and almost everyone likes to drink.

He opened a nightclub that had all of those. He called it the Penthouse because there was a two-storey building attached to the gym and cab company and he lived on the top floor. You don't have to have your head in the clouds to say you are living high up. The second floor was high enough for him to use the name and the great thing about names is that when you name something it becomes that.

Giving a cheery salute, Joe stands in front of the Penthouse. Some feared him, many loved him, but most were in awe of the godfather of this hub of Vancouver nightlife.
Photo by John Denniston, PNG

People become their names and their names become them. Look at anyone. They are their name. The same goes for buildings and countries and sports teams and nightclubs.

The Penthouse became a name that became a brand and you knew what it was selling. You could meet what we once called ladies of the night. Funny that only twenty years before the Penthouse opened they were called day ladies because the row of brothels on Alexander Street generally closed their doors at night so the ladies could get some rest.

Anyway, back to the Penthouse. If you just wanted to look and not touch (which would not get you in nearly as much trouble) you could do the looking most nights in the club. And since for a long time you were not really allowed to drink in the club because they did not have a licence for that you would also have to do the listening—for the warning bell.

Up on the roof was the spotter, and when he saw approaching police he would push a button that rang a bell inside the club and everyone would slip their mickey-sized bottles of rye into metal sleeves under the table.

The police would come in and look around and see no bottles on the tables and Joe would shake hands with them and folded pieces of paper with the Queen's picture on them would move from one hand to the other. It was good to know that law and order could be achieved in such a gentlemanly fashion.

Times changed and the police changed and younger police wanted to get rid of all corruption. They charged poor Joe with living off prostitution. That was because women of great beauty but low standards would meet men with some money and equally low standards in the club and they'd go somewhere else to do something for which the men would pay the women.

Then the women would go back to the club but like everyone else they had to pay a charge to get in. It was two dollars. Joe claimed it was the policy of the club to charge at the door no matter who you were and that he did not know who was working and who was not.

"It was just a question of boy meets girl," Joe Philliponi told the judge, portraying the strip joint as an innocent lonely hearts club. The judge was unconvinced. He convicted five of the accused of conspiring to live off the avails of prostitution and sentenced Joe and one of his brothers to jail. It was good to know that law and order could be achieved just by stretching the law.

After the Penthouse was closed the women who had worked there moved to the street and all sorts of bad things happened to them. Some caught colds from standing in the rain. Others were murdered. Neither of these things happened when everyone knew who everyone was and who was doing things with whom before they did them.

It is bad that law and order can be destroyed by strictly enforcing law and order.

That is enough philosophizing but it is just strange that the outcome of closing a place in which no prostitution occurred ruined the lives of many prostitutes.

Ultimately an appeal court overturned the convictions and the Penthouse got its business licence back, and then one of the most delightful nights of my long life happened there. I have told this story many times to my friends. If you have heard it then you are a friend and you can skip it—or enjoy it again. No, you don't get part of your money for this book returned if you already know the story.

You see, I have a friend who is also a reporter. He was getting to know Joe during the later years of his life and he loved meeting with this local legend. Half of the legend was that Joe was the Godfather of the shady side of Vancouver life and half was that he was the worst dresser in town, wearing checkered pants and striped jacket over a fat tie when skinny ones were in style. Godfathers don't care what others think.

Anyway, one day Joe asked this younger reporter if he would like to bring his wife and children to the club. "It's a clean show," he said in a guttural blend of Italian, English and coal dust on his vocal cords.

The young reporter was thrilled. His family would get a rare treat. But when they arrived there was already a line down the street. These were the people waiting to get in because the club was already filled.

He took his kids to the back of the line and felt bad. It would be hours before they would get in and his kids would never stand still that long and besides some of the other people in the line looked like they were Mafiosi wannabes.

He did not know that Joe was watching. From his office in the top floor Joe could look out at a half-dozen mirrors. Some were curved so he got a wide-angle view and some reflected into each other so he could see around the corner of the building. There were no TV monitors to look at. He could just look out and see whatever he wanted to see.

And on this night he saw the young reporter. He walked down the stairs and out of his private door. The crowd made way for him like he was a prince or a king or maybe just a kindly godfather. "Hey, Joe." "Hello, Joe." "Remember me, Joe? My uncle's father-in-law used to work for you."

Some reached out to touch him but he stopped for no one. He was about five feet five, no matter which way you measured. He did not actually walk. He waddled. But there was something very powerful and determined about his waddle. He was not like a chubby man. He was a round bulldog.

He walked to the end of the line and graciously introduced himself to the reporter's wife and children. Then he took each of the kids by the hand and led the family past the line, which was now quiet. No one was going to disturb Joe when he did not want to be disturbed. That would be silly, or crazy.

Then in through his private door. The place was packed and noisy, and the kids, who were in grades two and three, looked back at their parents. Is this what big people do?

Joe walked them to the front of the stage, raised one of his hands, snapped his fingers and then pointed down. Before he lowered his arm a waiter with a table over his head had squeezed through the crowd and put the table down just where the finger had pointed. A few people sitting near there were encouraged to make room.

Then Joe held the chair for the reporter's wife. When everyone was seated Joe put a white towel over his arm and asked to take their orders. The kids asked for burgers and chocolate milkshakes.

Joe left and passed by me while I was standing near the kitchen watching it all.

"Milkshakes," he muttered. "What's a milkshake?"

He told one of his small army of workers, "Two milkshakes, chocolate, and hurry."

"Where do I get that?" the soldier asked.

Mistake. When the boss, the really big boss, tells you to do something the answer is "Yes, sir." That is always the answer. Have you never been in the army, I thought while looking at the poor, seriously demented fellow who had asked Joe, "What's a milkshake?"

Joe stopped, turned, glared, raised the same finger he had used to order the table, raised it slowly, pointed it between the eyes of the fellow, tilted his head and whispered, "Don't forget, chocolate."

I don't think the poor fellow's shoes touched the floor before he was out the door and halfway down the block. I could hear him yelling, "Where do I get chocolate milkshakes, please? Someone tell me, please, or I will die."

A very short time later Joe walked to the reporter's table holding a tray up high on the tips of his fingers like a waiter. On it were burgers and chocolate milkshakes. "Thank you," both kids said.

Joe smiled, a true, sincere, absolutely warm smile. He never married. He never had kids. He looked very happy.

There was more than class in the Penthouse that night. It was a good night.

A few years later a really bad guy got into Joe's room late at night and with

Joe's younger brother Ross and a group of friends and family stand in front of the club on a chilly day in 1957. It really was a family business. In fact, it still is.
Danny Filippone and Arsenal Press

his gun out made him open the safe. He took everything, told Joe to get on his knees, which was not easy for an old, squat man to do, and the really bad man shot Joe in the head.

He was caught. He is still in prison, saying now that he is old and sick and should get out, because he is old and sick. That is a problem with really bad people. They think they should get things they took away from others.

The nightclub is now owned by Joe's nephew, a devout family man who walks his dog around the neighbourhood.

There is one last thing that makes the Penthouse different from all the other old nightclubs. It is still there.

THE FUTURE

t is impossible to report on how things will be—reporters only write about things that have been—but after more than a century and a half of watching this city, watching the hate and the prejudice, the heroes and the kindness and the craziness, I can, carefully, predict a few things.

Everyone says Joe's Cafe at Commercial Drive and William Street has the best cappuccino in town. Joe was a bull fighter in Portugal before he came to Vancouver. Do you really want to argue with someone who has gone eye to eye with more than a thousand pounds of muscle and horns?

Photo by Philip M. Tong

It all comes out of the last Italian Day celebration on Commercial Drive. The street was packed. There was music everywhere and the most popular song was "That's Amore." You know: "When the moon hits your eye like a big pizza pie…" That's a great song. I understand it.

There was dancing in the street. Almost every restaurant and coffee bar had tables out front where wine and beer were making people happy, at least until it ran out.

But what was best was that along with the Italians there were many people who used to be called yellow. They are no longer called that. Some of them wore T-shirts that said they were "Italian for a Day."

And there were many brown people, which they are no longer called. They wore turbans while eating Italian sausages. And there was a smattering of black people who are returning to the city.

There were many white people, some of whom were walking with yellow and brown and black people, and they were pushing baby carriages carrying children who will less and less attract attention as their numbers grow and prejudice fades. In fact, I see a whole new blend of people arising who just by being proud of themselves will fix much of the pain of the past.

And then there were the drummers outside Joe's Café. Joe has been on Commercial Drive for more than forty years. He came from Portugal. He was a bullfighter there until he lost to a bull that dug a horn into his stomach and almost killed him.

After he healed, Joe was on his way to Mexico to fight more bulls—that's like the minor league of baseball—but he stopped off in Vancouver to see a friend who had a coffee shop. Joe went to work for him and a few years later he bought the shop.

He never got to Mexico. He never takes a vacation. In fact he almost never takes a day off. The people who come into his coffee shop are his family, he says. Some of them can't afford coffee so he buys it for them.

He had a stroke one night in his shop. He was lucky it happened there. His family around the coffee cups called 911 and the ambulance driver knew just where the place was. Joe was in the hospital for months. That is the only time he's been away from his family.

He now spends his days in the shop letting others make the cappuccinos and lattes, but he watches and says hello.

He is as much a part of the history of this city as those who cut the trees and dug the ditches. He gave it soul and character. He gave it himself.

On Italian Day he was watching some Panamanians and Colombians who were new to the city and had made his shop their home. They were outside on the sidewalk playing their drums, all hand drums. A half-dozen of them got a rhythm going without discussing what song or what rhythm they would play. Drummers do that.

Then a white man with a white beard sat down and asked for one of the drums. He had incredible rhythm, for a white man. A black man came out of the crowd and borrowed another drum from one of the players. He, too, had incredible rhythm. The two of them set the pace for the others.

Watching them was a woman with one of those face coverings, the kind where you only see her eyes. She did what everyone does when they hear good drumming. She started moving, swinging her hips. Her friend with the same kind of face covering did the same.

The husband of one of them stepped closer. He was wearing a cowboy hat. He started moving, too, but we are not all created equal when it comes to rhythm. No matter where they are from, men don't move as well as women.

The drumming stopped and, with everyone else, they clapped.

If this is the new Vancouver and British Columbia I can predict the future is pretty good.

PS: Stop by Joe's. The old, old sign in his window says The Best Cappuccino in Town. It is.

And PPS: Because this history lesson that is not a history lesson has tried to give you a few tidbits of information, here is one more.

The word *cappuccino* comes from an ancient order of Italian monks called the Capuchins (they wore hooded habits, and *cappuccio* means hood in Italian). They lived in poverty. They begged and worked the land. The tops of their heads were shaved and were browned by the sun. The hair that surrounded the brown dome grew white with age. Below that was the distinctive red-brown hooded habit they all wore.

A cup of cappuccino: brown cinnamon on top of white foamed milk on top of red-brown coffee. The little Capuchin. Well, that's the version a friend of mine from Rome told me so it must be true.

There is nothing dull about the story of people.

And now I am going to have a cappuccino in Joe's and watch the next hundred years go by.

Index